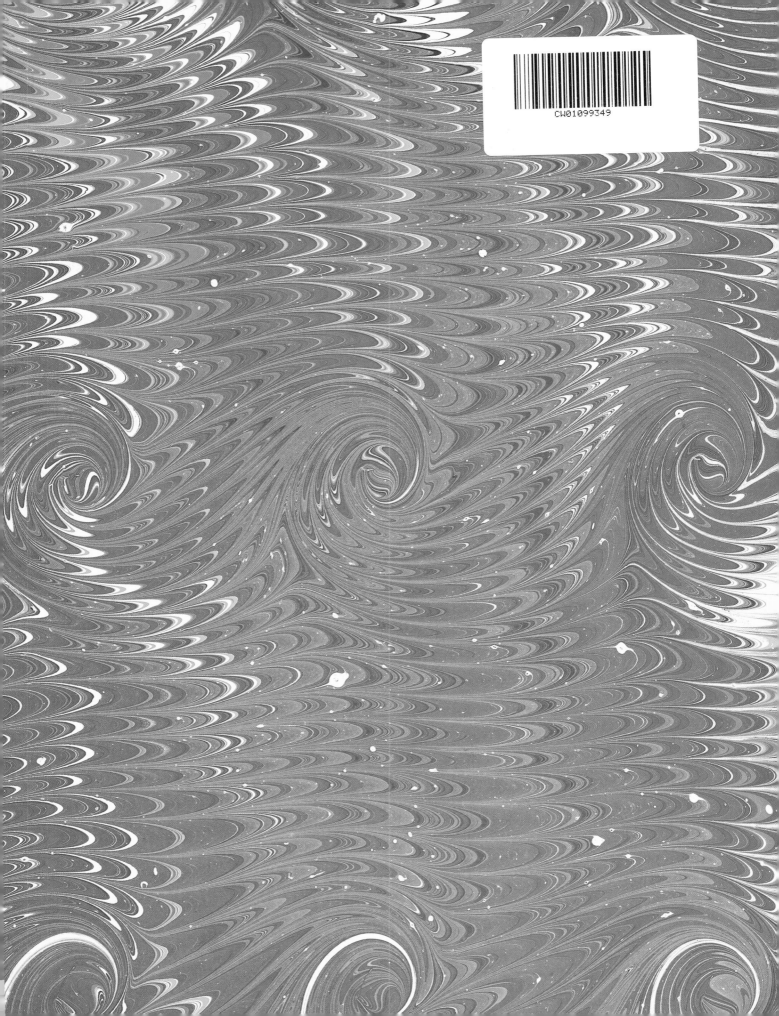

John Smith.

Paperweights from Great Britain
1930-2000

John Simmonds

Schiffer Publishing Ltd®

4880 Lower Valley Road, Atglen, PA 19310 USA

Dedication

This book is dedicated to my
wife, Rita, with love, for giving
me that first paperweight.

Note: Items in the photographs are from the author's
collection unless otherwise noted.

Library of Congress Cataloging-in-Publication Data

Simmonds, John.
        Paperweights from Great Britain 1930-2000/
John Simmonds.
        p. cm.
        Includes bibliographical references.
        ISBN 0-7643-1074-7 (hc.)
        1. Paperweights--Great Britain--Collectors and
collecting--Catalogs. I. Title.
NK5440.P3 S56 2000
748.8'4'0941075--dc21   99-057143

Designed by "Sue"
Typeset in Korinna/Zurich BT
ISBN: 0-7643-1074-7
Printed in China
1 2 3 4

Published by Schiffer Publishing Ltd.
4880 Lower Valley Road
Atglen, PA 19310
Phone: (610) 593-1777; Fax: (610) 593-2002
E-mail: Schifferbk@aol.com
Please visit our web site catalog at www.schifferbooks.com
Please write for a free catalog.
This book may be purchased from the publisher.
Please include $3.95 for shipping.

In Europe, Schiffer books are distributed by
Bushwood Books
6 Marksbury Ave.
Kew Gardens
Surrey TW9 4JF England
Phone: 44 (0)208-392-8585; Fax: 44 (0)208-392-9876
E-mail: Bushwd@aol.com
Free postage in the UK. Europe: air mail at cost.
Please try your bookstore first.

We are interested in hearing from authors
with book ideas on related subjects.

Contents

Acknowledgments

In producing a book of this nature, one quickly realizes how extremely helpful one's friends and acquaintances are in giving information, access to their records, and help with allowing items to be illustrated.

I am, of course, indebted to all of you, and the makers and others mentioned herein, for the many ways in which they have given freely of their time, to contribute to the work.

My special thanks go to the various people behind the scenes who have been associated with the ancillary aspects of producing a book of this nature. These include:

Dr. Richard C. Woodford

Dave Webber

Anne Metcalfe

Norman Faulkner

Charles Hajdamach of the Broadfield House Glass Museum for permission to quote the section for Paul Ysart 1971.

Linda Quin

Alan Quin

And my daughter, Karen.

Finally, a thank-you must go to Peter and Nancy Schiffer and the staff of Schiffer Publishing Ltd. for so expertly and promptly guiding me through the necessary procedures.

My grateful thanks to you all.

Prices and Values Guide

All prices are quoted in U.S. dollars, using a conversion of $1 = £0.67 sterling.

Prices can show considerable variation within a given country, apart from worldwide considerations, and are intended to be used solely as a guide. Unless otherwise stated, the values assume that the articles are in good condition, and are purchased from a dealer. Every care was taken in preparing the values given by checking with dealers, auction trends, and private collectors. However, the author accepts no responsibility for similar paperweights or related items that are bought, or sold, for different sums.

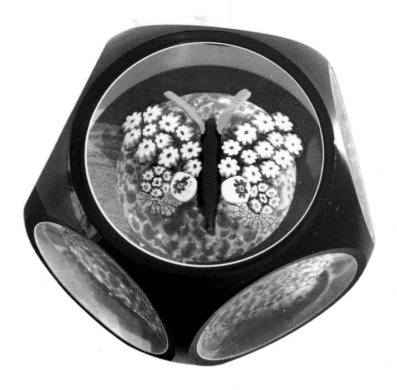

Introduction

Twenty-five years ago, when I began collecting glass paperweights, knowing virtually nothing about the subject, I was desperate to find out as much as possible about my new hobby.

Relatively few books on paperweights had been published before 1974; and as my first acquisition was a modern British paperweight (Caithness Reflections), my lengthy contact with libraries and book dealers was largely in vain. In fact, there was no book available which would tell me very much about my newly acquired paperweight. Having purchased a second paperweight, I was intrigued with its certificate, which finished with the words PH CANE.

Who was this person PH CANE? A hasty call to Caithness Glass followed, and Colin Terris quickly told me what a cane was. Steadily my collection grew, but I quickly found that each new addition brought with it a host of unanswered questions.

If only I had had a book that could have given me even some of the answers, I would have been very happy and much more knowledgeable. It would also have enabled me to purchase a rare Ysart bird worth $1000, which I passed by simply because I did not possess the knowledge to know otherwise. We all have regrets. I could have bought that paperweight for $45.

1969 saw the birth of the Planets by Caithness Glass, and with this event came the start of a whole new, large generation of paperweight collectors. Like myself, they were intrigued by these modern, and often abstract, designs.

I quickly came to realize that the needs of other collectors were much the same as mine, and relentlessly started noting down anything I had heard about the subject. Thus, the seeds of this book had been sown.

There is no doubt that the Ysart family had been largely instrumental in being the forerunners of the paperweight making scene in Britain, and my work begins there. An important aspect of the work has been an endeavor to try to catalog many of the paperweights, and related items, produced by a wide range of modern British manufacturers. For example, over four hundred Ysarts, one hundred and thirty Whitefriars, eighty Strathearns, and two hundred and fifty Caithness paperweights, and related items are listed, often with some indication of their features and value.

As my knowledge, and awareness, of the subject grew, so I began to appreciate how naïve it was to think that everything ever produced could be documented. The desire for completeness is of course a strong one. However, this has to be tempered with compromise, and I am well aware of the fact that the listings are still but a beginning.

In addition to providing illustrations and details of paperweights that the novice will spot, I have endeavored to show a reasonable number of rare, and possibly unique, items which have seldom or never been seen before. Thus, such rare paperweights as the Paul Ysart butterfly signed and dated 1937, the Salvador Ysart butterfly over double swirl latticinio ground, and the Whitefriars Royal Visit and magnum pedestal weights are included here.

We have Paul Ysart to thank for training many of today's great artists, including Peter Holmes, William Manson, and Colin Terris. Just as Salvador Ysart inspired and trained his sons in the art, so the reader can see the influence William Manson is having on his son and daughter. Read how John Deacons was inspired by early 19th century artists.

Most makers have interesting, often humorous stories to tell. This is certainly the case with Fred Daden, a skilled Whitefriars maker, introduced here for the first time to collectors. Thus, a little bit more of the jig-saw puzzle is completed.

With the vast army of collectors worldwide, it is becoming increasingly difficult to see, let alone to own, some of the many interesting glass paperweights, regardless of their value. Consequently, if this book enables them to see just one weight they have never seen before, or provides a piece of information to further their own understanding, then my efforts will not have been in vain.

Fig. 1. Dropping molten glass into a star shaped mold.
Courtesy of Perthshire Paperweights Ltd.

Fig. 2. Pulling a glass cane. Courtesy of
Perthshire Paperweights Ltd.

Chapter 1

The Manufacture of Glass Paperweights

Witnessing the manufacture of fine glass paperweights from beginning to end is an exceedingly fascinating and absorbing subject. Ideally, it needs to be seen a number of times, and preferably tried, in order to have a full appreciation of the process and skills required.

Clear glass

Considering firstly the manufacture of the clear glass itself, or metal as it is sometimes termed. The main ingredient is silica sand — this has to be of the highest quality if, after fusion with the other chemicals, top grade paperweights are to result. Caithness, for example, obtain theirs from Loch Aline in Argyll, Scotland. Perthshire's also originates from north west Scotland.

Caithness original formulation was:

Silica sand	65%
Sodium carbonate	14%
Calcium carbonate	6%
Potassium carbonate	6%
Lead monosilicate	4%
Sodium nitrate	4%
Arsenic	1%

After thorough mixing, the ingredients are melted in a furnace. This takes about fourteen hours at temperatures up to 1400°C. Furnaces vary in size, but it is not uncommon for a sizable manufacturer to melt a batch weighing up to three-quarters of a ton.

Irregularities in the batch are removed by boiling. This actually means stirring or agitating the melt. This can be done by the old traditional method of using a long iron bar tipped with a short log of silver birch that has been previously soaked in water. Almost instantaneously a huge bubble rises and breaks through the surface, clears the glass, and sends blasts of flame out of the furnace.

Canes

Three types will now be detailed: millefiori, silhouette, and portrait.

Millefiori

The manufacture of canes, the individual design elements, which are glass rods often of circular cross section, typically proceeds as follows.

A pontil rod is dipped into the tank of molten glass and a small amount of glass, known as a gather, adheres to the end. If a layer of color is required this can be done by rolling the layer in colored powdered glass or dipping it into molten colored glass. It is then shaped into an approximate cylindrical shape by rolling to and fro over a smooth flat block of iron known as a marver. Holding the pontil rod vertically the glass worker then pushes the molten gather into an iron mold that has the pattern that is to be reproduced suitably cut on the inner surface, figure 1. At this stage the molded shape is typically up to three inches in diameter and about six inches long.

After removing the molded shape and re-heating, a second pontil rod is attached to the opposite end and the two operators quickly run apart from each other, stretching the glass as they go, until it is perhaps thirty feet long and about 0.25" in diameter (figure 2). Whatever pattern was made is now perfectly miniaturized, although usually only a few feet at the center of this pulled cane will be of sufficiently good quality to end up being used in the paperweight.

For a single pattern thus formed, say an 8-toothed cog, such canes are referred to as simple. Complex canes are formed by taking a number of similar or differently patterned simple canes, binding them together, re-heating and again pulling to repeat the above mentioned process, figure 3. This procedure is sometimes repeated several times in order to produce the highly complex and colorful canes shown in figure 4.

Fig. 4. A good selection of Perthshire canes including portraits, and filigree.

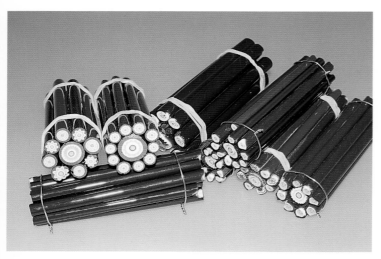

Fig. 3. Bound canes, ready for heating prior to pulling. Courtesy of Perthshire Paperweights Ltd.

Filigree and latticinio canes are made by lining a vertical iron collar with thin rods of colored or white glass, at even distances around the circumference, prior to introducing the clear mavered gather. Prior to pulling the cane, one end is attached to a small hand operated device that can rotate the cane while the operator at the other end walks away, see figure 5. The result is the familiar twist, common to many weights of traditional design.

Fig. 5. Twisting, and stretching a cane to make a filigree design. Courtesy of Perthshire Paperweights Ltd.

Silhouette

Made by the same process as millefiori canes, the cross section of the design is shaped within a suitable mold, only this time instead of say a geometric shape it could be an animal, bird, or a host of other things. The silhouette is usually in a single color surrounded by another color with which it contrasts.

Portrait

Here the design may again be an animal, bird, or some other figure but unlike the silhouette canes, the portrait type will be multi-colored. These are made by bundling together many very thin colored glass rods (about 0.03" – 0.06" diameter), to form a sort of mosaic image of the required design. After heating, the mass of rods fuse together and are pulled just like other canes. The selection of colors often presents its own problems, as different colors can expand and contract at different rates. Despite these limitations, portrait canes are capable of being produced which show an incredible amount of detail. Examples are shown in figures 6 to 8.

Fig. 6. Portrait canes (Perthshire) of a church, a butterfly, and Donald Duck.

Fig. 7. Portrait canes of a lion, horse and jockey, and frog.

Fig. 8. Detailed portrait canes, including golfer (middle of bottom row). Courtesy of Perthshire Paperweights Ltd.

9

Lampwork

Lampwork designs are made by heating and manipulating small pieces of glass with tweezers and other small tools. The glass is often in the form of thin glass rods, and these are heated with a blow-torch where the gas can be adjusted as necessary to give a very fine precision flame. The process is repeated until the complete design motif has been built up as in figure 9.

Fig. 9. Lampwork flowerhead receiving its finishing touches. Courtesy of Perthshire Paperweights Ltd.

Sulphides

These are technically demanding, if for no other reason than the fact that the composition of the sulphide is critical if differential thermal expansion of it, and the glass, are to be minimized. Chemically these cameos, as they are sometimes called, do not in fact contain a sulphide.

The first stage of manufacture is to make a model five times the size of the final sulphide in modeling clay. From this a plaster cast is made. Using the plaster cast a bronze mold is made and suitably dressed and polished. The bronze mold is mounted in a reduction lathe, which enables an exact miniaturization to be made, one fifth of the size, in steel. Finally, a plaster cast is made from the steel mold.

The specially formulated glass-clay paste is then poured into the plaster cast, pressed and heated to form the final sulphide which will later be incorporated into a paperweight. Most sulphides are white, colored designs being very rare.

Having given some details regarding the manufacture of canes, lampwork designs, and sulphides, the process by which these, either singly or in combination, are brought together to form the final paperweight will now be described.

Assembly

Canes are cut into slices about 0.06" – 0.13" thick and using tweezers, are placed upside down in a shallow circular iron dish or mold (figure 10) to form the design. For an intricate design this alone may take an hour. After heating the design and placing an iron collar over the mold a gather of glass on the end of a pontil rod is quickly but very surely lowered into the collar to pick up the design (figure 11). More glass is then gathered on top of the design to form what will eventually become the upper, clear dome of the paperweight.

Fig. 10. A millefiori set up. Pieces of cane being placed in a metal mold. Courtesy of Perthshire Paperweights Ltd.

By skillfully rolling the pontil rod over the arms of his chair the operator is able to maintain an even, circular profile. With a suitable wooden block, or carefully shaped pad of wet tissue paper, the operator wipes against the dome to give it its smooth surface (figure 12).

Using a tool known as priscillas, the operator narrows in the glass at the back of the design (figure 13). When sufficiently cool, a sharp tap causes the weight to break off and be caught in a suitable receptacle. From here the weight is taken to an annealing oven where it is allowed to cool slowly back down to room temperature. This last stage, taking up to twenty-four hours, is essential if subsequent shattering of the glass caused by internal stresses is to be avoided.

For those weights which are to be faceted, up to four different grades of grinding wheel and polishers are typically used, commencing, for example, with a diamond laced wheel and finishing with cerium oxide on a felt wheel for the final polish.

Although lampwork weights are made in the same general way, unlike the millefiori canes, the design is placed facing upwards prior to the initial placement of a gather of glass.

Fig. 11. Lowering of pontil rod and gather to pick up the design. Courtesy of Perthshire Paperweights Ltd.

Fig. 12. Shaping the dome while slowly rotating the pontil rod. Courtesy of Perthshire Paperweights Ltd.

Fig. 13. Narrowing in to form the base. Courtesy of Perthshire Paperweights Ltd.

Overlays

Overlay weights pose additional problems and are produced in various ways. Firstly, a small gather of clear glass is blown to form a bubble, rather like a hollow weight. A servitor with a rod tipped with glass, usually white, then carefully places the white gather onto the top of the bubble. After cutting away surplus white, the remainder is pulled and shaped over the clear bubble. This sandwich of color is then heated at the glory hole to enable an even flow of the white over the clear glass to be achieved. Following further work to ensure as even a coating as possible, the servitor and gaffer then repeat the pro-cess with the colored layer. After further blowing and shaping, the servitor places a very small gather of clear glass on the top of the multi-layered col-ored bubble. This bubble is then cracked free, and upon re-heating, the sharp, rough end becomes smooth and now appears like a bowl.

This bowl now has to be kept hot and in good shape to await the arrival of the weight which is to be overlaid. The hot weight is then lowered into the hollow overlay cup, where the marrying of the two together for similarity of size demands a good eye. Finally after applying a coating of clear glass from the furnace, the weight receives its final shaping and is then cracked off ready for annealing.

12

Cutting facets on overlay weights, as shown in figure 14, can present special problems, as, initially at least, the operator is to a degree working where the opaque layers obscure a good vision of the internal design and blind cutting is often resorted to.

Cutting printies around the sides and star cutting the base may well require two to four hours of work. Bearing all these factors in mind, it is not difficult to see why good overlay weights command a high price.

Fig. 14. Cutting facets on a blue, and white double overlay. Courtesy of Perthshire Paperweights Ltd.

Abstract designs

Along with the appearance in 1969 of the first Caithness abstract weights came the intrigue as to how these weights were made. Indeed, the techniques and materials adopted for some of the modern weights remains either a closely guarded secret, and/or a privileged skill of the expert paperweight makers who produce the weights.

Certain basic know-how applies, of course, to abstract weights just as much as it does to conventional weights, namely, the manner in which a weight is built up in stages, formation and polishing of the dome, faceting, and so forth. With regard to other information, fortunately a considerable amount of detail has now been released and is of obvious interest to the collector.

For example, by August 1979 Caithness had issued to members of the Caithness Paperweight Collectors Society an illustrated article detailing in thirty-one steps the production of their 'Snowflower' paperweight. Since 1981, Caithness have regularly published excellent articles[1-4] covering the manufacture

of a wide range of their paperweights. Figure 15, for example, shows the manufacture of ice dance.

Some abstract paperweights, form an excellent example of the way in which modern materials have been used successfully in conjunction with traditional techniques to produce results hitherto unachievable. A prime example of this is to be seen in the material which Selkirk Glass used to make the igloo/cavern effect that virtually makes an inner dome of their 'Ice Pool' weight (1979).

As might be expected, some techniques and effects consume much time and effort to perfect. Typical of this group is the translucent gold color developed and used by Peter Holmes in Selkirk's Argonaut, Midas, and Sceptre weights, and Ink bottle, all introduced in 1981. This effect alone took Peter Holmes at least two years of experimentation to achieve the desired color and stability. Early evidence showing the development of this color effect is to be seen in the same company's 'Space Pool' weight issued in 1978, where the gold effect is utilized in the lower bubble. Later examples of gold colored weights are Aztec and Labyrinth.

13

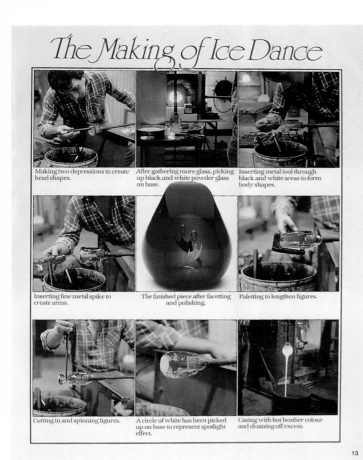

The Making of Ice Dance

Making two depressions to create head shapes.

After gathering more glass, picking up black and white powder glass on base.

Inserting metal tool through black and white areas to form body shapes.

Inserting fine metal spike to create arms.

The finished piece after facetting and polishing.

Paletting to lengthen figures.

Cutting in and spinning figures.

A circle of white has been picked up on base to represent spotlight effect.

Casing with hot heather colour and draining off excess.

13

Referring to chapter 7, the reader will see that hypodermic needles are used to pierce and expand specific air bubbles within a weight.

For more detail on the techniques used to make more traditional weights see McCawley[5], Kovacek[6], and Selman[7].

[1]Caithness Glass Ltd. Newsletter, September 1981.
[2]Caithness Glass Ltd. Newsletter, Spring 1982.
[3]Johnson, Glenn S. *The Caithness Collection.* U.S.A. 1981.
[4]Reflections. Journal published by Caithness Glass Ltd. for members of the Caithness Collectors' Club.
[5]McCawley, Patricia K. *Glass Paperweights.* London: Charles Letts Books Ltd., 1982.
[6]Kovacek, Michael. *Paperweights.* Vienna: Michael Kovacek, 1987.
[7]Selman, Lawrence H. *The Art of the Paperweight - Perthshire*. Santa Cruz, California: Paperweight Press, 1983.

Fig. 15. Eight stages of making Caithness' Ice Dance. Courtesy of Colin Terris, Caithness Glass Ltd.

Fig. 16. Paul Ysart during retirement at Wick, 1990. Courtesy of Colin Terris, Caithness Glass Ltd.

14

Chapter 2
Paul Ysart - his Father and Brothers

Often described as the 'father' of modern glass paperweights in Great Britain – the man who resurrected many of the skills from the mid-19th century era, Paul Ysart (figure 16) has represented all that is best in the production of weights spanning a period of more than five decades.

Prior to the publication of *Ysart Glass*, this doyen of paperweight makers' life history had only been briefly covered by other authors. The following abridged chronological listing gives some idea of this maker's background and career.

1904
Pablo (Paul) Moreno Ysart born in Barcelona, Spain. Like many great artists, it is hardly surprising that Paul's career was to be one of total involvement in glass, for his father (Salvador) and grandfather were both master glass blowers. Salvador's glass making tools dating from circa 1915 have been preserved and were on public view at Stuart Strathearn Ltd., Crieff, Scotland.

1915
The Ysart family emigrated to Scotland, via Lyons, Marseilles and Paris; and Salvador joined the Edinburgh and Leith Flint Glass Company (now Edinburgh Crystal). At the tender age of eleven Paul commenced his apprenticeship with this Company.

1916
The family moved to Glasgow, and worked for a glass company named Cochrane, which is no longer in existence.

1922
Family move to Perth and joined John Moncrieff Ltd. glass works.

1924
The Monart[1] range of colored glass vases, bowls, and lamps was developed by Mrs. Moncrieff and made by the Ysarts – hence the name Monart. Pieces were widely exported to the U.S.A. A few odd paperweights were probably made at this time, but only those made by Paul were to be of any real significance.

1938
Paul already making quality paperweights. Two examples featuring butterfly motifs were illustrated in the first edition of Bergstrom's book *Old Glass Paperweights*.

1946
Salvador, and Paul's brothers, Augustine and Vincent, left Moncrieff and formed a new Company at the Shore, Perth, known as Ysart Brothers Glass, naming their glass Vasart. Meanwhile Paul made some of his finest paperweights. Ysart's brothers made some millefiori weights but these were far below the quality of Paul's.

1955
Salvador died.

1956
Augustine died. Vasart Glass formed.

1962
Paul joined Caithness Glass Co. Ltd. at Wick in May as personnel officer, but paperweight production remained foremost in his mind. He was contracted to produce 288 weights per month, but the actual number he produced is unknown.

In the next seven years he was to produce over twenty different types of weights, and made an agreement whereby Paul Jokelson acted as sole distributor for his weights in the U.S.A. These weights contain a PY cane, and were sometimes sold in an appropriately marked box.

During the early 1960s, H.M. The Queen Mother made an official visit to Caithness Glass and to mark the occasion Paul made two perfume bottles, one of which was presented to her. It is believed that the design was a rose motif in the stopper and the base, together with a PY cane. (H.M. Queen Elizabeth II and H.M. The Queen Mother have a collection of Monart and Vasart items).

1964
Vasart Glass Company was re-formed, taken over by Teacher Ltd., and started trading in January 1965 as Strathearn Glass Ltd., managed by Stuart

Drysdale, who was later to form Perthshire Paperweights Ltd. A brochure issued by Strathearn stated 'The new company employs the same craftsmen under the guidance of Mr. Vincent Ysart.'

1971

Paul formed his own studio at Harland, Wick, Scotland.

1973

His secretary was a Mrs. Hendry.

1975

Paul formed Paul Ysart Glass Co.

1977

Paul formed Highland Paperweights Ltd. Because of his agreement regarding weights sold in the U.S.A., he also formed Highland Glass for the marketing of his weights in the U.K. These weights have an 'H' cane.

1978 – 81

Michael T. Vaughan acted as Paul's agent.

1979

Paul retires.

1991

In August, the staff of Broadfield House Glass Museum were fortunate to make the acquaintance of Mr. Robert Gunn of Lybster. He had set up and financed the Harland venture in 1971 and continued to act as backer until about 1975. Consequently, in 1991, Charles Hajdamach of the Glass Museum

Fig. 17. Bert and Louise Gunn. Bert is holding a millefiori, and a floating dahlia head weight. Photo taken in September 1991. Courtesy of Broadfield House Glass Museum, Dudley.

made two visits to meet Bert Gunn and his wife Louise (figure 17). The first visit took place between Friday 20 and Monday 23 September when Bert described many aspects of the venture. During that visit it was possible to find and identify the building at Harland farm where the weights were made, but it was not possible to arrange a meeting with Paul Ysart at his nursing home in nearby Wick. The second visit took place from Monday 11 to Wednesday 13 November. During both visits many weights were examined, all made at Harland, and which Bert Gunn had kept since that date. (All of the weights in the selling part of the Paul Ysart exhibition at Broadfield House Glass Museum, discussed below, were acquired from Bert Gunn on those two visits.)

From conversations with Bert Gunn various new pieces of information can be added to the Ysart/Harland episode. Gunn first heard of Paul Ysart through Gordon Brown who worked for Caithness Glass. "I searched round for several weeks to find a suitable place to start a paperweight factory and eventually I came across these old Air Force buildings outside Wick. They were used as radio stations and were built by friends of mine in Edinburgh, W. and G.R. Watson. When I saw them they were just the right size so I spoke to the farmer and asked him if he would lease the buildings to me. That's how we got started in paperweights at Harland, hence the "H" cane in the weights." Advice and equipment was sought from furnace builders Seismey and Linforth and the factory was operational within about two months. Paul Ysart made his own canes; the colors came from a German firm. Two or three assistants helped Ysart including William Manson. Paperweights were only produced in very limited numbers. Other products included bottles, decanters, and perfume bottles with canes inside. Designs were masterminded by Ysart. On one occasion Bert remembers going to Paris with Paul Ysart to meet Jokelson who still bought weights from Harland. Other weights were sent to Spinks in London, some to an agent in Glasgow, and others to Scotland Direct, a retailing outfit in New Lanark. Bert and Louise's daughter, Louise, often helped part-time in the packing shop.

Bert Gunn's overriding recollection of the whole period is of the "number of tricks that went on" including one attempt to poach Ysart from Harland. His general memories of Ysart are of a character who was very temperamental, who would easily fly off the handle and who fell out with everybody. The owner of the Harland site in 1991, Mr. Brims, remembers Ysart as a suspicious character worried that someone would steal his ideas. At that time Ysart and his wife lived in a council house in Lyth, and he drove each day to the workshop. Local anecdotes also recollect some sympathy for Ysart's wife. The end of Ysart's connection with Bert Gunn suggests that there is more than a grain of truth in these views. Before Ysart left the glasshouse finally, he threw a spanner into the glass pot to ruin the batch. Gunn called in the police chief and from his investigations it transpired that another officer had been trying to poach Ysart. Finally Gunn sold all the equipment and canes to Caithness Glass and packed the remaining stock away. He estimates that his loss on the venture ran into tens of thousands of pounds. His own building business kept him away from the glass works and his absence opened the door to various misdemeanors. Although glad to be rid of the business and reluctant to discuss too many of the problems, Bert Gunn appreciates and enjoys the beauty and skill of the paperweights, which would not have existed but for his financial support.

Paul died on December 18, 1991, at Pulteney House Nursing Home in Wick, Scotland, aged eighty-seven.

1992
The Broadfield House Glass Museum, Kingswinford, West Midlands held an exhibition of forty-five Paul Ysart paperweights[2]. At the same exhibition a listing of about two hundred and sixty weights was made available, these being the ones that Bert Gunn had carefully packed away in the mid-1970s. All were available for purchase at prices ranging from $75 to 420, and a good number were on public display. The selection included the main types of weights made at Harland e.g. Harlequin, Double harlequin, Fountain, Fountain with latticinio and scrambled base, Millefiori, Butterfly, Crown, Scrambled Dome, Scrambled Dome with ribbing, Floating Fish, Fish in Sand, Floating Dahlia Head, Floating Dahlia Flower, Dahlia Flowers in Sand, Heart, and Millefiori miniatures. A few weights had faceted cut ovals or are sliced across the top.

Unlike many of today's manufacturers, Paul Ysart did not issue brochures covering his weights. Instead, a select group of fine art dealers, that distributed his weights, would often feature them in their own catalogs and publicity adverts. Similarly, he kept no record of the limited or unlimited weights he issued; indeed, like paperweights made during the 19th century, a given design was rarely reproduced twice exactly the same. It is therefore impossible to list weights with any degree of completeness.

Ysart weights very rarely carry any identifying marks on the base and likewise accompanying certificates were never issued. The only exceptions were probably the few weights made for relatives and friends, which Paul would sometimes sign and date on the base.

An important and possibly unique paperweight is shown in figure 18. This butterfly is most unusual in that it has "P Y" and "19 37" incorporated into the wings. The flat, ground base is scratch signed "P. Ysart." Perth Museum acquired this exceptional weight at a local auction in 1993.

Fig. 18. Exceedingly rare signed, and dated butterfly, PY 1937. Paul Ysart. Dia. 3.55". Height 2.35". Courtesy of Perth Museum and Art Gallery, Perth and Kinross Council, Scotland. $1800/2200.

Labeling

Although virtually no weights were engraved or signed on the base, paper labels were clearly applied to some weights at the time of manufacture.

Some weights had a Monart label on the base. Besides this type two other designs were also used each carrying the initials "PY" and "Made in Scotland;" one of these (probably the earlier) was rectangular, while the other was circular. Caution is required however if trying to tie up the label with the possible date of manufacture, as occasionally whatever label was to hand would be put on a weight, and not necessarily agree with the period of manufacture. The fairly rare label shown in figure 19 is for Highland paperweights, the company Paul formed at Harland in 1977.

One known signed weight is a three dimensional red aventurine bodied fish above a rock ground set with a PY cane. The purple ground of this weight has been signed "P. Ysart" with a stylus. It fetched $600 at auction in 1994.

Figures 20 to 24 illustrate various Ysart weights showing the use of millefiori and lampwork, and figure 25 pictures some canes.

Maintaining secrecy is nothing new to glassmakers, and this is one reason why Paul would often make paperweights on Sunday mornings – he could usually guarantee that he would not be interrupted. In order to maintain secrecy, it was not unknown for him to plunge a nearly completed weight into a bucket of water if some unexpected person should suddenly appear on the scene. Another reason for the Sunday working was that he could have the sole access to a pot of glass for weights and experiments without fear of hindrance.

He did however allow himself to be filmed in 1971 (making a goblet) when he appeared together with Colin Terris, Peter Holmes, and William Manson in a program which was subsequently broadcast on British television.

Two years later on April 28, 1973, the newspaper *Daily Record* featured an article about Paul and his work. The accompanying picture showing him and his weights was somewhat surprising in that there were a high proportion of crowns shown – surprising that is in view of the relative scarcity of Ysart crowns.

Fig. 19. A relatively rare Highland label on a post 1977 paperweight. Courtesy of a private collector.

Although more commonplace now, Paul was one of the first modern makers to put a millefiori and lampwork design within the stopper of a millefiori inkwell.

The question is often asked regarding the number of paperweights Paul made during his long career. A precise answer cannot be given, but it is believed to be in excess of five to ten thousand. (In 1977 the *P.C.A. Bulletin* put his output at fifty per month). While the specific designs are unknown, it is known that in 1968 Paul's weights were being sold to the U.S.A. from approximately $25.

Fig. 20. A typical butterfly with a deep red aventurine body. Clear ground. Paul Ysart. Dia. 3". Height 1.8". $1000/1200.

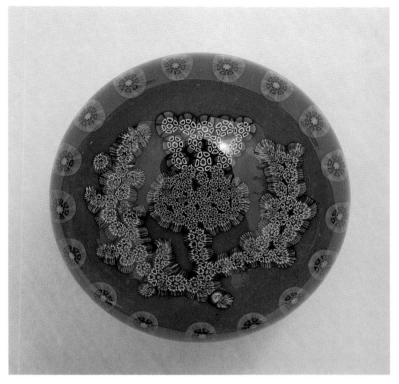

Fig. 21. Thistle design in millefiori on turquoise ground. PY cane. Paul Ysart. Dia. 3.25". Height 2.05". $600/800.

Fig. 22. Heart designs on blue and black grounds. Unsigned. Probably only about 100 were produced. Paul Ysart. Dia. 3". $550/750 each.

Fig. 23. Bouquet of well balanced design. Paul Ysart. Pre-1945. A fine pre-1945 piece. Pontil mark. Dia. 3.27". Height 2.25". $700/950.

Fig. 24. Bottle with PY canes in stopper and base, and an excellent range of canes. Some damage – reflected in its value. Probably pre-1945. Paul Ysart. Dia. 3.75". Height 4.75". $250.

Fig. 25. Complex canes, c. 1970, Paul referred to these as stones. The center stone in the top row contains over one hundred and thirty separate canes. Dia. 0.5". Courtesy of Colin Terris, Caithness Glass Ltd.

Canes

By far the most common cane shapes used by Paul Ysart are the cog and the star. Cogs appear in a very wide range of colors with 6, 8, 12, 16, 18, and 20 teeth. Six- and eight-point stars are frequently seen in virtually every millefiori weight. Five-point stars also exist.

Other cane profiles include concentric circles, and an octagon often seen inside an 8-toothed cog. A further cane with a rather strange appearance can be seen in figure 26. This consists of varying numbers of small rods fused around the perimeter of a circular rod – the final slice usually having a squashed spider-like appearance.

Fig. 26. Star and concentric millefiori patterns, pre-1945. Note the blue and mauve spider-like canes. Paul Ysart. Dia. 3.15". $400/500 each.

It is not uncommon to see distorted cogs, and yet somehow this can occasionally add to the appeal of a design, which sometimes has cog canes laid on their side.

A portrait cane of a butterfly is known, but these are very rare. An example is shown in figures 27 and 28. Salvador and Paul's brothers occasionally used a silhouette of a butterfly, but being of a single color this is less complex than Paul's. A spade cane was also made by them, and figure 29 illustrates these relatively rare designs.

Fig. 27. Rare scrambled millefiori with three butterfly portraits. Green jasper ground. Pontil mark. Paul Ysart. Dia. 3.5". Height 2.6". $1000/1300.

Fig. 28. Close up of Paul Ysart butterfly portrait cane shown in previous illustration.

Fig. 29. Butterfly and spade silhouettes in a close millefiori weight. Salvador or Paul's brothers. Courtesy of Anne Anderson.

Compared, therefore, with antique weights by the French makers, the range of different shapes utilized by Ysart is relatively small. However, it is the wide range of colors and designs which compensate for the limited number of shapes. Complex circular canes formed from six or more cogs or stars are common, and appear in a vast range of color combinations. A cross-like cane is another design occasionally seen (figure 30).

Latticinio is commonly used, as is filigree in a range of different colors including aventurine. These more frequently twist anti-clockwise (down towards the left). The number of strands most commonly used in latticinio are 4, 5, 8, 9, and 10.

A characteristic feature of Ysart's weights is that the canes and lampwork were invariably set in flush with the ground giving a very smooth profile when viewed from the side.

Two types of signature cane were used, as shown in figures 31 and 32. "PY" was used in some early weights (1930s), but after 1971 was reserved exclusively, in theory, for those exported to the U.S.A. In the *P.C.A. Newsletter* No. 117 (February 1995), it was revealed that Paul used two different methods to produce his "PY" canes. Details of both methods are given; and the newer method was probably not employed until after 1971. With the advent of Paul's studio at Harland, the "H" cane was adopted. Many weights had no signature cane.

A very few weights exist which carry a "Y" cane. These are pieces made by Paul's father, Salvador, and examples of such weights are shown later.

Fig. 30. Typical millefiori with radial filigree spokes. Pink and white cross type cane is at right hand side. Pre-1945. Paul Ysart. Dia. 3.4". Height 2.3". $350/450.

Fig. 31. PY signature cane used by Paul Ysart in some weights, with good complex canes. This example is in the stopper of the bottle shown in figure 24.

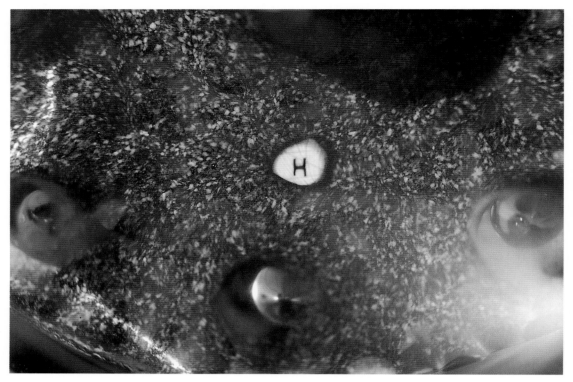

Fig. 32. H cane used by Paul Ysart at his Harland site from 1971 to 1975. This one is in a harlequin weight.

Early and late weights

Differentiating between weights made during the early (1930s and Monart) and later (Caithness, Harland) periods is not easy but can be generalized as follows.

Early weights sometimes tend to have a lower dome and a distinct un-polished pontil mark. Radial shrinkage lines can usually be seen coming away from the pontil mark (figure 33). Inside the circular line of the pontil is often rough, and has the appearance of many fine crystals and/or jagged facets. Another very relevant factor is the color of the glass in the dome. This is often somewhat dark and varies from one weight to another from gray to blue to yellow/brown hues. The color is most easily seen by taking a side view of the weight against a white background (figure 34).

Fig. 33. Pontil mark on the base of an early Paul Ysart weight. Note the many radial lines – a common feature on Paul's weights.

Fig. 34. Dark mauve dome glass, on weight with central clusters of canes including PY.
    Flat base. Pre-1945. Paul Ysart. Dia. 3.1". Height 2.4". $800/1000.

Later weights tend to have high domes of low color and bases tend to be ground flat and polished.

Examination under ultraviolet light also tends to show differences between early and late weights (see Chapter 13).

Subject range

Paul Ysart's weights cover a very wide range of subjects in millefiori and two- and three-dimensional lampwork. As the reference listing shows, subject matter ranges from concentric, scattered, and patterned millefiori work to butterflies, flowers, fish, mice, parrots, snakes, and sulphides.

Sulphides

Sulphides invariably present difficulties, and Ysart sulphides are rare. In the 1920s and 1930s, many housewives kept up the Scottish habit of whitening their front doorsteps. The whitening agent was available from local hardware stores, and Paul discovered that if he mixed this with water to make a paste and allowed it to dry, he could create his own sulphides which did not crack and were totally compatible with the glass that John Moncrieff of Perth produced at that time.

Furthermore, Paul tried coloring the resultant sulphides with metal oxides. A sulphide, conceivably by Paul Ysart is shown in figure 35. This piece, the clear glass of which is distinctly yellow, is believed to date from the 1920s or 1930s and was, prior to the 1960s, owned by someone having close connections with Scotland.

Fig. 35. Rare colored sulphide of ducks. Yellow tint to dome. Possibly 1920s or 1930s by Salvador or Paul Ysart. Courtesy of Colin Terris, Caithness Glass Ltd. $600/800.

A sulphide made by Paul in the 1930s is shown in figure 36. Rather appropriately this 2.5" dia. weight shows the Scottish emblem – the thistle, and was acquired in 1995 by a museum for $590.

Other known sulphides, with one example shown in figure 37, are as follows. (All except number five are believed to have been made in the 1930s.):

1. A head wearing a green and white striped turban, set on a blue ground and surrounded by an orange filigree with many yellow spots. Signed, but no PY cane. Value $975 in 1995.
2. H.M. King George VI and H.M. Queen Elizabeth set on a blue ground with eight peripheral canes. PY cane. Value $1275 in 1995.
3. Robert Burns set on a dark ground. Circle of peripheral canes in various colors. Value $260 in 1995.
4. Eagle, facing right, within a red and white torsade; all on a dark ground. Signed. 3.5" dia. Value $1320 in 1997.
5. Woman's head, facing left, set on a dark ground. Peripheral canes include a PY. 3" dia. Value $1320 in 1997. This is one of three weights featuring the same sulphide, which were probably made in 1946 or 1947. For more details see the P.C.A. Bulletin 1983, page 29.
6. Woman's head, facing left, set on a clear ground with twelve peripheral canes in white and yellow, and a PY cane.
7. Horse's head, facing left, set on a dark ground with a circle of peripheral canes including a PY cane.

Fig. 37. Sulphide of woman's head facing left. Dark ground. PY cane. Paul Ysart. Dia. 3". Courtesy of Sweetbriar Gallery Archive. $1350/1500.

Difficulty of manufacture

Not too much is known about which weights Paul found most difficult to make, but it is a fact that he was very excited when he produced a floating trout, and then topped this by making a weight with two trout.

Crowns are not common. It is not known whether Paul found these difficult to make. Magnum weights are also relatively rare and were probably made for friends. An example is shown in figure 38.

Faceting

It is very rare to see any Paul Ysart weights that have been faceted. The reason so few were faceted is not known. One known example of a weight having a top facet shows a blue flower within a circle of canes. This is illustrated in Paul Jokelson's book, *One Hundred of the Most Important Paperweights*, plate 99.

Forgeries

The art world has long been plagued by fakes and forgeries. Fortunately for the collector, the field of glass paperweights has been relatively free from this problem.

Sadly, however, forged weights purporting to have been made by Paul Ysart have appeared

Fig. 36. Colored thistle sulphide. Signed. Original label. Paul Ysart. Courtesy of Sweetbriar Gallery Archive. $600/700.

Fig. 38. Magnum showing a wide range of variously colored filigree. Pre-1945. Magnum weights are relatively rare. Paul Ysart. Dia. 4.25". Height 3". $500/650.

on the market in recent years. These weights are thought to have been made between late 1987 and 1989. A fairly large number (possibly about one thousand) were produced and appeared at large auction houses as well as other outlets such as antiques fairs.

Quality was variable, some being poor while others were of good workmanship. To further add to the confusion many of the forgeries contain original Ysart (but not Paul Ysart) canes from the Vasart factory.

Fortunately there are usually a number of ways to distinguish forgeries from genuine weights, and these can be summarized as follows:

1. PY cane.

Close examination will reveal that in forgeries (figures 39 and 40) the Y is set lower than the P, whereas in genuine weights the P and Y are effectively level with each other, compare with figure 31. In forged canes the letters are often shown in different colors such as an orange P and a red Y. Genuine canes usually have the P and Y in red surrounded by white with green on the outside.

Fig. 39. A fake Paul Ysart floral weight. Ground out pontil. Dia. 2.7". Height 1.65". $200/300.

Fig. 40. PY cane in a fake Paul Ysart weight. Note the Y set low, and the 20-point cog cane.

2. Cog cane in which PY is placed.

Forged cogs usually have twenty points. Although Paul Ysart used twenty point cogs, it is believed that he made far greater use of sixteen point cogs.

3. Base.

The center of the base of forgeries is slightly concave where the pontil mark has been ground out, and fine parallel lines made by the grinding wheel are visible even to the naked eye.

4. Color of glass.

Not an absolute test in itself, but the dome is always of crystal clear glass, and not tinted as per early Ysart weights.

5. Dome height.

The height of the dome is typically much lower in forgeries, this often having the effect of minimizing the magnification of the motif.

6. Filigree or Latticinio spokes.

Where radial spokes are employed Ysart typically used 12, 14, or 18 pieces whereas in forgeries 20 or more are normally present.

7. U.V. Fluorescence.

Under U.V. light the fluorescence of forgeries is usually quite different to that of the genuine article. (See chapter 13.)

Many collectors of Paul Ysart paperweights are keen to have a forgery in their collection, if only for purposes of comparison and as a talking point. Their value is typically up to about $220.

Detailed review of Paul Ysart weights by type

No.	Design	Date manufactured, where known	Value $ in year stated
	General millefiori		
1.	Heart, open design of cogs within an outer circle of blue and pink canes. Purple ground. Pontil mark.	ca. 1940	150/1982
2.	Star, 6 point orange, with pink, and white cogs forming infill pattern. Blue ground. Pontil mark. 3.15".	Pre-1962	150/1982
3.	Concentric millefiori of stars and cogs in outer circle of yellow canes. Speckled purple ground. Pontil mark. 3.15"	Pre-1962	150/1982
4.	Concentric millefiori with cogs, peripheral cogs interspersed with white latticinio.		
5.	Concentric millefiori of circular complex canes.		
6.	Concentric millefiori. Four rows with blue center cane. 4 + 1 faceting.		
7.	Concentric millefiori. Four rows mauve, blue, green, and purple containing cogs.		
8.	Concentric millefiori. Central mauve and blue set up within circle of green canes divided by gilt aventurine and latticinio twists. Opaque pink ground. 3".		22/1978
9.	Concentric millefiori. Central set up of blue and turquoise canes within an outer circle of alternate green and ochre canes divided by latticinio cable. Opaque blue ground. 2.9".		22/1978
10.	Concentric millefiori, predominately red, green, blue, and white on white ground.		
11.	Concentric millefiori. Central red and white cane within circle of lime-green canes. Green and red canes at periphery divided by latticinio thread. Opaque turquoise ground. 3.25".		24/1979
12.	Patterned millefiori. Central white, blue, and pink canes surrounded by six large green set-ups. Black ground. 3".		60/1978
13.	Patterned millefiori. Large orange canes at periphery divided by colored and gilt latticinio. Translucent dark blue ground. 3.5".		100/1979
14.	Patterned millefiori. Clusters of five canes radiating from central pink and white set up. Mottled translucent pink ground. 3".		60/1979
15.	Patterned millefiori. Central clump of colored canes within circlet of orange and yellow set ups. Eight large white peripheral canes divided by gilt and white, yellow and orange latticinio. Blue ground. 3.25".		70/1979
16.	Patterned millefiori. Large blue central set up surrounded by two circles of white and pairs of turquoise canes divided by latticinio ribbon.		20/1979

No.	Design	Date manufactured, where known	Value $ in year stated
	Opaque blue ground. 2.35".		
17.	As above, but on a pink ground. 2.35".		20/1979
18.	Star pattern millefiori. Six point close pack design with six pink and white peripheral circular canes. 3".		
19.	Star pattern millefiori. Six point, mainly white and pink cogs, with six peripheral green and yellow canes. Dark blue mottled ground.		
20.	Star pattern millefiori. Five point, pink and white cogs. Five peripheral green, white, and pink canes. Light blue ground.		250/1980
21.	Star pattern of colored set-ups in blue, pink, and white. Green ground. 3".		25/1971
22.	Star pattern millefiori of brightly colored canes, within garland of hollow orange canes divided by colored latticinio, cobalt blue ground. 3.25".		55/1978
23.	Star pattern millefiori. Five point, large green and white cogs. Five large complex peripheral canes. Blue ground.		
24.	Panel weight. Alternate red and green panels divided by blue spokes forming a hexagon. Light colored ground.		
25.	Panel weight. Twelve segments in turquoise, around central designs of seven units. Aventurine spokes.		
26.	Scattered millefiori and latticinio.		
27.	Close millefiori cluster within circle of pink canes. 2.75".	1965	
28.	Clusters of canes, various colors. Smokey ground. 2.75".	1965	
29.	Harlequin. Multi-colored canes. Peripheral bubbles, and central bubble. H cane.		30/1978
30.	Clusters of canes in green, pink, and blue. PY cane.		345/1978
31.	Close set millefiori, multi-colored canes within circle of pink and white canes.		210/1978
32.	Multi-colored canes in center within circle of white and blue canes divided by yellow ribbons. Blue ground.		
33.	Millefiori central cluster, pink and blue canes in garland. 2.9".		60/1974
34.	Millefiori central cluster within outer garland of alternate pink and green canes. PY cane. 3.15".		66/1975
35.	Millefiori, central group of close packed canes within peripheral circle of pink canes. PY cane.		85/1974
36.	Concentric millefiori. Five circles of canes on dark green ground. PY cane. 3.75".	1950-80	
37.	Close pack millefiori at center includes a PY cane.	1940	

Outer ring of blue/white and ochre canes. 3".

38. Spaced millefiori. Five large pink canes at the points of a pentagon. Blue and white cane at center. PY cane. Dark ground. 5 + 1 faceting, 3". — 1950-80

39. Close concentric millefiori. Four circles, including one of green/white/red cogs about a central complex cane. PY cane. 3". — Pre-1980

40. Latticinio scramble with prominent orange and blue canes. — Pre-1962 — 75/1990

41. Four concentric circles, two of which are latticinio twists with alternate canes in green and pink. Large central cog. — Pre-1962 — 75/1990

42. Concentric millefiori. 3 rows about a central complex cane. Predominantly orange, green, and yellow canes.

43. Concentric with alternate red ochre canes and latticinio twists around the circumference. Dark ground.

44. Central cluster of complex canes within outer garland of orange star canes interspersed with others. Dark ground.

45. Spaced concentric. 2 circles with a total of 12 canes about a central complex cane; all set on yellow and white filigree ground. PY cane. Flat base. 2.9".

46. Concentric millefiori. Canes at perimeter interspersed with 12 latticinio spokes. Clear ground.

47. Spaced millefiori. 5 large complex canes surround a central white cog with 12 points. 5 green and white perimeter cogs. Blue ground.

48. Central cluster of many different canes set close. Outer ring of 32 alternating latticinio and cog canes. Blue ground.

49. Circle of 15 pink cogs around a pink snowflake design. Surrounded by 22 alternating latticinio and green and white cogs. Dark ground.

50. Assorted colored cogs surrounding central floret. Twenty-eight alternating latticinio, and pink and blue cogs at circumference. Blue/gray ground. Pontil mark. 3"

51. Concentric with 4 circles predominantly in pink, blue, mauve, and white canes. Clear ground.

52. Five large mauve canes about a small central cluster. Alternating canes and latticinio at circumference. Dark ground.

53. Central cluster of blue and white canes within an outer garland of large canes. Dark ground.

54. Three concentric circles of canes, predominantly green and pink cogs. Five central pink canes enclose a blue cross design. Mauve ground. 3.5" Pontil mark. — Pre-1962 — 115/1990

55. Three concentric circles of canes, the outer one with turquoise and white cogs alternating with yellow and blue latticinio. Central peach and yellow cane. Blue ground. Pontil mark. 3.15" — Pre-1962 — 115/1990

56. Central cluster of green, white, and pink canes. Alternating white and pink canes at periphery. Translucent green ground. Pontil mark. 3.15" — Pre-1962 — 115/1990

57. Magnum consisting mainly of latticinio in at least 10 color combinations and blue and white cogs. Deep turquoise ground. Pontil mark. 4.35" — Pre-1962 — 165/1990

58. Orange, yellow, and white filigree rising from a red ground. Made with and without an H cane. Tall form weight 2.5" — Post-1977

59. Spaced millefiori of 12 canes about a central complex cane. Yellow ground. H cane. 3" — Post-1971

60. Circle of cog and complex canes about a central green complex cane. 6 peripheral complex canes. Green filigree ground. Flat base. H cane. 2.75" — Post-1971

61. Two circles of mixed cogs about a central complex cane. Alternating pink cogs and yellow filigree, 20 in total, at periphery. Black ground. Pontil mark. 3"

62. Six pointed star of closely packed canes with six green, red, and white peripheral canes. Pale blue ground. 2.75"

63. Six point snowflake design in large canes. Six large cogs at periphery. Sodden snow ground. PY cane 3.15"

64. Polychrome cluster of canes set within a circle of — Pre-1970

green canes PY cane. 2.75"

65. Close millefiori with an outer circle of yellow and white canes. PY cane. 3.15" — Pre-1970

66. Close millefiori of assorted canes including three butterfly silhouettes. Green jasper ground. Pontil mark. 3.15" — 260/1991

67. Fourteen peripheral green and white cogs laid radially and alternating with orange and white cogs. Four blue cogs at center surrounded by eight green cogs, and a circle of pink cogs, and orange, and yellow canes.

68. Central cluster of canes within a circle of 12 pale cream cogs. 12 latticinio spokes with gold aventurine and canes around periphery. Pontil mark. 3" — 1930s

69. Central yellow and orange cog cane surrounded by five complex canes and then a circle of 15 cog canes. All within an outer circle of complex pink cog canes and latticinio. Translucent blue ground. 2.95" — 385/1991

70. Unusual design of 3 'C' scroll type designs of pink cogs and complex cogs set around a central group of canes. Dark blue ground. PY cane. 3" — 290/1991

71. Close millefiori center cluster including a PY cane, set within a circle of alternating blue and puce cogs. High amethyst dome. Flat base. — 435/1991

72. Concentric with blue and white cogs alternating with latticinio in outer row. Next row alternating pink and green, then a circle of white canes about a central 6 point yellow/orange star. Dark ground. — 345/1991

73. A central close millefiori cluster suspended within a basket of alternating orange, green, and white cogs, and white and yellow cogs. — 400/1991

74. Central cluster of canes with a peripheral circle of orange, red, and blue canes. PY cane. 3" — 8/1950

75. Central cluster of complex canes within an outer circle of alternating green/white and pink, and white, and pink canes. Dark blue tinted glass. Flat base. PY cane. 3.05" — 1930s — 345/1992

76. Spaced millefiori of 5 large clusters about a central blue and white cane. Five large green, white, and yellow cogs around perimeter. Light blue mottled ground. Pontil mark. 2.65" — 220/1991

77. Super magnum, 6 point star design of complex canes interspersed with 6 large green and white cogs. Six large yellow peripheral canes. Amber flash ground. Over 5" in dia., and 3" high. Made for the New Zealand importers John Paine during the 1930s. Now in a private collection in New Zealand. PY cane close to a large cog. — 1930s

78. Six pointed star with a yellow floret at each intersection. Translucent brown ground. Printed paper label marked 'Moncrieff Scotland'. PY cane. 4.9" — 110/1976

79. Heart, open design of pink cogs and a central complex cane. Outer circle of alternate yellow and orange canes. Dark blue ground. 3" — Pre-1962 — 600/1995

80. Heart, open design of pink cogs and a central blue flower. Circle of alternate pink with orange, and blue canes. Royal blue ground. 3.15" — Pre-1962

81. Heart, filled in design with PY cane, set above a basket of white filigree. — 450/1989

82. Star pattern with 6 points. Interspersed with 6 large green and white cogs. Buff colored ground. — 420/1989

83. Spaced concentric. Outer ring of white cogs alternating with complex green and white cogs central PY cane. Deep purple ground. — 375/1989

84. Concentric millefiori of 2 circles of complex canes predominantly green and pink, set about a central complex cane.

85. Heart, open design with PY cane at top. Set above white filigree basket. 2.75" — 1976

86. Heart design with 24 cog canes and another cane at the center, all within a circle of canes. Dark ground. 3" — 67/1978

87. Heart design of 18 complex canes with a further cane at the center. Within a garland of alternating green and white cogs and complex canes. Dark ground.

29

No.	Design	Date manufactured, where known	Value $ in year stated
88.	Heart design in canes. Ten peripheral canes. Dark ground.		
89.	Spaced concentric with central pink, orange, and white cane surrounded by 5 green canes and a circle of cobalt blue canes. Within a basket of white latticinio and 9 amethyst canes. PY cane 2.8"		680/1993
90.	Magnum open concentric with complex cog canes in fuchsia, orange, blue, and green interspersed with white, orange, and chartreuse filigree. Dark green ground. PY cane 4.15"		1100/1993

Flowers

No.	Design	Date manufactured, where known	Value $ in year stated
91.	Red flower with 6 petals. Stem and leaves set above 12 latticinio spokes. Pale blue ground. PY cane.		
92.	Five petaled blue and white clematis with 5 leaves and a stem. Circled by large complex green, white, and yellow cogs and smaller orange cogs and other complex canes. Blue ground.		
93.	Bouquet of seven lampwork flowers and leaves, surrounded by circle of mauve and white complex canes. Pink ground. PY cane.		510/1989
94.	Pink flower with five petals and central PY cane. Set on cruciform[3] of iridescent green/gold leaves. All on a cushion of alternate maroon and white filigree.		450/1989
95.	Pink flower with central millefiori cane, with leaves and stem. All within ring of complex canes. Four large and four small side facets and one top facet. PY cane. Deep purple ground.		560/1989
96.	Six petaled pink clematis with gold flakes, central complex cane. PY at center of flower. Iridescent green leaves. Opaque orange ground with white filigree spokes and 6 canes around circumference.		465/1989
97.	Six petaled purple flower, central cane in yellow white, and green. Circle of canes in lime, white, and maroon. Salmon ground.		375/1989
98.	Bouquet of 7 flowers with leaves and stems. PY at center of central flower. Stave basket of yellow and white filigree, enclosing four rods of gold flake.		560/1989
99.	Bouquet of 3 flowers in red, blue, and white, with PY cane at center of red flower. Set in white filigree stave basket.		510/1989
100.	Pink flower with 6 petals. Complex star cane at center. Leaves and stem. White filigree basket.		375/1989
101.	Blue and white striped double clematis with 10 petals. Leaves with PY cane at base of stem. Royal blue ground.		520/1989
102.	Coral colored double clematis with 10 petals. Central white cane. Four leaves with PY cane at base of stem. Set on basket of two types of white filigree.		470/1989
103.	Six petaled pink clematis with central complex cane. Six leaves and PY cane at base of stem. Textured sandy ground.		285/1989
104.	Two flowers; purple and white with purple, with complex central canes. Two buds, leaves, and stems. PY between stems. Outer circle of spaced canes. Lacy cushion.		465/1989
105.	Bouquet of 5 small flowers and stems. Two complex canes at base of stems. Circle of canes containing 5 white and yellow which alternate with green and orange.		
106.	Pink and gold flower with 10 petals. Four leaves and stem. Circle of pink canes. Blue ground.		
107.	Pink clematis with 6 petals, complete with stem and leaves. Set on cushion of radiating filigree twists including threads of green aventurine. PY cane. 2.75"		480/1989
108.	Five petaled white flower with gold aventurine stripes, and central blue cane. Seven leaves and stem. Set within outer garland of alternate blue and pink cog canes. Dark ground.	1968	12/1970
109.	Pink flower, 5 petals and 8 leaves. PY cane	1963	
	at base of stem. Circled by pink and red canes. Green ground. Caithness 1963 on base.		
110.	Bouquet of 5 small flowers and 1 large blue flower. PY cane. White filigree basket. 3"	1960/80	
111.	Pink flower with 5 petals. Leaves, stem and PY cane. White filigree basket. 3"	1963	
112.	A cruciform of overlapping green leaves, the central point with a pink cane inscribed PY. Ground of radiating hollow yellow and white latticinio. 3.5"		530/1990
113.	Central posy with pink and white flower and smaller flowers on a ground of white and yellow filigree. PY cane. Pontil mark. 3.5"		250/1990
114.	A posy of pink, purple, and white flowers with a pink ribbon within a garland of pink and white canes. PY cane. 3.15"		300/1990
115.	Clematis type flower and 5 smaller flowers within a garland of pink and white filigree staves. PY cane. 3"		215/1990
116.	Bouquet of 5 flowers within white, yellow, and blue perimeter canes. Dark ground.		
117.	Magnum of blue, mauve, and pink 5 petaled flowers within outer garland of canes. Dark ground. Pontil mark. 3.75"	1930s	
118.	Cream clematis with 5 petals within garland of cogs and complex canes. Dark ground.		
119.	Pink clematis with 5 petals, and a yellow center; within an outer garland. Dark ground.		
120.	Four leaf clover within a garland of 20 alternating cog canes. Translucent ground.		500/1995
121.	Red flower with 5 petals, with stems, bud and leaves. Dark blue translucent ground. Pedestal base. PY cane. 2.75"		765/1990
122.	Flower with 5 cream petals and 5 leaves. Yellow center. Two concentric rows of canes - blue, and orange. Blue ground. Pontil mark. 3"	Pre-1962	210/1990
123.	Two yellow roses, stems and 8 leaves on black ground. Pontil mark. PY cane. 3"		
124.	Pansy with 2 blue and 3 orange and black petals, stem and 6 leaves. Blue ground. Pontil mark. PY cane. 2.75"	1930s	
125.	Yellow dahlia with 10 petals, stem and 3 leaves. Green cog and pink peripheral canes. Lilac ground. Flat base. PY cane. 2.75"		
126.	Flower with 10 mauve petals, stem and 3 leaves within a circle of pink canes. Brown ground pedestal. PY cane. 3.75"		
127.	Flower with 6 pointed yellow and red petals with stem and leaves. Red and white jasper ground. H cane. 2.75"	Post-1971	
128.	Flower with 4 striped orange petals, stem, leaves and bud. 8 additional leaves at periphery. On scattered latticinio ground. Flat base. 2.75"		
129.	Blue striped white flower with 5 petals, stem, and 9 leaves. 8 blue canes at periphery. Set on radiating latticinio and red ground. PY cane. 2.75"		
130.	Blue flower, stem, and leaves set over a basket of green/white cogs and filigree. PY cane. 2.75"		
131.	Red and cream flower with 12 petals, stem, and leaves over latticinio basket. Pontil mark. PY cane. 2.75"		
132.	Five petaled pink and yellow flower with stem and 8 leaves set over a basket of green and white cogs. Pontil mark. PY cane. 3"		
133.	White flower with central red complex cane, stem and 3 leaves over a basket of red cogs and latticinio. Pontil mark. PY cane. 2.75"		
134.	Flower with 5 orange striped cream petals and 5 leaves. Blue, white, and gold ground. 8 peripheral bubbles. H cane. 2.75"	Post-1971	
135.	Gold aventurine striped turquoise flower with 10 petals. Stem and leaves. Red and white jasper ground. Flat base. PY cane. 2.9"		
136.	Bouquet of flowers with large central 5 petaled flower. Stems tied with ribbon. Yellow and white jasper ground. 2.75"		
137.	Flower with 10 red striped white petals. Peripheral circle of green complex canes. Smokey gray ground. Pontil mark. PY cane. 3"		

138. Small 5 petaled white flower at center of crucifix form of green leaves. On radiating latticinio set on a red ground. PY cane. 2.75"[3]

139. Seven flowers and stems set in a blue vase shaped and colored in the Monart style. Black ground. Pontil mark. PY cane. 2.75". This is one of only about 6 weights made with a Monart vase in the design. — 1930s

140. Large 6 petaled blue flower, leaves, and 9 small flowers set on black ground. PY cane. 3". Paper label over pontil. — 1930s — 825/1992

141. Blue flower and blue bud on tall stems in a red vase. Dark green moss ground. 3.25" — Pre-1977

142. Bouquet of 6 flowers and stems with 2 pink canes at base. Pink ground. Flat base. PY cane 2.75"

143. Ten petaled white flower. Six peripheral canes all on scrambled filigree ground. Flat base. H Cane. 2.75" — Post-1971

144. Yellow flower set with a garland on transparent cobalt blue ground. 3" — 375/1986

145. Orange flower on yellow ground with latticinio. — 430/1986

146. Two clematis, blue and ochre set in garland of dark-green and ochre canes, one with PY cane. Semi-translucent pale green ground. 2.75" — 360/1990

147. Beige clematis with petals striped in red and orange. Central green and white cane, 3 leaves, garland of green, white, and mauve canes. Dark Ground. PY cane. 3" — 525/1990

148. Purple clematis with 10 petals about a central white cane. 3 ribbed leaves. Contained in a basket of green-centered amber canes. PY cane. 2.75" — 540/1990

149. Loose bouquet of 5 flowers and a bud tied with blue cord. Contained in a basket of lime-green, turquoise and latticinio hollow canes. PY cane. 2.9" — 720/1990

150. Orange striped yellow flower with 5 petals, stem and 8 leaves. Set above basket of pink cog canes. Pontil mark. PY cane. 2.75"

151. Bouquet of 5 flowers in blue, mauve, and pink with 2 green canes at base of stems, 20 peripheral canes in 5 groups of 3 white/orange and 1 yellow. Black ground. Pontil mark. 3.15" — 1930s — 230/1991

152. Bouquet of 6 flowers in various shades of pink, blue, and yellow. 11 latticinio spokes with gold aventurine cores alternating with 11 canes around periphery. Clear ground. Pontil ground out. 2.9" — 1930s

153. Pink and orange striped double clematis with 10 petals. Leaves. PY cane at base of stem. Blue and white jasper ground. 3.05" — 530/1991

154. Bouquet of 6 flowers and 3 veined leaves. Set within a basket of canes. 2.9" — 580/1991

155. Bouquet of 5 flowers in blue, yellow, and pink. 2 white/orange cog canes at base of stems. 20 peripheral canes in white, yellow, and green. Blue ground. Pontil mark. 3.15" — 1930s — 230/1991

156. Yellow flower with green aventurine leaves, within a circle of pink cogs including a PY cane. Mauve ground. — 450/1990

157. Five petaled blue flower and leaves within circle of pink complex canes, and a circle of green and orange cogs. Light blue ground. — 300/1990

158. Five petaled pale blue flower, 8 leaves and stem within circle of pink and white canes. Blue ground. — 435/1991

159. Five petaled cream flower with 4 leaves within circle of mauve canes and another circle of green and orange canes. Dark canes. — 345/1991

160. Central bouquet of flowers with long leaves tied with an aventurine bow. PY cane. 2.75" — 10/1950

161. Pink flower with 10 petals in two tiers, with white and orange center. Stem and three leaves. Light blue mottled ground. PY cane. 2.05" — 570/1992

162. Two flower bouquet. An orange and yellow striped flower and a yellow flower with gold aventurine stripes. Two buds, stems and leaves. — 330/1992

Mottled pink ground. PY cane. 2.65"

163. Blue and yellow flower with stem and leaves made by Debbie Tarsitano, circled by 11 pink, white, and orange complex star canes made by Paul Ysart. Clear ground. DT and PY canes. 2.75"

    A bouquet made by Debbie in the early 1980s had an Ysart cane at the center of a flower. Value $700. — 520/1992

164. Bouquet with large central purple clematis and 11 small flowers. Leaves and stems. Set on a filigree basket of 9 yellow and 9 white staves. Pontil mark. PY cane. 3.35" — 520/1992

165. Blue flower with 5 petals, on stem with 9 leaves within a circle of blue and white complex canes. Mauve ground. Top facet. PY cane. 3" — Pre-1966

166. Blue flower with 8 petals, stem and 3 leaves set into a three dimensional latticinio and cane basket. Pontil mark. 2.5" — 285/1991

167. Pink flower with 5 petals and central cog cane, stem and 8 leaves. Peripheral circle of alternating orange cogs and latticinio. Dark ground. Flat base. 3" — 370/1992

168. Double clematis with 12 blue striped white petals on a stem with 3 leaves. Outer circle of blue and white cog canes. Opaque black ground. PY cane. 2.9" — 670/1992

169. Purple thistle with green leaves all in cane work. Outer circle of 17 canes. Turquoise ground. PY cane. Flat base. 3.25" — 490/1992

170. Bouquet of 8 small flowers set within long leaves tied with a red aventurine bow. Clear ground. PY cane. — 490/1992

171. Purple thistle with 12 canes forming the flower, the design with leaves made entirely of canes. Black ground. Dark tinted dome. Flat base. PY cane. 2.75"

172. Bouquet of 5 flowers on four slender leaves with orange centered purple canes both sides of the stems. Translucent emerald green ground. PY cane. 3" — 290/1982

173. Clematis with 10 pink ribbed petals and 3 leaves on the stalk, within a garland of alternate pink and ochre canes. Translucent dark green ground. PY cane. 3" — 405/1985

174. Three large 5-petal flowers in pale mauve, pink, and light blue, each surrounded with leaves and alternating with 3 purple and white canes. All within a garland of alternate blue and white canes. Translucent dark brown ground. PY cane. 3.75" — 970/1985

175. Bouquet of 5 flowers and a bud in blue, purple, and pink with 5 leaves. Stalks tied with blue ribbon. Peripheral circle of 8 large pale blue and green canes. Translucent pale gray/blue ground. PY cane at center of one flower. 3" — 485/1985

176. Bouquet of 6 flowers in lavender, blue, pink, and white with 4 leaves. Stalks tied with blue ribbon. Peripheral circle of red, white, and turquoise canes. Translucent gray/green ground. PY cane at base of flowers. 3" — 485/1985

177. Flower with 6 shaded pink and yellow petals, stalk and a total of 8 leaves. Set in a basket of hollow yellow and white filigree tubes. PY cane. 2.9" — 540/1984

178. Flower with 5 blue striped white petals, stem and 7 leaves. Peripheral canes alternating in lime green, cobalt blue, red, and white. Translucent cobalt blue ground. PY cane. 3.05" — 410/1987

179. Bouquet of 5 small flowers in pink, lilac and yellow the stalks tied with a gilt aventurine bow. Spirally twisted lengths of filigree in white and green radiate from the bouquet. Translucent red ground. PY cane. 2.75"

180. Bouquet of 6 flowers in blue, white, and mauve with stems and 6 leaves. Stems tied with blue ribbon. All within a basket of turquoise and white cog canes. PY cane.

181. Five petaled salmon pink flower, stem, and 8 leaves encircled by green, orange, white, pink, — 770/1993

and yellow canes. Translucent wine colored ground. PY cane. 3"

182. Slightly unusual flower with 7 pistachio, orange and white striped petals interspersed with 7 leaves. Three further leaves on the stem. Red and white jasper ground. PY cane. 3.25" — 550/1993

183. Double clematis with 10 ridged pink and blue petals in 2 tiers, and a stem with 2 leaves; all floating within a white latticinio basket. PY cane. 2.9" — 600/1993

184. Bouquet of 3 flowers in blue, yellow, and pink with long stems within a circle of complex canes in green, chartreuse, and lavender. One further cane is placed each side of the stems. Cobalt blue ground. PY cane. 2.9" — 770/1993

185. Five petaled pink flower with 8 leaves and stem, floating in a white latticinio basket with 5 pink, white, and orange cane spokes. PY cane. 2.75" — 825/1993

186. Pink flower with 5 striped petals with red, white, and green central cane. Stem and 8 leaves. Peripheral circle of 16 complex pink, white, and green cog canes. Translucent green ground. PY cane. 3" — 700/1993

187. Orange flower with 5 petals with central red and white cog cane, with stem and 8 leaves. Set above a basket alternating with 2 white latticinio tubes and 1 light blue and white twist. PY cane. 2.8" — 600/1993

188. Red flower with 10 petals. Stem set with leaves. All within a white latticinio basket containing 5 spaced green spokes. PY cane. — 675/1993

189. Pink flower with 5 petals, aventurine stem with leaves, all within a garland of large blue and small white canes. Translucent blue ground. 3" — 135/1976

190. Five petaled royal blue clematis with red center and 5 leaves. Two outer circles of green and white, and blue and white cog canes. Opaque black ground. PY cane. 3.25" — 1650/1990

191. Ten petaled maroon double clematis with gold aventurine stripes. Surrounded by spokes alternating between pink and purple with white latticinio. Tan textured ground. PY cane. 2.9" — 715/1990

192. Turquoise clematis with 6 gold striped petals. Stem and leaves. Red and white jasper ground. PY cane. 2.9"

193. Cruciform of leaves with a complex lavender, light blue, and white cog, and PY cane at center. White lace ground. 5 + 1 faceting. 3.5" — A weight of very similar design sold for $2720 in 1996

194. Five petaled salmon colored flower with a central violet cog cane. Five leaves. All within 2 circles of pink, white, and gold canes. Black ground. PY cane on base. 3" — 680/1993

195. Pink and red double clematis with 10 petals, stem and 2 leaves. Peripheral canes of alternating cross and cog design are violet, white, and green. Black ground. PY cane. 3" — 625/1993

196. White flower with 10 ridged petals around a pink, orange, and white cane. Stem and 3 leaves. Within a basket of complex fuschia cog canes. PY cane. 2.9" — 850/1993

197. Flower with 10 white, blue, and lavender striped petals, stem and 8 leaves. Outer circle of alternating caramel and green complex canes. Black ground. PY cane. 3.05" — 625/1993

198. Flower with 10 ridged pink petals, stem and 3 leaves. Peripheral circle of blue complex cog canes alternating with white filigree and lace with goldstone rods. Mottled translucent blue ground. 3.5" — 625/1993

199. Thistle and leaves all in purple and green millefiori canes. Black ground. PY cane at base of stem. 2.35" — 650/1997

200. Bouquet of 6 flowers in orange, yellow, blue, pink, and white with stems and leaves. 24 peripheral canes alternating in blue and pink. Translucent gray ground. PY cane. 3"

201. Five petaled pale blue flower with stem and 7 leaves, above latticinio basket interspersed with 5 gold aventurine rods. PY cane. 2.95" — 1100/1994

202. Six petaled pink flower with stem and 3 leaves — 735/1994

encircled by 12 canes in pink, yellow, pale green, white, and royal blue. Mottled translucent pink ground. PY cane. 2.9"

203. Triple flower. Blooms pale blue, salmon pink, and mauve with five leaves all within a garland of alternate green and white canes. Translucent amber ground. 3.75" — 360/1978

204. As above, but with garland of pink and white canes. H cane — Post-1971

205. Nine flower bouquet. Pink, yellow, blue, and white flowers tied with pink and blue ribbon. Five leaves. Mottled dark blue ground. 3" — 105/1979

206. Striped blue flower, 6 petals, on radiating lace ground. PY cane near base of stem.

207. Striped pink flower, 5 petals. Eight leaves and H cane near base of stalk. All on radiating white and yellow lace ground. 2.75" — 120/1978

208. Bouquet of 5 flowers and a bud on brown and cream stalks within a circle of red, white, and blue canes. Smokey ground. PY cane. 2.75" — 1965

209. Five striped petals, pink flower with 9 leaves. Beige jasper ground. PY cane. — 160/1978

210. Ten petaled blue flower on green jasper ground. Peripheral circle of 8 bubbles. — 60/1978

211. Striped 5 petaled yellow flower with 5 leaves. Eight green and 4 white latticinio spokes. Mauve ground. — 65/1978

212. Yellow and red striped flower with 10 petals. Flower surrounded by 12 spokes of blue, white, and green latticinio. Mauve ground. H cane 2.75" — Post-1971 105/1982

213. Bouquet of 6 flowers and buds, with leaves. Stems tied with ribbon. Very dark blue ground. — 324/1982

214. Thistle and leaves, all in green and mauve millefiori. PY cane at base of leaves. Dark ground. Flat base. 2.75" — 1930s — 400/1982

215. Ten petaled pink flower with stem and 3 leaves set within basket of pink centered yellow canes. — 260/1982

216. Ten petaled pink flower with bud and 3 leaves on stem, set within basket of alternate green and white canes and latticinio. PY cane.

217. Two different flowers and buds, pink and white, on blue ground. PY cane. — 1975

218. Pink striped white flower with 5 petals plus leaves. Sand colored ground. H cane. — 120/1982

219. Spray of 6 flowers pale blue, dark blue, white, and lime green with 4 leaves, within a latticinio basket. PY cane. 3" — 190/1978

220. Pink flower surrounded by pink, red and white canes. Thin purple ground. PY cane at base of stem 3.5" — 75/1979

221. Spray of bright colored flowers. Green leaves tied with pink ribbon. Dark blue ground. 2.75" — 60/1972

222. Yellow clematis within a surround of blue and orange canes. Opaque blue ground. 3" — 27/1971

223. White clematis are 10 striped petals, and orange center. Three leaves. Outer garland of blue, pink and white set-ups. Deep blue ground. 3" — 140/1974

224. Pink flower set within blue and orange florets. Green ground. 3" — 22/1978

225. Pink clematis with white striped petals. Eight leaves. Opaque pink ground. PY cane. 3.15" — 75/1978

226. Flowers with striated pink, white, and mauve petals floating above a flecked opaque green ground and surrounded by air bubbles. PY cane. 2.75" — 75/1978

227. Group of florets within a garland of canes. PY cane. 3" — 45/1970

228. Flat spray of 5 florets and 5 leaves within a basket of alternate puce and white latticinio. PY cane 2.15" — 180/1978

229. Blue flower with 6 petals, and 1 bud. Six peripheral blue canes. All set on white latticinio. H cane.

230. Six flower bouquet, one with PY cane, and leaves set within basket of orange canes.

231. Yellow striped green flower. Five petals and 5 leaves with 4 other leaves on stem. All set on white latticinio.

232. Brown and pink striped 5 petaled flower with central cog cane. Surrounded by alternating spokes of white and blue latticinio. Turquoise ground.

No.	Design	Date manufactured, where known	Value $ in year stated
233.	Six petaled pink flower with brown stripes and central cog. Six leaves plus 4 on stem. Green and white jasper ground.		
234.	Blue clematis with 5 petals, 5 leaves plus 4 on stem. All floating in white latticinio basket. PY cane.		
235.	Five petaled white flower with stripes set on a crucifix form of leaves with PY cane. Six white peripheral canes. Blue ground pedestal base[3].		750/1994
236.	Clematis with five striped pink petals and five leaves plus four on stem. Set on green and white latticinio crown. PY cane.		
237.	Dahlia with 10 mauve petals, and white central cane. Three leaves on stem plus PY cane. All suspended above white latticinio basket.		

Butterflies

No.	Design	Date manufactured, where known	Value $ in year stated
238.	Pink bodied butterfly with orange antennae and pink, mauve and white wings. Circle of complex and cog canes. Pink ground. PY cane.		
239.	Three butterflies in pink, green, and blue with antennae around a pink lampwork flower. Circle of yellow canes at periphery. Clear ground.		
240.	Orange bodied butterfly with red tipped antennae. Wings outlined with blue/white and green/white cog canes. Pink complex canes are at the center of each wing. Dark ground.		
241.	Dark bodied butterfly with 7 yellow spots. Red eyes. Mottled green cane wings. Peripheral canes in green and white. PY cane. Caithness 1963 scratched on base. 3"	1963	
242.	Dark bodied butterfly with orange tipped yellow antennae. Spotted pink and amber wings. Circle of canes with a PY. Mottled blue ground.	1950-70	
243.	Orange bodied butterfly with wings of pink complex canes. Yellow antennae. All over a basket of white filigree with PY cane.		520/1989
244.	Dark bodied butterfly with green, yellow, pink, and white wings. Circle of green and pink complex canes. Blue ground.		
245.	White winged butterfly with 4 small flowers, 15 leaves and stem. All within circle of pink canes. PY cane. Dark ground.		
246.	Orange bodied butterfly with millefiori wings. Chain garland encircles butterfly. Blue ground. 3.75"	1935-40	
247.	Rust colored butterfly with 8 yellow spots on wings. Circle of spaced green and white star canes. PY cane. Blue ground. 2.75"	1976	
248.	Multi-colored butterfly and spray of pink flowers on translucent aubergine ground. PY cane. 3.15"		280/1990
249.	Pink butterfly and sprays of pink flowers on aubergine ground. PY cane. 3.15"		300/1990
250.	Green bodied butterfly with pink wings and a spray of pink flowers. Blue and white pebble ground. PY cane. 3.35"		280/1990
251.	Aventurine bodied butterfly with wings of white stardust canes, each wing containing a PY cane. Aubergine ground. 3.15"		250/1990
252.	Two butterflies, and a dragonfly with mottled yellow wings. PY cane at base of dragonfly's tail.		
253.	Cerise bodied butterfly. Green, white, and yellow front wings, and blue and white back wings. Outer circle of 28 canes of latticinio, complex canes, and cogs – mainly alternating. Blue ground.		
254.	Two-tone blue striped bodied butterfly with light brown and pink antennae. Green wings have white and orange centers. Set within a garland of complex green and white cogs. Clear ground.		
255.	Butterfly with white wings and brown body and yellow and red antennae, near a brown branch with 4 pink flowers and 15 leaves. Outer circle of pink canes. Dark ground. PY cane. 3.75"		1365/1990
256.	Copper aventurine-bodied butterfly with pink wings with yellow and black dots and 16 mauve canes on edges of wings. Orange antennae. Border of alternate orange/white and green/white cog canes. Blue translucent ground. Pontil mark. 3.75"	Pre-1962	480/1990
257.	Yellow butterfly set within a garland of pink canes.	Pre-1970	

No.	Design	Date manufactured, where known	Value $ in year stated
	PY cane. 2.65"		
258.	Orange bodied butterfly. Wings in white and orange, and orange antennae. All within a basket of white and black canes. PY cane Pontil mark. Made for Frank Eysner who worked at Caithness with Ysart. 2.75"	About 1960	780/1990
259.	Aventurine-bodied butterfly with pink and blue wings and green antennae, within two concentric rows of red and pink canes. Opaque green ground. 3.5"	Pre-1962	480/1990
260.	Dark bodied butterfly. Blue wings have 4 green and 6 pink spots. Large peripheral cog and other canes. Dark ground.		300/1982
261.	Dark bodied butterfly with orange complex and cog cane wings. Yellow and red antennae. Mottled lilac ground. Pontil mark. 2.75"		
262.	Red aventurine-bodied butterfly with cane wings predominantly yellow. Yellow and red antennae, all within a circle of orange and pink cog canes. Dark blue ground. Pontil mark. 3.65"		
263.	Dark bodied butterfly with yellow and pink wings. White and red antennae. Within a circle of green and white, and pink canes. PY cane. Clear ground. Flat base. 2.75"		
264.	Dark bodied butterfly with pink and amber cane wings. White and red antennae. All within a circle of orange and white canes, 30 in all. A further cane is signed PY. Black ground. Pontil mark. 2.5"		
265.	Orange bodied butterfly, with white wings having 8 green spots. Orange antennae. Twig with leaves and 4 blue flowers. Sandy ground. PY cane. Flat base. 3.25"		
266.	Butterfly set with a garland of canes on transparent smoked ground. 3.15"		475/1986
267.	Amber aventurine bodied butterfly with orange and white antennae. Ochre and pink wings with lime and amber spots. Lime green, pink, and white peripheral canes. Clear ground. PY cane. 2.75".		
268.	Aventurine bodied butterfly with brown and blue cane wings, each with a PY cane. 2.9"		
269.	Double overlay. Large butterfly made from canes. PY cane	Pre-1939	
270.	Gold bodied butterfly with royal blue and green wings encircled with complex canes. Pale blue ground. PY cane. 3"		530/1991
271.	Aventurine bodied butterfly within a circle of pink canes. PY cane. 2.75"		9/1950
272.	Green bodied butterfly with purple, orange, and yellow spotted pink wings. Yellow antennae. Ringed by green, red, and orange canes. Mottled blue ground. 3.05"		610/1992
273.	Brown and orange-bodied butterfly with spotted blue and green wings hovering near a stemmed plant with three pink and yellow flowers. Blue jasper ground. PY cane at center of one flower. 3.25"		705/1992
274.	Iridescent gold bodied butterfly with orange antennae and pink, white, and yellow cane wings. Set within a latticinio basket. PY cane. 2.05"		850/1992
275.	Orange-bodied butterfly with orange tipped antennae. Yellow cane wings also contain six complex canes. Pontil mark. Dark ground. 3.25"		200/1991
276.	Butterfly with spotted red aventurine body and red antennae. Mauve and orange millefiori wings. Outer circle of 30 cogs and complex canes, plus a PY cane. Dark amethyst ground. 3"		550/1992
277.	Red aventurine-bodied butterfly with green wings spotted with aventurine and orange canes. Red tipped white antennae. Peripheral canes in pink, white, and latticinio. Flat base. 3"	1930s	300/1992
278.	Pink-bodied butterfly with gold aventurine spotted pink wings and yellow antennae; together with 4 pink flowers on stems with 15 leaves. Wine colored translucent ground. PY cane. 3.05"		670/1992
279.	Gold aventurine bodied butterfly with yellow antennae. Two-tone blue and white wings are spotted. Near the insect are 4 pink flowers with		770/1992

stems and 15 leaves. Dark translucent charcoal ground. Top facet. PY cane. 3.15"

No.	Design	Date manufactured, where known	Value $ in year stated
280.	Red aventurine bodied butterfly with orange tipped yellow antennae. Cane wings are white, yellow, and blue. Outer circle of pink, green, yellow, and blue complex canes. Opaque green ground. PY cane. 2.95"		1135/1992
281.	Red aventurine bodied butterfly with green and claret wings, within a basket of purple circled lime-green and white tubular canes. 2.9"		355/1982
282.	Green aventurine bodied butterfly with red tipped lime green antennae, and orange and white wings, within garland of ochre, pink, yellow, and white canes. Translucent brown ground. 3"		260/1985
283.	Pale blue bodied butterfly with pink wings and lime green antennae, within garland of 7 large pink and white canes. Translucent brown ground. PY cane. 3.05"		485/1984
284.	Three butterflies with pink and green aventurine bodies. Wings in pink, blue, and lime green. Central white and black cane and 3 smaller canes. Garland of orange and white canes. Black ground. PY cane. Monart period. Gilt label. 3.05"		865/1985
285.	A green, blue, and brown butterfly with aventurine markings and orange antennae, near a floral spray. Red and white jasper ground on a dark footed base. PY cane. 3.15"		636/1984
286.	Aventurine bodied butterfly with blue wings within a circle of yellow and purple canes. Crushed raspberry ground. 3.35"		90/1977
287.	Butterfly with burgundy body and caramel wings above a central cluster of multi-colored canes, from which radiate sky-blue and pink elongated canes. Ochre ground. 3.15"	Pre-1977	
288.	Aventurine bodied butterfly with 2 blue and 2 green wings and yellow antennae, within an outer circle of pale blue and white stardust canes, broken up every two canes by one large royal blue cane. 3"	Pre-1977	
289.	Aventurine bodied butterfly with pink and blue wings. Rich opaque blue ground. 3"		255/1976
290.	Green bodied butterfly with pink and white millefiori wings and red tipped orange antennae within circle of complex pink and white canes. Translucent green ground. PY cane. 3.15"		935/1990
291.	Butterfly with striped caramel body, and red and orange head and antennae. White wings have green and copper aventurine spots. Floating in white latticinio basket. PY cane. 2.95"		740/1993
292.	Orange bodied butterfly with yellow antennae. Two green and 2 orange wings with gold aventurine spots. Encircled by an unusual orange and yellow filigree torsade with green spots. Black ground. 2.3"		800/1993
293.	Dark blue bodied butterfly with pink and brown wings, set within two concentric circles of canes in salmon pink, claret, dark blue, and green. Clear ground. PY cane. 2.9"		
294.	Aventurine bodied butterfly with brownish wings. Pale blue ground. Each wing has a PY cane. 2.75"	Pre-1966	75/1966
295.	Ruby aventurine bodied butterfly. Green wings are spotted with blue, pink, white, and vermilion. Encircled by green, pink, royal blue, and chartreuse canes. Powder blue ground. PY cane. 2.8"		910/1994
296.	Brown bodied butterfly with pink wings spotted with green aventurine, and 5 yellow and orange petaled clematis with stem and leaves. Blue and white jasper ground; and cobalt blue pedestal. Top facet. PY cane. 3.3"		790/1994
297.	Red and white winged butterfly, with red antennae. Set within circle of red and white canes. 3.25"		60/1971
298.	Pink and white winged butterfly with white and red antennae. Peripheral circle of multi-colored canes. Smokey ground.	1965	
299.	Orange bodied butterfly within blue and pink garlands. Blue ground.		
300.	Orange bodied butterfly with pink wings and yellow antennae. Peripheral circle of pink canes.		
	Blue filigree cushion.		
301.	Pink and orange winged butterfly with green antennae, within circle of pink cogs. Pink ground. PY cane. 2.9"		120/1978
302.	Blue winged butterfly with green and red antennae within a circle of various canes. Dark ground.		105/1978
303.	Dark aventurine bodied butterfly with bright wings surrounded by 8 orange set ups within a garland of similar canes. Black ground. PY cane. 3"		105/1978
304.	Dark bodied butterfly with spotted white wings in green and white basket. PY cane.		
305.	Magnum weight with aventurine bodied butterfly with green wings. Translucent red ground.		300/1978
306.	Aventurine bodied butterfly, with 2 blue and 2 green wings, within garland of large claret and white canes, on spreading cobalt blue foot. 3.75"		225/1978
307.	Three aventurine bodied butterflies about a central white cane, set within an outer garland of alternate white and orange canes. Black ground. PY cane. 3.5"		405/1978
308.	Red and yellow bodied butterfly with aventurine wings. Orange ground. PY cane. 3.15"		90/1980
309.	Butterfly within garland of red and blue florets. Pale blue ground. 2.65"		60/1980
310.	Green bodied butterfly. Ochre wings with blue-green aventurine spots. Orange antennae. All within garland of colored canes. Translucent dark blue ground. 3"		120/1979
311.	Green bodied butterfly with blue and white wings; set on white latticinio and yellow ground. Signature cane.		
312.	Blue bodied butterfly with blue and white wings on green jasper ground.		
313.	Mauve bodied butterfly with orange and red wings surrounded by circle of blue canes. All set on an undulating maroon cushion.		

Dragonflies

No.	Design	Date manufactured, where known	Value $ in year stated
314.	Green bodied dragonfly with red head and aventurine wings, surrounded by 6 complex pink and white canes. Upset muslin ground. PY cane. 2.8"		640/1990
315.	Red bodied dragonfly in aventurine, with green aventurine wings. Blue and white mottled ground. PY cane. Flat base. 3"		
316.	Dragonfly with green aventurine body. Red and white filigree wings. Smokey ground. 9 green and 1 pink peripheral canes with PY set into the pink cane. Flat base. 3"		
317.	Red and gold aventurine bodied dragonfly with green complex cane wings. Pink ground with 14 complex canes. PY cane. Flat base. 2.75"		
318.	Gold aventurine bodied dragonfly with orange and white complex cane wings. Set above yellow and white filigree basket. PY cane. Pontil mark. 3"		
319.	Dragonfly with green body, orange head, and yellow wings hovering over pink/white jasper ground.	1970	
320.	Iridescent red bodied dragonfly with yellow spots. Four iridescent gold wings. White and green floret both sides of the body. All within a circle of 10 complex canes. Lime green ground. PY cane. 3"		410/1991
321.	Dragonfly with gold aventurine body and wings. Red aventurine head with orange eyes. A complex cane is set each side of the body. Peripheral circle of canes. Cobalt blue ground. 3.25"		550/1982
322.	Green aventurine bodied dragonfly with red head and gold aventurine wings. Red and white jasper ground. PY cane. 2.95"		410/1992
323.	Red aventurine bodied dragonfly with green aventurine wings. Red and white jasper ground. PY cane. 2.95"		410/1992
324.	Dragonfly with 7 spots on its body, with yellow wings together with 2 butterflies with dark aventurine bodies one with mauve wings, the other with blue and mauve wings. Three individual canes separate the insects. Outer ring of canes, one with a PY cane. Dark		735/1992

ground. Dark dome. Pontil. 3.15"

325. Green bodied dragonfly with 6 yellow spots, and blue and white wings; circled by complex canes. Mottled red ground. Monart label. PY cane. 2.9"

326. Pink-bodied dragonfly with white latticinio wings with gilt inclusions, within a circle of large white and pink canes. Translucent brown ground. PY cane. 3.15" — 455/1985

327. Black spotted, green bodied dragonfly with orange head. Wings pale turquoise, pink, green, and white. Within garland of cobalt blue, crimson, and white canes. Translucent gray ground. PY cane. 3" — 570/1984

328. Red aventurine bodied dragonfly with yellow spots, green aventurine head with orange eyes. Four millefiori wings of pink and white canes. Set within a white latticinio basket. PY cane. 3" — 650/1993

329. Green bodied dragonfly with 7 yellow spots, gold aventurine wings, and red eyes. All within a white latticinio basket with 5 equally spaced pink, white, and black cog spokes. PY cane. 3" — 910/1993

330. Brown aventurine bodied dragonfly with 6 yellow spots. Red aventurine wings. Encircled with blue, white, green, and amethyst canes. Translucent dark green ground. PY cane. 3.05" — 855/1994

Fish

331. Two green aventurine bodied fish with pink spots above broken blue ground. — 1977

332. Gold bodied fish with red fins surrounded by eight bubbles. Blue ground. 2.75" — 110/1982

333. Green spotted red aventurine-bodied fish above a rocky bed in turquoise, green, and white. PY cane and signed on base. 2.75" — 390/1978

334. Green bodied fish with orange fins on white scrambled ground. Six peripheral canes and PY cane.

335. Turquoise bodied fish with orange spots above a blue and sandy pebbled ground.

336. Green and white bodied fish with green translucent fins. Yellow eye. Surrounded by a circle of 6 bubbles. Beige sandy ground. — 260/1989

337. Green bodied fish on jasper ground.

338. Two green aventurine fish, spotted, above rocks and shells on sea bed ground. PY cane. Flat base. 3"

339. Striped green fish with yellow eye facing right. 7 large green cog and 14 pink peripheral canes. Yellow ground. Flat base. PY cane. 3" — 1950s

340. Vertically striped red fish with white eye facing right. Green ground. White and pink peripheral canes. Flat base. PY cane. 2.75" — 1950s

341. Red fish with green scales and yellow markings. Multi-colored rock ground. Signature cane. — 470/1986

342. Pink fish with gilt aventurine fins within a garland of pink and ochre canes including a PY cane. Dark ground. 3" — 420/1990

343. Red bodied fish with dark fins, facing right. 6 peripheral canes. Sand colored ground. Signature cane. — Pre-1975

344. Black striped pink-bodied fish with iridescent gold fins and tail. Facing right. Set within a circle of 12 pink and maroon complex canes. Sandy ground. PY cane. 2.95" — 365/1991

345. Orange bodied fish with pink and white fins facing right. Set within a circle of 25 pink and white, and yellow and white canes. Dark blue ground. PY cane. 3.35" — 470/1992

346. Three dimensional turquoise fish floating above a gravel ground.

347. Fish with horizontally green striped body within a circle of canes. Yellow ground.

348. Two three dimensional fish. One with white spotted red body, the other in green aventurine. Both above brightly colored rocks and shells.

349. Pink fish facing right on a sand colored ground. Eight large bubbles around periphery.

350. Orange bodied fish with mauve fins facing right.

Eight peripheral bubbles. Pale green ground.

351. Orange striped fish with mauve fins facing right. Encircled by 6 large cog canes. Blue jasper ground. Signature cane.

352. Green bodied fish facing right with horizontal stripes. Red fins and lips, and yellow eye. Encircled by pink, green, and white canes. Yellow and white jasper ground. PY cane. 2.95" — 550/1994

Birds

353. Three ducks and a lily. PY cane. 3" — 1955/60 — 420/1982

354. Green bodied parrot with striped yellow wings, sitting on a brown branch with 9 leaves. Sandy jasper ground. PY cane. 5 + 1 faceting.

355. Blue bodied parrot with pink and white wings. Perched on a branch with leaves and a PY cane at one end. Mottled blue ground. Side and top facets. 3.15" — 880/1990

356. Green bodied parrot with pink wing, orange beak, and black eye, on a branch with 10 leaves. Blue and white jasper ground. Pedestal base. PY cane. 3.05" — 860/1990

357. Orange bodied parrot with yellow wings on a branch with leaves and white flowers. Yellow ground. PY cane. Flat base. 2.75"

358. Four blue bodied ducks, with pink wings and yellow bills above a blue and white jasper ground. Black pedestal base. PY cane. 3.5" — 570/1990

359. Three upright orange ducks with a flower. Graveled ground, and black foot. Faceted. 3.35" — 760/1992

360. Three orange ducks, 2 with pink wings and 1 with brown wings on a pond of crushed translucent blue glass. Floating pink flower with leaves. White glass stones sit at the bottom. Smokey ground. Footed. PY cane. 3"
A similar weight 3.5" in dia. sold for $1725 in 1997. — 990/1993

361. Three orange and pink ducks, floating above rock work with a signed water lily. Black ground. PY cane. 3.5" — 230/1977

362. Two green and blue ducks with red beaks, and a pink water lily with leaves, all on a translucent blue pond. Blue and white jasper ground with large white stones. PY cane. 2.75" — 825/1990
(A further weight containing 3 ducks has recently come to light. This has a PY cane set in the water, and a CG cane and Caithness label on the base. It was made between 1964 and 1970).

363. Blue bodied parrot with green wings and orange beak perched on a branch with 9 leaves. Red and white jasper ground. Made at Caithness Glass. PY cane. 3.25" — Post-1962 — 855/1994

Snakes and reptiles

364. Brown serpent with pink and cream spots. Green ground. PY cane. — 1975

365. Bright mauve bodied rattlesnake with green spots. Turquoise ground.

366. Red snake with cerise and chartreuse spots. White stones on green ground. PY cane. 3" — c.1970

367. Red bodied snake with white filigree coil. Yellow eyes. Coiling clockwise from the head. Green ground. PY cane. Flat base. 2.75"

368. Double snake pedestal weight. Two coiled snakes with yellow bodies entwined with pale green filigree. Red tongues. Green base and ground. PY cane. 3" — 975/1990

369. Green aventurine and yellow snake coiled anti-clockwise from the head. Green and white rock ground. Flat base. PY cane. 3"

370. Red aventurine and green salamander on sand colored ground with rocks. Made as a limited edition, but actual number made is unknown. PY cane. 2.5" — 1970

371. Red bodied salamander with green stripes, set on sandy ground with rocks. PY cane. Flat base and circular PY label. 2.65" — 1170/1992

372. Yellow snake with red mouth and black and white eyes, set on a sandy ground. Dark glass footed — 870/1984

No.	Design	Date manufactured, where known	Value $ in year stated
	base. PY cane. 3.15"		
373.	Tan colored snake with black and orange stripes and red dots. Green and white jasper ground. PY cane. 3"		625/1993
374.	Two three dimensional snakes, decorated with zigzags and spots. One reptile is orange and the other green aventurine. Both coil anti-clockwise from the head. Opaque green ground, and translucent gray pedestal. PY cane. 3.35"		

Animals

No.	Design	Date	Value
375.	Three white mice with cheese. Brown sandy ground. PY cane.	1975	
376.	White mouse with upright ears, and two pieces of cheese near to which is PY cane. Textured black over white ground. Flat base with PY circular label. 2.75"		840/1992
377.	Two white mice and two pieces of cheese on earth colored ground. PY cane. 2.75"		

Footed weight

No.	Design	Date	Value
378.	Yellow striped white flower with 10 petals. Leaves surround the flower and are also on the stem. Mottled red ground with foot.		

Wig stands

No.	Design	Date	Value
379.	Concentric millefiori wig stand. Four concentric bands of pink, yellow, and white , deep blue and yellow canes about a central orange set up within a circle of green and ochre canes. Translucent deep blue ground, the stem with swelling shoulder knop and the front inset with 3 claret and white canes. 7" high.		39/1973

Inkwells

Note: Those made by Paul Ysart differ from those made by his brothers in that they never had any decoration in the neck.

No.	Design	Date	Value
380.	Clusters of canes set into turquoise ground. Matching turquoise ground stopper. PY cane.		
381.	Six point star millefiori pattern on marbled orange ground. Stopper has concentric bands of white and green canes about a white center star. 3.75"		75/1979
382.	Close packed assorted canes completely covering the base and the stopper.		675/1978
383.	Commemorative to mark the visit of H.M. Queen Elizabeth the Queen Mother to Caithness during the 1960s. *(Said to be very similar to the one presented to the Queen Mother).	Post 1962	1300/1981*
384.	Inkwell with 10 petaled pink flower in circle of red, white, colorless, and amber canes. PY cane. Blue ground. Stopper with similar canes.	1950/60	
385.	Ink bottle with spaced complex canes in base and stopper. PY cane in bottle. 5" high.		
386.	Footed ink bottle with outer ring of green, red, and white cogs in base and stopper. Central clusters of close millefiori with PY canes in stopper and base. Pontil mark 4.75" high x 3.75" dia.		
387.	Ink bottle with close millefiori canes in base and stopper set within an outer ring of green/white/red cogs all on a white ground. 5" high.		560/1991
388.	Ink bottle and stopper with white grounds completely covered with a wide range of close millefiori canes. Flat base. 5.5" high.		
389.	Inkwell with a pink fish in an opaque leaf green base ringed with large complex canes in pistachio, pink, blue, white, and green. The stopper with canes of similar color also on a green ground. Height 5.15"		1760/1993

Doorknobs, etc.

No.	Design	Date	Value
390.	Doorknob with canes set on blue ground. Brass mount. 3"		

Crowns

No.	Design	Date	Value
391.	A swirl of alternate white with green and white with red filigree (10 of each) radiating from a central bubble. Blue ground. 3.25"	1930-40	
392.	Crown with alternate green filigree, white over red, and red, white, and blue twists, 20 in all. Central bubble. Transparent ground. 3.25"	1930-40	
393.	Staves of alternate blue/white, green/white, and red/white filigree around a central bubble. 2.75"		
394.	Staves alternating in pink and green, 6 of each.		
395.	Staves in buff, green, and pink.		
396.	Lime green, yellow, and pink staves twisting down to the right with latticinio in bands of four twisting to the left. Pontil mark. Although within each length of filigree the threads usually twist down towards the left, the pieces, as a whole, can swirl to either left or right. It is interesting to note that this filigree is the same as used for the body of some snakes.		285/1991

Sulphides

No.	Design	Date	Value
397.	A woman's head facing right set on a dark ground. Eight peripheral canes.	1930	
398.	A swan in Paul Ysart's personal collection.	1930s	
399.	Sulphide of a female's head, facing left, with flowers in her hair, all on a powder blue ground. Signed on the back of the sulphide. Surrounded by 12 predominantly white canes. All set in clear glass. PY cane. 3.2"[4]	1946 or 1947	1500/1995
400.	Sulphide of a horse's head, facing left, with a bridal in its mouth. Encircled by pistachio, pink, green, and white canes. Black ground. PY cane. 3.25"	Pre-1962	975/1996
401.	Painted sulphide of a basket of flowers with brown basket with roses and other blooms in red, yellow, blue, and white over a sky blue ground. All within a spiraling blue and pink torsade. Signed. 2.75".		1100/1994

Metal regimental badges

No.	Design	Date	Value
402.	Army Service Corps badge set on jasper ground. No pontil mark. 3"	1930s - 1940s	8/1980
403.	Royal Engineers badge set on jasper ground. Pontil mark. 3"	1930s - 1940s	50/1995
404.	Canada badge set on white ground with assorted canes. Eight peripheral bubbles. Pontil mark. 4.35" (This is believed to be by far the largest badge weight in existence).	1930s - 1940s	70/1989

Percentage breakdown by type

The 404 weights listed break down to the following percentages by type:

Type	Total No.	% of total
Floral	147	36.4
Millefiori	90	22.25
Butterflies	76	18.80
Fish	22	5.45
Dragonflies	17	4.2
Birds	11	2.7
Snakes and reptiles	11	2.7
Ink bottles	10	2.5
Crowns	6	1.5
Sulphides	5	1.25
Metal regimental badges	3	0.75
Animals	3	0.75
Doorknob	1	0.25
Footed weights	1	0.25
Wig stand	1	0.25

"H" cane weights

The following few examples give some idea of weights that were issued containing "H" canes.

	Price in 1978, $
Floating fish on jasper ground	52
Starfish on lime green jasper ground with lace twists.	60
Floating pink clematis on sand ground	67
Clematis on latticinio with barber pole effect	90
Harlequin single, and double.	
Pink fish on lime ground within circle of eight complex canes.	

Salvador Ysart

An experimental cup made by Salvador in 1923 contains a millefiori 6-point star cane, and an early bowl contains filigree canes made by him.

In view of his overall background he clearly had the necessary skills to produce paperweights, but the extent to which they interested him and the priority he attached to them, is perhaps an entirely different matter. For instance, he protested when Paul was keen to pursue his own individual interest in the subject.

How many weights Salvador made is unknown, but he most certainly did make some. Those that have been positively linked with Salvador are the rarest and most sought after, and contain a distinctive "Y" cane. (figure 41). At the time of writing, only about eight of these are known to be in existence. Those seen by the author, have all been close concentric millefiori types. Figure 42 shows typical examples.

Fig. 41. Large Y cane at center of concentric millefiori weight. Salvador Ysart.

Fig. 42. Two fine, signed close concentric weights. Those signed with a Y in the center are impressive, and particularly rare. Salvador Ysart. Probably pre-1945. Dimensions are virtually identical, and both have pontil marks. Dia. 3.25". Height 1.9". $900/1100.

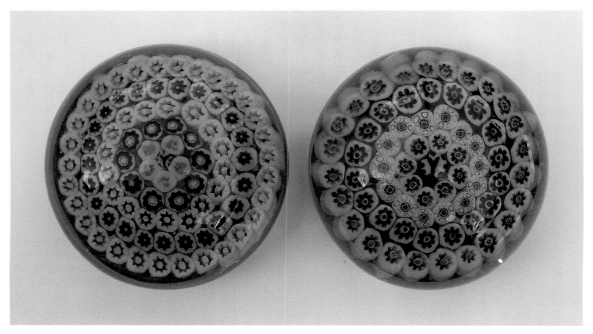

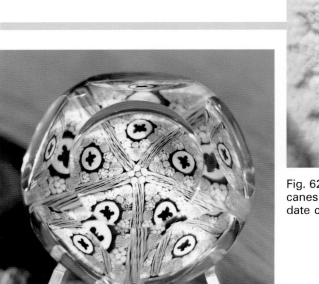

Fig. 62. Close up of central canes in a P25 design. 1978 date cane. Whitefriars.

Fig. 61. Butterfly silhouettes, with subtle use of a range of colors. Pattern PS202. 1977 date cane. Whitefriars. Dia. 3". $300/350.

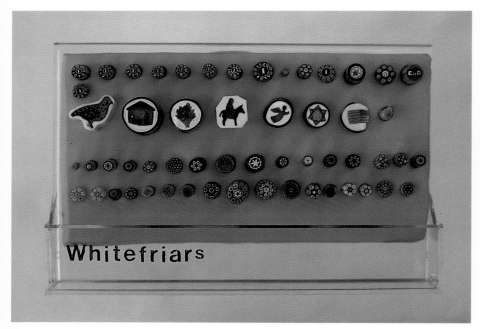

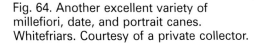

Fig. 63. A selection of canes. Dates in top row, and portraits in second row. Whitefriars.

Fig. 64. Another excellent variety of millefiori, date, and portrait canes. Whitefriars. Courtesy of a private collector.

Chapter 3

Whitefriars

Whitefriars Glass is known to have been established by 1680 and in all probability its beginnings date back even further. The glassworks site near the River Thames, London, had originally been occupied by the Carmelite Fathers, whose white habits made the monks known as White Friars. After a few other owners the business was taken over in 1834 by James Powell and Sons, and for five generations the firm traded as James Powell and Sons, before becoming Whitefriars Glass in 1962.

With several thousand formulations for different colored glasses, it is hardly surprising that the company have supplied stained glass for use in great cathedrals throughout the world including St. Paul's Cathedral, London and the Anglican Cathedral, Liverpool as well as, of course, using their own colors in their paperweights. Other glass products, besides paperweights, which featured in the company's history include special colors for glass eyes, miners lamps, vacuum flasks, optical glass for gun sights and telescopes, watch dials, thermometer tubing, and experiments in toughened glass[1].

In 1923 James Powell & Sons moved to a new factory at Wealdstone, Harrow, and in keeping with one of the many ancient traditions associated with glass making, a brazier was carried from the old works to ignite the first furnace at Wealdstone. Quality of ingredients is important when making the finest glass and Whitefriars imported silver sand from Fontainebleau, France, claiming it to be the best in the world. This was washed, sifted, and dried prior to mixing with the other ingredients, which guaranteed the consistently brilliant low color associated with English crystal glass.

Regarding the production of glass paperweights, the presence of an 1848 date cane, and the similarity of cog canes in certain weights, led authors of some earlier books to believe that paperweights were being made by Whitefriars in the first half of the 19th century. However, a considerable amount of recent research by various workers would suggest that this was probably not so. The earliest authenticated references to paperweights actually made by Whitefriars are believed to be those referred to in the company's catalogs, now housed in the Museum of London. These reveal: 1938, a paperweight with high dome; and 1945, an *illustration* of a paperweight with a high dome. The museum also has a paperweight which is known to have been made in the early 1950s.

Between 1953, when Whitefriars produced their first limited edition weight, and 1980, they issued twenty-nine different designs in limited editions and a wide range of other weights. These are detailed later.

Readers seeking in-depth knowledge of the company should refer to the two excellent books published in 1996.[2] Sadly, Whitefriars went into liquidation in the autumn of 1980, the last weights were made on the morning of September 12. Thus ended their three hundred-year existence.

Canes

Paperweights made by Whitefriars were produced virtually exclusively from a rather limited variety of millefiori canes. While, however, the number of different shapes may be considered as being rather restrictive, this is compensated for by the very wide range of colors and combinations adopted by the company. Indeed, it is generally recognized that in terms of preciseness of the canes, and the beauty of the color combinations, modern Whitefriars weights rate very highly amongst all British manufacturers.

Even in their unlimited weights, the subtle use of a wide range of colors is frequently in evidence. As an example of this, consider the butterfly silhouette weight PS 202 shown in figure 61. Although the overall color effect of this weight is of blue butterflies within pale blue and pink canes, closer examination reveals the presence of pale green, mauve, and white canes, some of which contain six point stars. Figure 62 serves as a further example and shows the range of colors within the central region of the pattern of P25. Figures 63 and 64 illustrate a wide range of the canes present in Whitefriars paperweights, and star, cog, trefoil, and quatrefoil shapes have been widely used.

By far the most commonly used canes are cogs and stars. Five and six point stars are common, as are five, six, eight, twelve, and sixteen tooth cogs. A rare cane is the 'Clichy' style rose (Figure 65) which features in the center of designs PB300, PB301 (figure 66), and also at the top of a butterfly weight. According to Annenberg, the rose cane was a difficult one to manufacture. In relation to normal canes, five times as much was typically required to give the same amount of usable stock. Rose canes were produced in pink and blue. Other canes difficult to make included asymmetrical ones such as the partridge and leaves in the 1979 Christmas weight. The shaping of the pieces for the central motif of the Mayflower (1970) was also a problem.

Fig. 65. Pink rose cane, reminiscent of that made famous by Clichy in the 19th century. Whitefriars.

Fig. 66. Garlanded rose weight, pattern PB301. The six point yellow cog canes are reminiscent of Clichy pastry mold canes. 1979 date cane. Whitefriars. Dia. 2.5". Height 1.5". $300/400.

48

Together with Perthshire, Whitefriars was probably the only other British company at that time that made and utilized portrait canes. But whereas the former company invariably used rods, Whitefriars typically used stars set within tubes. The workmanship can be gauged when it is realized that in the right hand man alone of the 1976 Three Wise Men weight, shown in figures 67 and 68, seven different colors and more than two hundred and thirty separate canes have been used. Portrait canes were used extensively by Whitefriars in their limited edition issues to form motifs such as fish, birds, animals, people, and flags, etc. Figure 69 shows a wide range of these subjects. Occasionally a silhouette cane would be used, such as the butterflies in design PS202.

Fig. 67. Christmas 1976, Three Wise Men. One of six highly collectable Christmas weights. 1976 date cane. Whitefriars. Dia. 3". Height 1.85". $350/500.

Fig. 68. Close up of a portrait cane of one of the Three Wise Men, containing over two hundred and thirty separate pieces. Whitefriars.

Fig. 69. Portrait canes. Some of these, including the Queen's head, squirrel, and pansy, (bottom row) are particularly rare. Whitefriars.

Characteristics and cut patterns

Unlike any other company currently manufacturing paperweights in Great Britain, those made by Whitefriars were all based upon English full lead crystal (30% PbO). It is believed that in later weights this was reduced to 27%.

Modern Whitefriars weights have characteristic base profiles that set them apart from other maker's products. The circular base on which the canes are set is not only clearly visible underneath, but usually actually protrudes from where the outer clear glass dome commences. Furthermore, some of the canes often extend right through the circular set-up and can actually be felt. In very early weights, such as the 1951 Triplex and 1953 Coronation designs, the outer row of canes often give the impression of being longer than the other canes. This is not an illusion, as longer pieces were actually used. A profile of a typical Whitefriars base is shown in figure 70. A characteristic of the vast majority of this company's paperweights is that they have printies. The extensive range of the surface cut patterns is larger than that of any other British manufacturer, encompassing everything from a single printy to complete coverage of the surface. The company carried out their own faceting. Examples of this range of surface cutting together with their appropriate reference numbers are shown in figure 71.

Fig. 70. Typical base. Note the marked indentation between the clear glass, and the colored design. Whitefriars.

Fig. 71. Whitefriars specialized in a wide range of cut patterns. Company brochure, late 1970s.

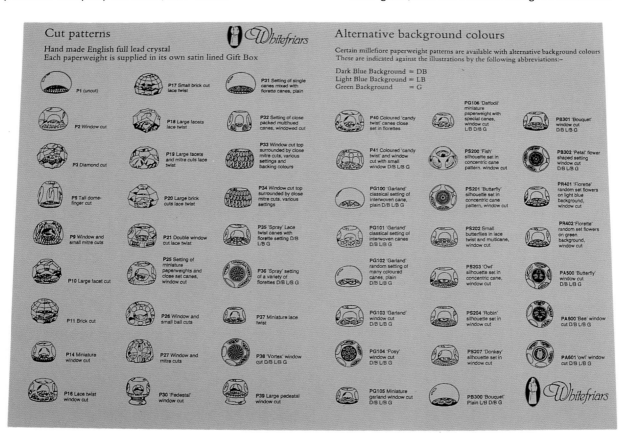

Fig. 72. Unusual, almost dumbbell shape, concentric millefiori. 1971 date cane. Whitefriars. Dia. 2.8". Height 2.45". $225/300.

One of the men responsible for faceting and polishing was Alan Sadler. Alan told the author that although officially a given cutting pattern was to be adhered to for a given weight, in practice, weights with a variety of surface imperfections were often cut with a non standard pattern, in order to give perfectly acceptable end products (see figure 72). Alan is now at Blue Crystal in London where he is closely involved with the restoration of paperweights.

Date canes

Modern millefiori weights all carry a date cane together with the symbolic representation of a White Friar, introduced in 1970. Date canes were inserted largely due to pressure from the USA which represented Whitefriars largest export market. The White Friar sometimes resembles a lower case 'i' or a white candle against a dark blue background and faces to the right. Similarly, dates are invariably white on a blue background. Note also that whereas in most late date canes the numerals are white set into blue, from 1970 - 72 the reverse was the case. The change to white numerals was made because it was felt that this combination blended in better with a wide range of designs.

Slight variations occurred in the manufacture of date canes. For example some 1978 and 1979 canes have four star rods to complete the peripheral circle, whereas others will be seen to contain five. Similarly the 1829 – 1979 cane exists with 2 or 4 star rods. While discussing dates it is of interest to note that one weight exists with two date canes namely 1974 and 1975. This faceted weight has latticinio rods laid as radial spokes amongst the other conventional canes. As an example of another wrongly dated weight, a Mayflower exists with a 1975 date cane, and was sold for $410 in 1999.

Production personnel

The men mainly associated with the production of paperweights are as follows:

Frank Hill was the principal cane and weight maker of the 1950s. Frank's servitor was Syd Shephard. Syd also made canes, and was, apparently, a great experimenter. Other names closely associated with paperweight production were Ronald Wilkinson, Fred Daden, Raymond Annenberg, and Alan Sadler.

Ronald Wilkinson, born in east London in June 1928, seemed destined to pursue a career in glassmaking. His father, grandfather, and uncles had all worked at Whitefriars. When he was a young lad Ronald and his family moved near to Wealdstone, and while he was only twelve years old he would play truant from school in order to acquire rudimentary knowledge about glass. Still only fourteen he began his employment at Whitefriars, and was quick to learn all the techniques necessary for him to eventually become a master glass blower. At the age of twenty-two Ronald became the gaffer responsible for a skilled team of operators. He stayed with Whitefriars until they closed in 1980, and later went to the Glasshouse at Covent Garden, London. Ronald died in 1991, aged sixty-three.

Fig. 73. A rare weight containing a portrait cane resembling Queen Elizabeth II. Date cane 1978. Whitefriars. Courtesy of Sweetbriar Gallery Archive. $600/700.

Ronald's personal collection of about sixty-five Whitefriars weights were ultimately purchased and resold in July 1998 by the dealer Sweetbriar Gallery. Many of Ronald's weights that he had collected were standard items both limited and unlimited. However, as might be expected he also had a few rare and some possibly unique items, which included the following:-

1. Central portrait cane which resembles the Queen in a coronet, with canes radiating from it. Dated 1978, it sold for $500. This is illustrated in figure 73.
2. Central butterfly in blue millefiori, trial issue – sold for $413.
3. Central butterfly in green millefiori, trial issue – sold for $413.
4. 1975. A single angel portrait cane at the center of concentric circles of canes – sold for $585.
5. 1975. A magnum mauve flash overlay, five and one faceting – sold for $600.
6. 1977. A prototype cut nativity – sold for $545.
7. 1978. Close pack thick garland with central 'Clichy' type rose – sold for $625.
8. 1978. A concentric, amber flashed – sold for $445.
9. 1979. A pedestal weight – sold for $663.
10. 1978. Central swan portrait cane, commemorative for Western Australia, made for Boan's – sold for $780. Obviously the highlight of the collection.

Fred G. Daden (Hon. FRCA) was born on February 20 1925. When his mother moved to Harrow, young Fred was looking for a job. The local labor exchange told him of a vacancy at Whitefriars, and as a result he joined the company in 1942. With the long and often awkward hours he hated the job to begin with, but soon came to love it. He left Whitefriars in 1969 to become a lecturer at the Royal College of Art.

During an interview with the author in November 1997, Fred (figure 74) was able to confirm that he had made many of the "EIIR 1953" weights, issued to commemorate the Coronation of Her Majesty Queen Elizabeth II. Although he cannot recollect anything about the "Triplex 1951" weights, he well remembers Whitefriars having a small furnace at the Festival of Britain Exhibition in 1951. Regarding weights with a central cane bearing initials such as "GEW," and "GF," these were said to be made to order for anyone who could afford them. Fred has a high regard for Bill Heaton under whom he trained. Bill left and went to the R.C.A., and upon leaving the R.C.A. it was Fred who filled his post.

Recalling the paperweights he made, Fred stated that he always preferred apple wood for blocking, and that he annealed his weights for about eight hours. In the 1950s the furnace was heated by coal and the lehrs by gas. Like all paperweight manufacturers Fred has many a tale to tell. He recalls how they used to trick new apprentices by covering a coin with a hot set-up. When he thought the coin was hot enough he would remove the set-up and ask an unsuspecting lad to pick up the coin to go and buy something! While at the R.C.A. he perfected the ability to make sulphides

Fig. 74. Fred Daden (photographed in 1997) – the master glass craftsman who made many of the Whitefriars Coronation weights in 1953. Courtesy of Fred Daden.

and produced a few, including one of a beetle and another of a lion. He traveled and was in demand for lectures and demonstrations in California, Australia, and New Zealand. An example of his work, a blue plaque, is in the Victoria and Albert Museum, London.

At the age of sixteen Raymond Annenberg joined Whitefriars in 1953, and was to become their chief cane maker in 1972. He is a man who can tell many an interesting story about happenings at Whitefriars. The following three stories quickly came to Raymond's mind during an interview. Firstly there was a bin in which canes were stored. A member of the management team would regularly inspect this as if to make sure that nothing was being stolen. Raymond said he felt certain that some of the management thought canes were being stolen – but in fact they were not. Somewhat annoyed at this regular inspection it was decided that the time had come to retaliate. So one day they fixed a dead rat to the bin in such a way that upon opening the lid the rat fell out causing the management quite a shock. The bin was never opened again. On a different occasion a member of the management team, thinking Raymond was keen to buy some canes – perhaps for personal keeping, said: "You can have some for £10 per pound." As quick as a flash Raymond got a one-pound note out of his pocket and said: "Yes, all right, I'll have some at ten pounds a £."

As a final amusing story, Raymond relates how one day he was asked to make, and then pull, a portrait cane of excessively large diameter. In keeping with normal practice, the portrait cane was surrounded by an outer coating. Raymond had told management that it would probably not be possible to pull the cane due to the problem of the outer layer staying much hotter than the inner portrait. However, at the manager's insistence the pulling went ahead while they watched. Despite doing his best, Raymond could see the outer coating peeling off away from the central design which promptly fell to the floor and smashed to pieces. Raymond said that under his breath he was saying: "I told you so!"

Aside from the humor, Raymond Annenberg is clearly a skilled paperweight maker. The design of P25, for instance, was his idea and he produced the prototype of this in soda glass. A further achievement Raymond quoted was pulling a three- to four-inch diameter portrait cane of an owl from its initial length of six inches to about forty feet. Partridge and pear canes he lists as amongst the most difficult he has ever pulled, so it is no surprise that the 1979 Christmas weight is one of his favorites.

He made for himself a 'Host of Angels' weight with a single large angel cane at the center. To differentiate it further from the commercial issue, this weight contains a 1974 date cane. As a further example of his expertise, he produced about fourteen glass swords. These are about three feet long and are topped with a design akin to a miniature paperweight, about one and a half inches in diameter, containing a large central portrait cane of a crown set into a royal blue ground.

In 1954 Geoffrey P. Baxter, Des.R.C.A., M.S.I.A., joined Whitefriars and stayed with the company until its closure. He became the company's chief designer. By the late 1960s he had a strong personal interest in paperweights, and subsequently became responsible for the design of many of their weights. When writing to the author in 1980 Geoffrey stated that paperweights were usually made at the beginning of the week. Born on February 12, 1922, Geoffrey Baxter died on August 22, 1995.

Regarding amusing happenings, Geoffrey's children, Richard, Anthony, and Helen, recollect being involved with school projects and electing to go to the factory to study the glass-making procedures. In due course, they were given a mold and had to set up the appropriate canes. Apart from satisfaction and knowledge gained, this also provided their pocket money. Meanwhile, Geoffrey's wife, Marion, can remember how they would both discuss ideas pertaining to the Christmas weights. Her own personal favorite, however, is not a Christmas weight, but the very attractive peacock design (figure 75) described later.

The company's technical manager was Brian Slingsby, whose wife, Sylvia, produced set-ups as a home worker.

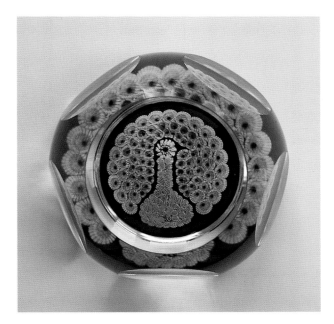

Fig. 75. Peacock on green ground. Only one ever made, using specially developed canes. 1978 date cane. Signed on base G. Baxter. Whitefriars. Ref. No. 22. Dia. 3.1". Courtesy of Geoffrey Baxter. $600/800.

Paperweights

Unlimited edition weights sometimes feature large central canes illustrating, for example, a robin, butterfly, fish, owl, or donkey. It is interesting to note that, for all their pictorial type weights (birds, animals, people, flags, etc.), Whitefriars formed these central designs from a closely packed pattern of colored cog canes as opposed to using the lampwork technique. Before pieces of some of the complex portrait canes could be used in a set-up, they often had to be ground flat to lose the irregular surface produced by the initial cutting.

Canes exist some of which have probably never been used in a completed paperweight. For example, a bird on a nest, the Queens head, Windsor Castle, a large White Friar, a dove, and the letters U.S.A. exist.[3] These are shown in figure 76. Of all the manufacturers covered in this publication, Whitefriars were unique in that, excluding the Christmas issues, virtually all of their limited edition weights were issued as commemoratives for special occasions. Examples include the sailing of the *Mayflower*, the Silver Jubilee of H.M. Queen Elizabeth II, the 1976 Olympic Games, and so forth. Rejection rate of the more difficult limited edition issues was often high – a figure of 50% not being uncommon.

Like all paperweight manufacturers, Whitefriars undertook considerable development work before many weights were of finalized design. In June, 1982, it was possible for collectors and members of the public to see evidence of such development and the resulting rare Whitefriars weights. This was brought about by the first exhibition arranged by the Cambridge Paperweight Circle, who exhibited a large number of rare weights. Because of the interest and importance of these weights, they are described below, so that a better appreciation may be had of the trials and problems encountered by the manufacturer.

These 31 weights were very kindly loaned by the late Geoffrey Baxter, and a fine selection of these is shown in figures 79-93.

Fig. 76. Very rare portrait canes, many were probably never used. Whitefriars. Courtesy of a private collector.

Ref. No.	Description	Year of Manufacture

*Denotes weights illustrated

1.*   Early experimental paperweight, blue/black and white. Only a few were made, faceted and un-faceted.   1954/56

2.*   Trial setting to test two new colors – straw and brown.   1954/56

3.*   Setting in a new trial color – coral. Only a small amount of cane was pulled from a trial melt which was never again repeated with the same quality of color. Only one weight was made.   1954/56

4.*   Setting to test trial yellow color, giving khaki yellow with blue-black four-way dip mold pattern. Eight coral canes set in small size canes. Signed G. Baxter.   1954/56

5.   Turquoise, browns, and greens, variation of six colors, random, undated.   1954/56

6.*   Random setting of blue bunched canes, interspersed with small red canes.   1954/56

7.   Early trial to include a date cane. A number of 1956 date canes within a setting of white bunch canes. Eight varied canes set round central red, white, and blue cane. Outer ring of white, and green. The figure 'five' is poorly formed.   1956

8.   Setting of small canes, random blue, green, and red with central 1956 test cane. The type of setting used as a basic pattern.   1956

9.   Random bunched cane setting including four 1956 dates, various gold, pink, blue, and blue/white bunches, set to test best position for date settings.   1956

10.   Test setting of pale enamel type colors. New canes at time of setting, dated 1970, first year of regular inclusion. Duck egg blue, pale blue, white/green center, and yellow canes with small red center.   1970

11.   The first dated limited edition '350th Anniversary of Sailing of the Mayflower to America'. Dated 1620-1970. Original pattern. The ship was made from seven separate pieces fused together.   1970

12.*   A one-off weight. Alternate concentric rows of two different yellow canes with coral colored, and white center cane. Window cut.   1972

13.   Trial setting with cotton twist and bunched canes in purple, green, and pink. A one-off weight.   1972

14.*   Fish shoal. Only one was ever made.   1976

15.   Pattern No. P25. Large cane bunches set in concentric pattern.   1975

16.   1975. Christmas limited edition of 1000. Host of Angels.   1975

17.*   Stars and Stripes Flag. Limited edition sold only to the U.S.A., to commemorate the American Bicentennial of Independence, dated 1776-1976. This is the original weight set by the designer. Forty-four only numbered to the U.S.A.   1976

18.   Liberty Bell. American Independence paperweight dated 1776-1976   1976

19.*   Partridge in a pear tree. This is the original trial weight for the 1979 Christmas limited edition. The weight was set, and made in 1976, dated, plain. The infill green canes are weaker in color than those which appeared in the weights that were eventually issued for the edition.   1976

20.*   Jubilee crown. A color variant of the standard issue. Only two were ever made in these colors   1977

21.   Large butterfly set in blue and pink with yellow flower, surrounded by single row of green cane cogwheel. One of the first of pattern PA500/G made. Set by the designer.   1978

22.*   Peacock. An experimental setting in specially made canes. Dated. Only one was made as it was too difficult to produce commercially.   1978

23.*   Commemoration of the founding of Western Australia. A limited edition of fifty weights made for Myers of Australia. The central cane is of a black swan surrounded by fine pink, dark purple, red, and an outer row of green single canes, all set concentrically. Weights are dated 1829-1979. Faceting is 5 + 1 or 6 + 1.   1979

24.*   A variation on number 23 above, this limited edition was produced for Boan's of Australia. The black swan cane appears at the center, set in concentric circles of single canes, two rows of dark blue, one each of purple red-gold, and pale green (outer). 5 + 1 faceting.   1979

Although examples of numbers 23 and 24 very rarely appear for sale, the former is considered to be the more attractive of the two designs, especially if it has the added bonus of the type of swan's beak that contains about fourteen pink and white cog canes. Plain and pink beaks appear to have been used at random in both designs, and examples are shown in figures 77 and 78.

Ref. No.	Description	Year of Manufacture
25.	1979 Christmas limited edition weight. Partridge in a pear tree, including final new development of infill of leaf shape green cane in a brighter color.	1979
26.*	Pedestal paperweight. One of only two ever made at Whitefriars, the weight is 5.25 inches diameter, and features a central Whitefriars 'Clichy' type rose in red. The rose is surrounded by twelve concentric circles of canes in colors which include red, white, blue, turquoise, mauve, and straw. The Whitefriar cane is set in the tenth row from the center. Height 5.25"	1979
27.*	Radiating lace twist setting with alternate rows of single pink canes with white row and row of pink rosettes. At the center is a Whitefriars type 'Clichy' rose. Made for the American market. Pattern No. P43A.	1979
28.*	One of twenty-four weights made on the morning of September 12 1980, the last day of working hot glass at Whitefriars. The last hot glass items to be made before glassworking ceased at midday. Dated 1980.	1980
29.	Pink and white candy-twist on green backing. Limited edition made for Smithsonian Institution, U.S.A. Alternate rows of four white bunch canes with pink center and pink rosettes. Dated 1980. Set by the designer.	1980
30.	1980 Christmas limited edition, Christmas bell.	1980
31.	Experimental pansy. A large pansy is set centrally and surrounded in white enamel and dark blue, set in concentric circles of straw, pale green, purple, and pink single canes. Only one was made.	

Fig. 78. The same design as in Fig. 77, but note the plain beak. Courtesy of Geoffrey Baxter. $750/850

Fig. 77. One of only fifty made for Myers, commemorating the founding of Western Australia, (150th Anniversary). Dated 1829 – 1979. Note the pink canes in the beak. Whitefriars. Dia. 2.95". Height 1.9". $800/1000.

Fig. 79. Early experimental weight. 1954 – 56. Whitefriars. Ref. No. 1. Dia. c. 3". Courtesy of Geoffrey Baxter. $300/350.

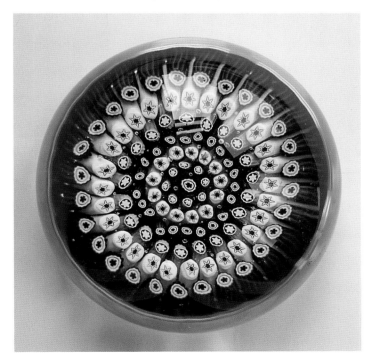

Fig. 80. Trial piece to test straw and brown colors. Rough pontil. 1954 – 56. Whitefriars. Ref. No. 2. Dia. 3.25". Courtesy of Geoffrey Baxter. $300/350.

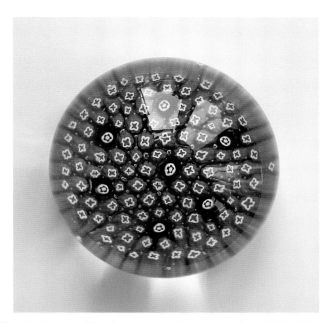

Fig. 81. A one-off weight to test the coral color. 1954 – 56. Whitefriars. Ref. No. 3. Dia. 2.75". Courtesy of Geoffrey Baxter. $300/350.

Fig. 82. Test piece for khaki yellow color. Rough pontil. 1954 – 56. Signed G. Baxter. Whitefriars. Ref. No. 4. Dia. 2.9". Courtesy of Geoffrey Baxter. $350/450.

Fig. 83. G. Baxter signature on base of Fig. 82. Courtesy of Geoffrey Baxter.

Fig. 84. A test piece for yellow, and coral canes. 1972 date cane. Whitefriars. Ref. No. 12. Courtesy of Geoffrey Baxter. $300/350

Fig. 86. The original Stars and Stripes flag set by the designer. Whitefriars. Ref. No. 17. Dia. 3". Courtesy of Geoffrey Baxter. $350/500

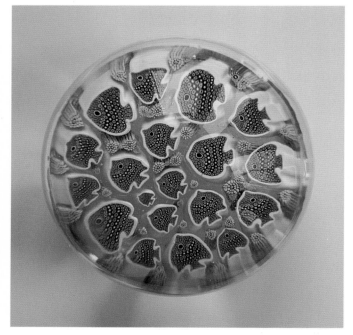

Fig. 85. Shoal of fish. Clear ground. A one-off, beautiful weight. 1976 date cane. Whitefriars. Ref. No. 14. Dia. 3.05". Courtesy of Geoffrey Baxter. $350/500.

Fig. 87. Partridge – the original design made in 1976. The issue appeared in 1979. Dated 1976. Whitefriars. Ref. No. 19. Dia. 2.95". Courtesy of Geoffrey Baxter. $500/700.

Fig. 88. Jubilee crown. One of only two made in these colors. 1977. Whitefriars. Ref. No. 20. Dia 3.2". Courtesy of Geoffrey Baxter. $450/550.

Fig. 89. Western Australia commemorative made for Boans. 1979. Whitefriars. Ref. No. 24. Courtesy of Geoffrey Baxter. $700/900.

Fig. 90. Magnum pedestal, 12 row concentric with central rose. Dated 1979. Only two were ever made. 16-point star cut base, signed G. Baxter. Whitefriars. Ref. No. 26. Dia. 5.25". Height 5.25". Courtesy of Geoffrey Baxter. $1700/2200.

Fig. 91. Top view of rare magnum shown in Fig. 90. 1979 date cane in the 10th row from the center. Courtesy of Geoffrey Baxter.

Fig. 92. Radiating lace twist with central rose. Dated 1979. Maker's pattern No. P43A. Whitefriars. Ref. No. 27. Courtesy of Geoffrey Baxter. $350/500.

Fig. 93. One of twenty-four weights made on the last day. Dated 1980. Dia. 3.05". Whitefriars. Ref. No. 28. Courtesy of Geoffrey Baxter. $600/800.

The values of these weights, many being one-offs, is difficult to assess if only because such pieces are rarely offered for sale. As guidance however, values ranging from $300 to 2200 each (depending upon design) are probably realistic.

Other extremely rare, or one-off, weights are known to exist. For example, figures 94 and 95 show the only known piece bearing the central cane "Royal Visit." It is not known for which occasion this was made, but it is known that, whereas Her Majesty Queen Elizabeth II has not visited Whitefriars, Prince Philip and Prince Charles did pay visits on November 10, 1960, and March 7, 1962, respectively. Furthermore, in March, 1957, HRH Princess Alice visited Whitefriars and was given some "charming souvenirs" which she displayed at Kensington Palace.

The general coloring of the weight, and in particular the surface appearance of the central cane, and the way in which it protrudes low into the base, compares well with the Coronation EIIR design issued in 1953. At the center of the Royal Visit cane are four badly distorted digits. Repeated careful examination of these has

convinced the author that they are in fact probably '1951'. If this is correct, then the weight may well have been made for a member of the British Royal Family, who visited the Festival of Britain Exhibition held in that year. The weight was once owned by a lady who was probably a relative of a Whitefriars employee. In view of the potentially highly significant importance of this weight, it has a value of $800 to 1200.

Right:
Fig. 94. Royal Visit. An exceedingly rare, early design. Dated 1951. Probably produced for a member of the British Royal Family, maybe for a visit to the Festival of Britain, 1951, where Whitefriars had a stand. Pontil mark. Whitefriars. Dia. 2.95". Height 1.75". Historically important. $800/1200.

Fig. 95. Close up of Royal Visit cane. Central date 1951 is very indistinct.

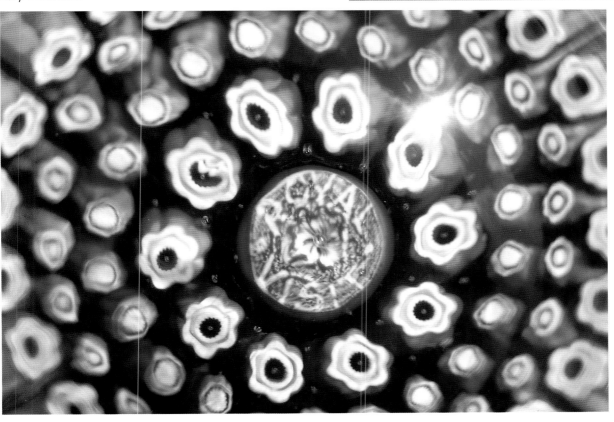

Then there are the Triplex weights. Whitefriars experimented with toughened glass, but their relationship with Triplex, who produced vehicle windscreens, is unknown. Equally it is known that Triplex and Whitefriars both exhibited at the South Bank Exhibition (Festival of Britain), London in 1951. At least five Triplex weights with a central 1951 date cane are known to exist, but how many were made in total is unknown. The different colorings of the weights shown in figure 96 tend to suggest that they were perhaps experimental pieces. Note the similarity of the date cane to the central cane in the Royal Visit weight described above. Triplex weights typically have rough pontil marks. These weights rarely appear for sale, thus when they do come up at auction one can expect to pay a relatively high price. In 1996 an example sold for $375.

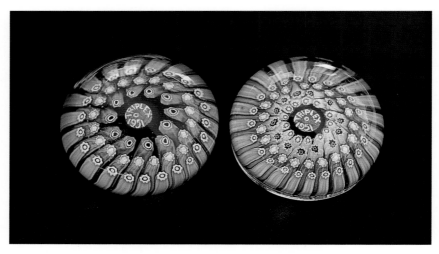

Fig. 96. Triplex weights. Other than the Royal Visit, these are possibly the only other weights known that are dated 1951. Probably less than about twenty exist. Pontil mark. Whitefriars. Dia. 2.75". Height 1.6". $350/500 each.

Another weight, very much in the style of the Coronation EIIR 1953, Royal Visit, and Triplex weights with respect to the type of canes, is a concentric design containing a silhouette of a heart in the central cane. The red heart is surrounded by five circles of canes in white, blue, red, white, and blue. In view of the color scheme, and the possibility that it was manufactured between 1951 and 1953, suggests that the weight may well be a one-off piece. This weight was sold for $150 in 1994. Figure 97 shows a weight containing numerous heart canes. At least one other variation of the 1977 Royal Silver Jubilee Crown is known. For example, an un-faceted weight exists with the usual design, but the canes are set high above the blue ground in an unconventional manner. The base is more or less conventional. The weight, which sold for $200 at auction in 1994, was probably yet another example of an experimental or prototype piece. Further examples known, where the central cane is marked in the style of the Royal Visit and Triplex weights, are initialed "GEW," "GF," and "SAL." The "SAL" weight, a five-ring concentric with pink, blue, and white canes, appeared at an auction in 1978. None of these weights contain a Whitefriar cane.

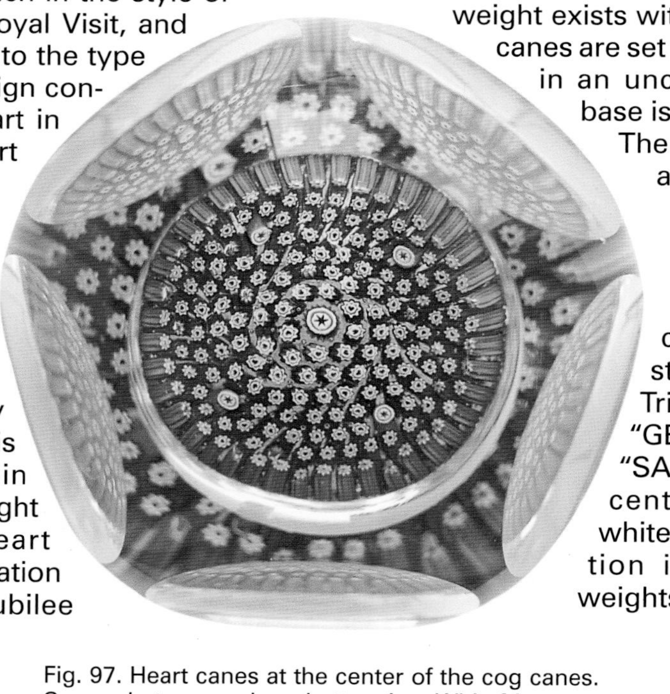

Fig. 97. Heart canes at the center of the cog canes. Somewhat unusual, and attractive. Whitefriars. Courtesy of a private collector. $175/300.

An important and rare weight containing the letters "EC" at the center is shown in figure 98. Only fourteen of these were made, and one was given to every member of the Executive Council of the Company at the annual general meeting in 1978. The example illustrated has five and one faceting, and exchanged hands in the 1990s for in excess of $350. The cane of the Mayflower appears at the center of one weight which is faceted all over, apart from the base which is of characteristic shape. Around the central cane are concentric rows of canes, the first of which has been noticeably distorted during manufacture. As it contains no date or Whitefriar cane this could well be an experimental piece.

Fig. 98. EC. One of fourteen weights produced for members of the company's Executive Council. Dated 1978. Whitefriars. Courtesy of a private collector. $400/600.

Central cane detail of EIIR 1953, Royal Visit, Triplex 1951, and GEW weights

It should be noted that the central identifying canes of these weights differ markedly from conventional (later) Whitefriars date canes, in that the design does not go right through the cane. The design is purely on the surface with the underneath of the cane being perfectly plain.

A detailed examination of a typical Triplex 1951 cane reveals a central circular opaque white rod. Around this is the layer of royal blue which can be quite thick. The blue extends as a thin coating over the upper surface. The blue was then literally scratched off, as necessary, to expose the white and form letters and numerals. As each cane was made individually it was very labor intensive compared with the use of a conventional date cane.

Overlays

In theory, overlays are unknown, apart from those made after 1981 by Caithness Glass and bearing the Whitefriar emblem and date cane. Although overlays were never officially issued by Whitefriars, the company clearly undertook some development work in the field, because in 1978 a blue overlay, listed as a factory reject, was on the market at $15.[4] Two more blue-flash

Fig. 99. A relatively rare blue flash overlay. Whitefriars. Courtesy of Sweetbriar Gallery Archive. $400/500.

overlays were auctioned in 1997 for $417 and $440.[5] An amber-flash overlay also exists. Figures 99 and 100 show two examples of flash overlays. A white overlay, sold by a dealer in 1996 for $300, was a close concentric about two inches in diameter and containing a 1972 date cane. This has two rows of printies on the side and one on top. The surface is of dirty appearance, and it has been said by a Whitefriars operator that these were made by rolling the weight in powdered white glass. According to Raymond Annenberg, they had problems with overlays as the overlay typically was too thick.

Fig. 100. An attractive amber flash overlay. Whitefriars. Courtesy of a private collector. $400/500.

Further experimental pieces include:
1. A small blue bird on a nest, placed centrally on the ground and made in the style of a portrait cane.
2. A large face of a ginger cat on a white ground. This was made by using the technique of incorporating a suitable transfer of the design into the glass. The weight has five and one faceting.
3. Five large pieces of portrait cane of a crown set into a circle on the ground.
4. A standard size weight with a large central portrait cane of a butterfly surrounded by concentric rows of small mauve, pale yellow/green, and pale blue canes. Dated 1975. Pontil mark.

Sub-standard weights (seconds) are known to have been sold. For example, in December, 1977, the following appeared in one dealer's stock list:

Bouquet window cut (PB301)	$45
Garland plain (PG102)	$38
Random setting	
window cut (PR400, PR401, or PR402)	$30

Seconds, which were typically sold to the staff, had a "S" engraved on the base. How many trade shows Whitefriars exhibited at is unknown, but exhibit they did. For example, designs PA500, PB302, and PG104 were three of several new designs first shown at the Hotel St. George, Harrogate in 1978. These were offered in a wide variety of color patterns.

Pattern reference numbers

As previously stated, various pattern numbers were used by Whitefriars to identify the type of surface cutting. Hereunder is a reasonably comprehensive list of these pattern numbers, the cutting to which they refer, and contents of the weight, where known.

Legend to background colors:
DB – Dark blue
LB – Light blue
G – Green
R – Ruby

Pattern No.	Design features	Issue Price in 1977 $	Value /in year stated
P1	Plain uncut dome	35	
P2	Window cut (side and top printies) 1977 date cane	39	
P3	Diamond cut	44	
P4	Finger cut	39	
P5	Finger cut, printie top, tall dome	41	
P9	Window and small miter cuts	47	
P10	Large facet cut	47	
P11	Brick cut	47	
P12	Cylinder-ball cuts	47	
P13	Cylinder-finger cut	47	
P14	Miniature window cut	35	
P16	Window cut-lace twist	50	
P17	Brick cut-lace twist	60	
P18	Large facets-lace twist	60	
P19	Large facets-lace twist and miter cuts, filigree spokes	60	
P20	Large brick cut-lace twist	60	
P21	Double window cut-lace twist	57	
P22	Miter cut cylinder	50	
P23	Large facets	50	
P25	Window cut-close set canes. 1978 date cane	60	120/1983
P26	Window and small ball cuts	44	
P27	Window and miter cuts	44	
P28	Cylinder-finger cuts	53	
P30	Pedestal-window cut (known to have been made in 1972 and 1976)	53	375/1994
P31	Single and floret canes, plain dome. 1977 date cane	47	
P32	Close packed multi-hued canes, window cut	72	
P33	Window cut top and close miter cuts. 1977 date cane	50	
P34	Window cut top and close miter cuts-lace twist	50	
P35	Spray lace twist canes with floret setting DB, LB, and G	62	
P36	Spray setting of variety of florets DB, LB, and G	47	
P37	Miniature lace twist	60	
P38	Vortex window cut DB, LB, and G		
P39	Large pedestal window cut		
P40	Colored candy twist canes close set in florets		
P41	Colored candy twist, and window cut DB, LB, and G		
P43A	Radiating lace twists. Central rose		

Pattern No.	Design features	Issue Price in 1977 $	Value /in year stated
PG100	Garland setting (classical), interwoven cane, plain dome DB, LB, and G. Star cut base	70	
PG101	Garland setting (classical), interwoven canes, side and top printies DB, LB, and G. Star cut base	80	
PG102	Garland random setting of many colored canes. 70 DB, Plain dome LB, and G		
PG103	Garland, window cut 80		
PG104	Posy window cut DB, LB, and G		
PG105	Miniature garland, window cut DB, LB, and G	60	
PG106	Daffodil miniature weight with special canes, window cut DB, LB, and G	60	
PS200	Fish silhouette set in concentric cane pattern, window cut. 1978 date cane	70	310/1997
PS201	Butterfly silhouette set in concentric cane pattern, window cut	70	330/1997
PS202	Five small butterflies in lace twist, and multi-cane, window cut. 1977 date cane	70	
PS203	Owl silhouette set in concentric cane, window cut	70	425/1992
PS204	Robin silhouette. Window cut	70	500/1993
PS207	Donkey silhouette. Window cut	70	
PB300	Bouquet. Plain dome. DB, LB, G, and R. Rose cane	70	600/1993
PB301	Bouquet. Window cut. DB, LB, G, and R. Rose cane	80	
PB302	Petal flower shaped setting. Window cut. DB, LB, and G	96	
PR400R	Florette random set flowers. Window cut. R	53	
PR401B	Florette random set flowers. Window cut. LB	53	
PR402G	Florette random set flowers. Window cut. G	53	
PA500	Large butterfly, window cut DB, LB, and G	96	725/1997
PA600	Large bee, window cut. DB, LB, and G	81	700/1993
PA601	Owl, window cut. DB, LB, and G	81	333/1993
CM625	Decanter with millefiori stopper	80	
CM637	Cut, square spirit decanter with millefiori stopper	80	
9739	Millefiori dish in various colors and patterns. Smooth profile. 4.5" diameter		
9754	Millefiori bottle, height 5.25," dated 1970	160	
9755	As per 9739, but periphery fluted with large facets		
9756	As per 9739, but periphery cut with a multitude of facets		
9850	Streaky weight	12	

Although of no known pattern number, a garlanded weight was produced with a central cane of a Jewish menorah. When this was first issued is not known, but at least one with 6+1 faceting exists dated 1980. This example fetched $315 at auction in 1991. A design also exists with a portrait cane of a squirrel. One known to the author with 5+1 faceting is dated 1978.

It is perhaps of interest to note how the retail price of Whitefriars weights, in common with many other manufacturers, increased in just a few years. The following are a few typical examples:

Pattern No.	Issue price $	Price 3 years later $
P2	39	44
P9	50	81
P16	51	59
P31	50	81
P36	47	63
P37	60	81
PG101	80	130
PG202	71	114
PL504	87	128

Limited edition weights

Year of Issue	Name	Edition	Pattern No.		Issue Price $	Value $ /in year stated
1953	Coronation EIIR	Officially unlimited but only 600-700 were actually issued				600/1999
1970	Mayflower	400 (at least 389 were made)				
1972	Royal Silver Wedding	500				
1975	Christmas, Host of Angels	1000	15		83	575/1995
1976	Olympic Games Montreal, XXI Olympiad	1000 (500 on clear ground 500 on blue ground)			75	300/1997
1976	U.S.A. Bicentennial Flag (for U.S.A. market only)	150				520/1997
1976	U.S.A. Bicentennial Bell (600 of these went to U.S.A.)	750				400/1993
1976	Christmas, Three Wise Men	1000	PL502,	717	83	750/1998
1977	Telephone Centenary	500	PL503		83	
1977	U.S.A. National Flag	500	PL504		87	600/1997
1977	U.S.A. Liberty Bell	100	PL505		87	
1977	U.S.A. American Eagle	100	PL506		87	
1977	U.S.A. Flag, Bell, and Eagle	100	PL507		87	
1977	Royal Silver Jubilee Crown	1500				
1977	Royal Silver Jubilee Cipher	1000	PL508		75	
1977	Royal Silver Jubilee Garland	1000			83	
1977	Royal Silver Jubilee White ribbon Twist	1000			102	450/1993
1977	Royal Silver Jubilee Garland Ink Bottle	50			300	
1977	Royal Silver Jubilee Decanter (Cipher)	50			150	
1977	Christmas, Manger	1000			102	420/1997
1978	Coronation Anniversary Crown	500	CA1, PL520		90	
1978	Coronation Anniversary Orb	500	PL521		90	
1978	30th Anniversary of the Foundation of the State of Israel	1000			75	400/1997
1978	Christmas, The Road to Bethlehem	1000	PL522		90	750/1997
1979	Founding of Western Australia (for Myers, Australia)	50				900/1999
1979	Variation on above (for Boan's, Australia)					
1979	Christmas, Partridge in a Pear Tree	612 issued			113	450/1999
1980	Pink and white candy twist, made for Smithsonian Institution, USA					
1980	Christmas, Bell	258	W29			600/1999
1980	Olympic Games, Moscow, XXII Olympiad	1000				400/1999

Fig. 101. Coronation weight. Collectors are often fascinated by the range of color combinations. A desirable early weight. Dated 1953. Whitefriars. Dia. 2.75". Height 1.7". $600/700.

Descriptions of a few selected weights

1953 Coronation weight

This concentric design typically has five circles of cog canes. At the center of the circles of canes is the EIIR 1953 motif. The weight can be plain or have five and one faceting (figure 101). While the weight rarely appears for sale, it is generally acknowledged to be of a lower standard of quality than the company's later weights. Various combinations of colors have been used to produce at least thirteen different forms of the weight.

Typical color combinations in Whitefriars Coronation weights (1953):

Circle next to EIIR cane	Next Circle	Next Circle	Next Circle	Circle nearest perimeter
Red	White	Red	White	Blue
White	Blue	Red	White	Blue
White	Red	Blue	White	Red
Red	White	Blue	Red	White
Red	White	Blue	White	Red
White	Red	Blue	-	White
White	Blue	White	-	Red
Red	Blue	White	-	Red
Green	Red	Blue	White	Red
Blue	White	Red	White	Blue
Green	White	Blue	White	Red
Blue	Red	Blue	White	Red

Another rare variety of this weight is believed to contain some yellow canes. Possibly the rarest combination of all is the six circle concentric which from the center is blue, white, green, white, red, and blue.

1970 Mayflower

Seven separate pieces of blue/black glass go to form the central Mayflower motif (facing left or right), and are set on a white background. This is surrounded by up to five concentric circles of canes in various colors including blue, green, mauve, yellow, and red. Date cane 1620-1970. Figure 102 shows an example.

Fig. 102. Mayflower. The first limited edition weight issued, and very popular. Like the Coronation weight, various color combinations exist. Dated 1620 – 1970. Whitefriars. Courtesy of Sweetbriar Gallery Archive. $400/600.

Fig. 103. Host of Angels. A fine example of the first Christmas weight. Dated 1975. Whitefriars. Courtesy of a private collector. $450/650.

1975 Christmas, Host of Angels

The central angel is surrounded by a circle of between ten and fourteen further angels, all depicted in portrait canes. Five side printies. See figure 103.

1976 Christmas, Three Wise Men

The three wise men, all in multi-colored portrait canes facing to the right, are set within a disc of blue star canes with an outer circle of pistachio cogs.

1976 U.S.A. Bicentennial Bell

A central silhouette cane of a bell encircled by five concentric rows of canes in pink, white, and blue. 1776-1976 date cane. Five and one faceting. Dia. 2.9".

1976 U.S.A. Bicentennial Flag

A large single flag is used, and the weight has five side printies. Some weights have six pink and white stripes in the flag, and some have seven. One example exists where the lowest pink and white stripes are normal when viewed from the front, but both are pink when seen through the base. Design is principally in pink, white, and blue, and the date cane is 1776-1976. Typical dia. is 3.15".

1977 U.S.A. National Flag

Three stars and stripes flags are set at the center of the design, and these are surrounded by six point star canes in blue and white. The outer ring of canes are red.

1977 Christmas, Manger

Mary, with the infant Jesus in a manger within a stable, is shown in a single portrait cane. Two angel portrait canes are set above. All within blue and pink canes.

1978 Christmas, The Road to Bethlehem

Portrait canes of Mary on a donkey and Joseph face to the right. Both are set on a blue cushion of canes with concentric circles of pink and blue canes.

1978 Thirtieth Anniversary of the Foundation of the State of Israel

A large six point blue and fawn portrait cane of a star is at the center of the design. It is surrounded by concentric circles of canes in blue and fawn, and a cane dated 1948-1978 is incorporated within a blue circle.

1980 Christmas, Bell

This is a relatively rare weight that was being made in the year the factory closed down. How many were actually made is unknown, but it is believed that the total number is probably less than two hundred and sixty. Figure 104 shows a large bell, in cane work, virtually filling the ground of this weight.

The development of this weight is of interest, as in the beginning Geoffrey Baxter had the idea of representing 'while shepherds watched their flocks by night' as the theme. However, when a white silhouette cane of a sheep was made, the result was

Fig. 104. Christmas Bell. Last of the Christmas weights, dated 1980, and possibly the most difficult to obtain. Whitefriars. Dia. 3.3". Height 2.1". $500/700.

not entirely satisfactory – it having been described as looking more like a poodle! One weight was made with the cane at the center. Unfortunately Whitefriars frequently tended to minimize the time, and money, devoted to the development of paperweights, and hence the idea of sheep was dropped.

1980 Olympic Games

This is not a particularly common weight, and although it is not known how many were issued it was probably significantly less than five hundred. Due to a dispute over the games with the USSR, it is known that at the time the U.S.A. was not showing much interest in this weight. The weight differs from the 1976 issue in having the intertwined canes in different colors. According to Raymond

Annenberg, Whitefriars had difficulty making the brown circle of canes (third from the left in figure 105). The ground color was a light transparent blue. Like the 1976 issue the date was made up of two separate canes, and the flame portrait cane was identical to that in the 1976 issue. Faceting is six and one.

Although the emphasis in this chapter has been on Whitefriars millefiori weights, one should not lose sight of the bubbled and spiral design weights which the company made.

Bubble designs are known to have been made in the 1930s, and those incorporating spiral motifs were made in the 1950s, and also shown in a catalog produced in the late 1970s. Figure 106 shows typical bubble weights. These were most commonly 3-3.5" dia., and in addition to clear glass were also issued in aqua, antique blue, gold, ruby, and sky blue. All except ruby were full lead crystal. Quite a large number of ruby weights do not contain the characteristic large central bubble. This arose as a result of a lapse in quality control. When issued in 1957 bubble weights cost $0.5, and in the same year spiral designs cost $1.2, and millefiori weights (of unknown design) $3. In 1979 bubble weights retailed at prices ranging from $7 - 10.

Weights containing spirals in one or more colors range in size from 2.75" to 5" in dia., and currently realize $22 - 37. Those containing spirals in red, white, and blue were either made in 1951 for the Festival of Britain, or more likely in 1953 the year of the Coronation of Her Majesty Queen Elizabeth II.

Fig. 105. Olympic Games 1980. The more desirable of the two editions (the 1st was 1976). Whitefriars. Dia. 3.3". Height 2". $350/500 .

Fig. 106. Two bubble weights. Also made in other colors. Post 1940s. Whitefriars. Dia. 3.5". Height 2.8". $30/40 each.

Certification

Issued on quality paper with many weights, the wording is as follows:

'Whitefriars millefiori items are collectors' pieces and will enhance in value over the years. They are made by highly skilled craftsmen in English full-lead crystal by a sophisticated method used in the factory for over a century. Incorporated within the design is the Whitefriars trademark together with the year of manufacture.' See figure 107.

Labelling

All weights were probably issued with an adhesive paper label. Some weights still have their original labels which were probably of two types:

A circular label used for the 1953 EIIR Coronation weights and maybe later. This label is rare.

A rectangular label.

Other weights

One of the joys of collecting Whitefriars paperweights lies in realizing the extremely wide range of unlimited edition designs that they produced. It is reasonable to assume that in all probability many of these patterns were not issued in very large numbers.

Fig. 107. Typical Whitefriars limited edition certificates.

Hence to many collectors the pleasure is not solely confined to building up a collection of the limited editions, but in additionally locating attractive unlimited pieces. These weights sometimes contain rare complex canes (such as a two-color cog filled with about twenty white tubes with turquoise centers) which seldom appear in limited editons.

The final illustrations, shown in figures 108 to 125, give some idea of the range of designs (limited and unlimited), and related objects available to the collector.

Fig. 109. A good six row concentric. Note the 1970 cane. This was the first year of regular inclusion, and the numerals are blue. Whitefriars. Dia. 3.1". Height 2.25". $225/300.

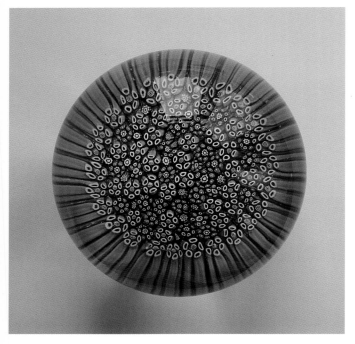

Fig. 108. An attractive early weight, made 1954 – 56. Pontil mark. Whitefriars. Ref. No. 6. Dia. 2.95". Courtesy of Geoffrey Baxter. $300/350.

Fig. 111. Weight with fish portrait cane. Although unlimited, portrait cane weights of this type are very popular. Maker's pattern No. PS200. Whitefriars. Dia. 3.2". Height 1.9". $350/400.

Fig. 110. An unusual shape from 1972. Note once again the date cane, set at the front of the white row, the numerals are still blue. Whitefriars. Dia. 3.25". Height 4". Courtesy of Sweetbriar Gallery Archive. $300/400.

Fig. 112. Very attractive white and gold star canes on clear ground. Another example of a quality design in an unlimited weight. Whitefriars. Courtesy of a private collector. $225/275.

Fig. 113. Circular Whitefriars label. Always look out for labels, as they can often enhance the value of a paperweight. The earlier design shown here is relatively rare. Much more common is the rectangular shape. Courtesy of Roy and Pam Brown.

Fig. 114. Typical Whitefriars portrait canes, showing detailed construction. Dia. c. 0.5".

Fig. 115. An example of a Whitefriars brochure, showing the attraction of collecting weights with a wide range of faceting designs.

Fig. 116. Probably an experimental piece associated with the rich red ground. Whitefriars. Dia. 3.2". Height 2". $100/150.

Fig. 117. An unusual weight, possibly experimental, with vertical latticinio giving an attractive lightness to the design. Whitefriars. Dia. 3.1". Height 2.05". $150/250.

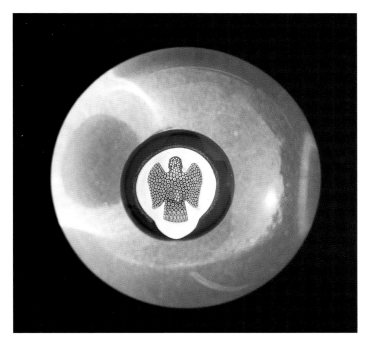

Left:
Fig. 118. Trial piece with a distorted angel portrait cane. Frosted flat base. Whitefriars. Dia. 2.4". Height 1.3". $60/100.

Fig. 119. One of the few transfer type weights. Silver Wedding of H.M. Queen Elizabeth II and H.R.H. Prince Philip. 1972. Whitefriars. Dia. 3.15". Height. 2.1". $80/120.

Fig. 120. Scratched Whitefriars logo, and number on base of weight shown in Fig. 119.

Fig. 121. A fine weight, design PB301, with a good range of canes, and a central rose. 1979. Whitefriars. Dia. c. 3". Courtesy of a private collector. $375/500.

Fig. 122. Royal Silver Jubilee Crown. A good commemorative weight, enhanced by the presence of its rarely seen mold. Whitefriars. Dated 1952 – 77. Dia 3.3". Height 1.9". $350/500.

Fig. 123. Christmas Manger, 1977. The third of the popular Christmas weights using portrait canes. Whitefriars. Dia. 3.1". Height 1.9". $400/600.

Fig. 124. Coronation Anniversary Orb, 1978. One of two designs issued to commemorate the 25th Anniversary. Dated 1953 – 1978. Whitefriars. Dia. 3.2". Height 1.9". $275/400.

Right:
Fig. 125. Christmas 1979. This is shown to illustrate the subtle difference between a final production issue, and its original trial piece in Fig. 87. Whitefriars. Dia. 3.1". Height 2". $400/600.

Readers seeking other informative data on, and illustrations of, Whitefriars paperweights should refer to the excellent articles by D. Webber in the Annual Bulletin of the P.C.A. 1997 – 99. These cover a wide range of unusual designs which include abstract, transfer and picture weights, doorstops, marbries, and experimental pieces that encompass trial Christmas themes.

[1]*Three hundred years of glass making*. Whitefriars publication.
[2]Evans, Wendy; Ross, Catherine and Werner, Alex. *Whitefriars Glass – James Powell and Sons of London*. London. The Museum of London. 1995.
Jackson, Lesley. *Whitefriars Glass – The art of James Powell and Sons*. Catalog of an exhibition held in Manchester, England from January 27 to June 30 1996.
[3]Brown, Roy. *Cambridge Paperweight Circle newsletter number 63, March 1998.*
[4]Pavitt, Trevor. *Paperweights – a bulletin for collectors, number 3, May 1978*. Darius Arts Limited, 105, Clerkenwell Road, London, EC1R 5BX.
[5]L.H. Selman Limited. *Spring 1997 price guide and mail auction, lot 245, and Fall 1997 price guide and mail auction, lot 272.*

Fig. 126. A wide range of common Strathearn millefiori
weights. Attractive, and an ideal weight for the beginner.
Courtesy of Sweetbriar Gallery Archive. $30/80.

Fig. 127. Dish of attractive shape, with millefiori
base. Strathearn. Length 7.4". Height 1.4". $55/70.

Chapter 4
Strathearn Glass

Members of the Ysart family, together with John Moncrieff, formed the first link in a chain of events that was to culminate with the formation of Strathearn Glass Ltd. Lawrence Selman gives the full history of this development[1], which can briefly be shown as follows.

In 1924 Salvador Ysart, his sons and John Moncrieff produced Monart Glassware. 1946 saw Salvador and sons Vincent and Augustine trading as Ysart Brothers Glass, and in 1956 as Vasart Glass Ltd. By 1963 William Teacher and Sons showed interest in Vasart Glass Ltd., and by 1964 the latter became Strathearn Glass Company. In 1980 the company was renamed Stuart Strathearn.

Strathearn Glass with Stuart Drysdale as manager, began production from its glasshouse on the banks of the River Earn in Muthill Road, Crieff, Scotland, in December 1964, and two of the craftsmen who were to become closely associated with the many and varied weights produced were Herbert Dreier and Donald McDonald. Production of paperweights ceased in 1980.

In common with most other paperweight manufacturers, Strathearn exported to France and the U.S.A.. Again, like many other British makers, the lead content of Strathearn's glass at 2.5% was low.

Their range of paperweights was far more extensive than is commonly imagined, and in addition to conventional concentric and spaced millefiori designs included a range of abstracts, lampwork, crowns, sulphides and overlays. Figures 126 to 128 serve to show a range of millefiori weights and other items prior to discussing specific details.

Fig. 128. Pair of door handles with spaced millefiori canes. Strathearn. Dia. c. 2.4". Courtesy of Sweetbriar Gallery Archive. $80/100 each.

Cane details

Cog canes are common and are found with 4, 8, 14, and 20 teeth.

Teeth of cogs can be pointed or rounded. Very rounded eight toothed cogs can sometimes look like a floral motif. Maltese cross canes are occasionally seen and were produced in various colors including black, white, and pale blue/gray.

Although the cog was fundamental to their millefiori designs, Strathearn would often use it in various colors and in many different ways to produce more complex canes.

This makers canes sometimes appear with a fuzzy and distorted outline, and the entrapment of fine air bubbles just above the top of some of the canes is frequently seen. Coated spherical bubbles will often be seen adhering to the sides of canes – notably those of a pale cream color – figure 129. However, examination of weights made during the last two or three years of their production would perhaps suggest that this fuzziness had finally been minimized or overcome.

Canes can also assume the appearance of a squashed pastry mold, reminiscent of those in some of the Clichy weights made in the 19th century. Strathearn frequently used long pieces of cane in their set-ups, and these often protruded well above the upper surface of the ground.

Fig. 129. Fuzzy edged cream colored cane. Note spherical globules, common to many early Strathearn weights.

Figures 130 and 131 show the 'S' signature cane, which was made in a few different colors, and a date cane.

Fig. 130. Red S signature cane in the base of a floral weight. Only some of Strathearn's weights were signed.

Fig. 131. Date 72, with red 7 and black 2. This one is at the center of a D4 flower (Ref. No. 75).

Sizes

Weights were produced in a range of sizes from miniatures, 1.65" in diameter, to magnums, in excess of 4".

Grounds

As well as clear, popular colors were royal blue, orange, brick red, turquoise, green, yellow, and pink. These are shown in figure 132 together with a green spatter ground which is believed to be somewhat rarer.

Fig. 132. One attraction of Strathearn weights is the wide range of colors used for their grounds. The center weight has a label – always a bonus.

Publicity brochures

Few brochures would appear to have survived, and figures 133 to 140 show those relating to pre-1979, 1979, and 1980.

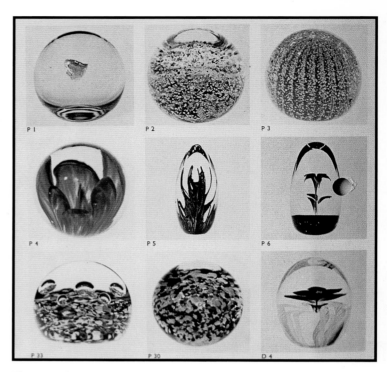

Fig. 134. A continuation of Fig. 133 showing various designs.

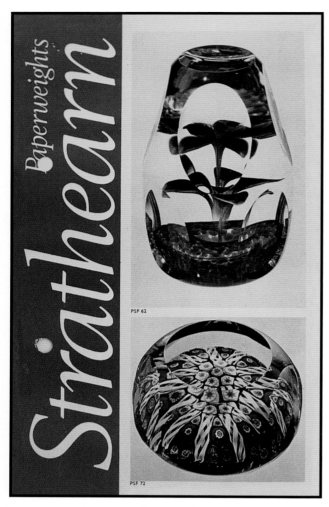

Fig. 133. Strathearn brochure. Collectors always like brochures. This is the earliest seen by the author. Probably pre-1978. $10.

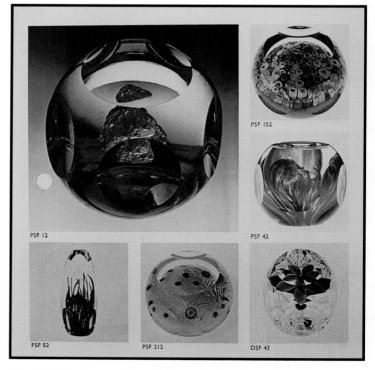

Fig. 135. Another section of the early Strathearn brochure.

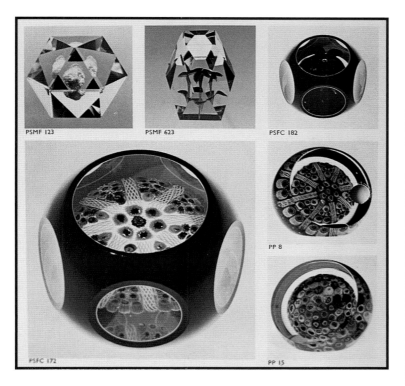

PSMF 123 PSMF 623 PSFC 182

PP 8

PSFC 172 PP 15

Fig. 136. Last section of early brochure.
Note the two blue overlays – these are
rarely seen.

Fig. 137. Strathearn brochure for 1979.

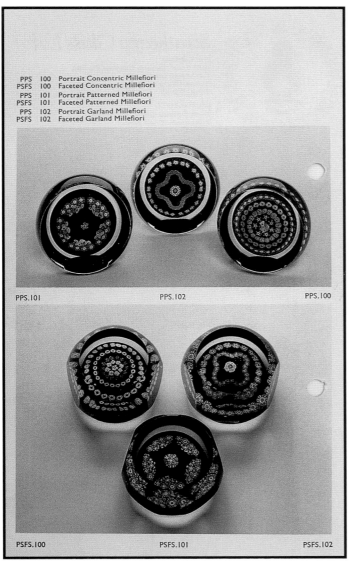

PPS 100 Portrait Concentric Millefiori
PSFS 100 Faceted Concentric Millefiori
PPS 101 Portrait Patterned Millefiori
PSFS 101 Faceted Patterned Millefiori
PPS 102 Portrait Garland Millefiori
PSFS 102 Faceted Garland Millefiori

PPS.101 PPS.102 PPS.100

PSFS.100 PSFS.101 PSFS.102

Fig. 138. 1979 brochure. Note facets on top
three weights enabling them to be stood
up.

P.39

P.4l   85 mm dia. 80 mm ht.   P.37   80 mm dia. 70 mm ht.   P.39   80 mm dia. 70 mm ht.

Fig. 139. Strathearn 1980 brochure, with the emphasis on abstract designs.

P.38   75 mm dia. 70 mm ht.   P.40   75 mm dia. 70 mm ht.   P.36   75 mm dia. 70 mm ht.

P.38

Fig. 140. Strathearn 1980. Probably their last brochure. Again the emphasis is on abstract designs.

List of Weights Issued:

Note: the word "portrait" in this chapter is the word used by Strathearn in their publicity brochures, and does *not* refer to the inclusion of portrait canes, as normally inferred when this term is used.

Reference No.	Name	Manufacturer's No.	Edition Limit	Issue Price, $
				*Denotes weights illustrated.
1.	Ice pool, Strathearn range*	P1	Unknown	12
2.	Stoer, Strathearn range*	P2	Unknown	Not known
3.	Sea urchin, Strathearn range*	P3	Unknown	Not known
4.	Orchid, Strathearn range*	P4	Unknown	20
5.	Tropic, Strathearn range*	P5	Unknown	Not known
6.	Flower, dated and signed, 2.5" dia. x 3.5" high	P6	Unknown	37
7.	Millefiori	P7	Unknown	13
8.	Millefiori	P8	Unknown	10
9.	Star	P11	Unknown	13
10.	Carpet	P14	Unknown	13
11.	Carpet	P15	Unknown	10
12.	Carpet, mini	P16	Unknown	9
13.	Lace Latticinio, large	P21	Unknown	24
14.	Aurora, miniature	P26	Unknown	6
15.	Aurora	P28	Unknown	10
16.	Floe, small, Arctic range*	P30	Unknown	Not known
17.	Force 1, large, Arctic range	P31	Unknown	21
18.	Force 2, large, Arctic range	P32	Unknown	Not known
19.	Force 3, large, Arctic range*	P33	Unknown	Not known
20.	Force 4, large, Arctic range	P34	Unknown	Not known
21.	Lava, Arctic range	P35	Unknown	Not known
22.	Whirlwind 3" dia.*	P36	Unknown	Not known
23.	Flower garden 3.25" dia.*	P37	Unknown	Not known
24.	Kaleidoscope 3" dia.*	P38	Unknown	Not known
25.	Sea Anemone 3.25" dia.*	P39	Unknown	Not known
26.	Cyclone 3" dia.*	P40	Unknown	Not known
27.	Coral fantasy 3.25" dia.*	P41	Unknown	Not known
28.	Millefiori, large. Date & signature cane	P7DS	3000 per annum	Not known
29.	Millefiori, small. Date & signature cane	P8DS	3000 per annum	Not known
30.	Millefiori, large. Portrait range	PP7	Unknown	Not known
31.	Millefiori, small. Portrait range	PP8	Unknown	Not known
32.	Millefiori, miniature. Portrait range*	PP9	Unknown	Not known
33.	Carpet, small. Portrait range*	PP15	Unknown	Not known
34.	Carpet, miniature. Portrait range	PP16	Unknown	Not known
35.	Lace, large. Portrait range	PP21	Unknown	Not known
36.	Lace, small. Portrait range	PP22	Unknown	Not known
37.	Portrait concentric millefiori 1979*	PPS100	Unknown	Not known
38.	Portrait patterned millefiori 1979*	PPS101	Unknown	Not known
39.	Portrait garland millefiori 1979*	PPS102	Unknown	Not known
40.	Ice pool, faceted*	PSF12	Unknown	52

Reference No.	Name	Manufacturer's No.	Edition Limit	Issue Price, $
41.	Stoer, faceted*	PSF22	Unknown	Not known
42.	Orchid, faceted*	PSF42	Unknown	Not known
43.	Flower, faceted, jumbo*	PSF43	Unknown	Not known
44.	Tropic, faceted*	PSF52	Unknown	Not known
45.	Flower, faceted, dated and signed*	PSF62	Unknown	Not known
46.	Millefiori, faceted, with lace, large 1976*	PSF72	Unknown	51
47.	Millefiori, faceted 1977	PSF72	Unknown	56
48.	Millefiori, faceted, small	PSF82	Unknown	Not known
49.	Millefiori, faceted, clear base, dated & signed	PSF102	Unknown	Not known
50.	Carpet millefiori, faceted, small*	PSF152	Unknown	Not known
51.	Lace, large, faceted*	PSF212	Unknown	Not known
52.	Lace, small, faceted	PSF222	Unknown	Not known
53.	Overlay butterfly, dated S76*	PSFC001	Edition limited but size unknown	Not known
54.	Overlay crown, faceted	PSFC162	Issued 1976, limited but edition not known	260
55.	Overlay millefiori*	PSFC172	Unknown	Not known
56.	Overlay flower*	PSFC182	Unknown	Not known
57.	Overlay lace	PSFC192	Unknown	Not known
58.	Crown	PSFC202	Unknown	Not known
59.	Faceted concentric millefiori 1979*	PSFS100	500	Not known
60.	Faceted patterned millefiori 1979*	PSFS101	500	Not known
61.	Faceted garland millefiori 1979*	PSFS 102	500	Not known
62.	Ice pool, multi facet*	PSMF123	Unknown	Not known
63.	Flower, multi-facet*	PSMF623	Unknown	Not known
64.	Concentric millefiori 1979*	SP100	500	Not known
65.	Patterned millefiori 1979*	SP101	500	Not known
66.	Garland millefiori 1979*	SP102	500	Not known
67.	Flower, faceted, jumbo	DSF43	Unknown	Not known
68.	Seaweed, faceted		Unknown	Not known
69.	Jumbo		Unknown	63
70.	Sulphide, S79 cane in base		Unknown	Not known
71.	Sulphide, faceted*		Unknown	Not known
72.	Sulphide, Napoleon		10 – 20	Not known
73.	Red and white spiral, S79 cane*		Unknown	Not known
74.	Quatrefoil, pink center cane S80*		Unknown	Not known
75.	Flower with leaves and radial latticinio. Dated and signed*	D4	Unknown	Not known

Fig. 141. Orchids in sepia and turquoise. Flat base. Strathearn. Dia. 2.8". Height 2.6". $60/80 each.

Specific details

Reference numbers are those used in the section (above) on List of Weights Issued:

1. Ice pool. A lump of Scottish quartz is suspended in clear glass.
2. Stoer. Scottish sand and granite are encased in clear glass.
3. Sea urchin. With the inner design resembling a sea urchin, the weight was produced in red and green.
4. Orchid. Depicts an open bud and was issued in sepia, turquoise, and madder. Figure 141 shows orchid in two of the colors.
5. Tropic. A tall drop-shaped weight with multi-colored fronds.
6. Flower. An open flower with leaves growing from a dark ground is featured in this tall, drop-shaped weight. Issued in turquoise, madder, and gentian.

24. Kaleidoscope. Abstract patterns of opaque colors on an opaque ground. Issued in pine green, chalk blue, sand yellow, and turf brown.
25. Sea anemone. Marine form rising from a bed of matching color, the weight was issued in lagoon green, Atlantic blue, rock shade mauve, and meridian yellow.
27. Coral fantasy. A coral like form rises from a weed green bed.
31. Millefiori, small. Sometimes referred to as a portrait weight, the weight has a small facet on which it stands, and is so placed that the millefiori pattern is virtually upright and facing the viewer. This weight has radial spokes of latticinio which center upon a circle of canes. The pattern is visible through a large facet.
33. Carpet, small. A further example of a portrait weight.

85

87

89

Other weights

Colin had some modern design ideas, and realized that the magnification, distortion, refraction, and diminution effects that occur in a paperweight, could lead to the manufacture of a new generation of weights. His ideas and experiments were to lead to the production of the Planets set one, and so the success story of Colin Terris and Caithness Glass Ltd. had begun.

These innovative designs had considerable impact upon the market, and in 1969 Caithness opened a factory in Oban, and appointed Colin Terris design director in 1970. In 1976 he became design and marketing director, and deputy managing director. Production went from strength to strength, and in 1979 a specially designed factory was opened on the outskirts of Perth. This was to be the most ambitious so far, and provides excellent facilities for visitors including a viewing gallery and shop. By 1995 around forty personnel were employed in the paperweight making department.

The first four paperweights Mars, Mercury, Saturn, and Venus (Planets set one) shown in figure 160 were boxed as a set. Eighty per cent of the edition was exported to the U.S.A. where they were quickly purchased by keen collectors. The majority of the remaining sets were sold in Great Britain. Thus glass paperweights showing a different adventurous approach had been launched.

To further understand the possible reasons for their success, it should be borne in mind that at about this time people were paying much attention to aerospace programs, culminating with the first landing on the moon in July 1969.

The final act by Caithness which cemented the interests of collectors was launched in 1976. This was the formation of the Caithness Paperweight Collectors Society. This was the first paperweight society in Great Britain, and as proof of its success the worldwide membership now stands at twelve thousand.

Fig. 160. Planets set 1. From top left to right Mars, Mercury, Saturn, and Venus. The first Caithness weights that were to inspire a whole new generation of collectors. Average dia. 3". Courtesy of Colin Terris, Caithness Glass Ltd. $2000/2700.

What the future holds for the society remains to be seen but enthusiasm is certainly not lacking. As early as 1981, the author was instrumental in suggesting that a paperweight design competition was held. The winner was David Green, with his design titled Persephone, figure 161.

At this point mention must be made of Peter Holmes another glass craftsman who was to create many of this company's early paperweights.

Peter Holmes, still only in his early twenties, had already completed his exacting training under Paul Ysart when he joined Caithness in 1969. By 1975 Peter headed the paperweight making team and was responsible for training four craftsmen. Another name was soon to emerge, namely that of William Manson. Here again was a young man whose work was quickly to be admired. His specialty was lampwork, and following his first paperweight Butterfly (shown in figure 162) he became associated with fine paperweights such as the Four Seasons, and El Dorado.

In 1981 Caithness announced that they had acquired much know-how, tools, and so forth from Whitefriars Glass Ltd. who had ceased operation the previous year. Thus the name Whitefriars Glass was to live on, and by December 1981 Caithness had issued Snow Crystal (figure 163), the first of a new range of Whitefriars paperweights. One difference is to be noted about Whitefriar style paperweights made by Caithness, namely, that the glass used is low lead, and identical to that used for their other weights.

Fig. 162. Butterfly 1974/5. The first butterfly weight made by William Manson. CG cane. Rarely available. Courtesy of Colin Terris, Caithness Glass Ltd. $350/450.

Fig. 161. Persephone. 1982. Abstract design by David Green. Winning entry of a design competition. Courtesy of Colin Terris, Caithness Glass Ltd. $90/120.

Fig. 163. Snow Crystal. 1981. An attractive design, achieved by careful placement of canes. Date cane. Courtesy of Colin Terris, Caithness Glass Ltd. $100/150.

In addition to limited and unlimited edition weights, one-off weights are sometimes issued. Some notable ones were issued from 1976 – 8, when the cost of commissioning such a piece was around $300. An example of a one-off piece is shown in figure 164. The company receives many inquiries to produce specially commissioned weights. Maybe one of the most technically challenging, and aesthetically appealing, is that shown in figure 165, which has successfully encapsulated a sample of North Sea oil. 1991 saw the production of a limited edition of magnum weights containing a central capsule of whisky, recovered from the wreck of SS Politician. Glass paperweights containing liquids of any kind are rare.

Fig. 165. North Sea Oil. Special commissions are undertaken by Caithness. This one is rare in that it contains liquid oil. Courtesy of Colin Terris, Caithness Glass Ltd.

Fig. 164. Strawberry Trifle. A superb, realistic one-off weight by Scott Miller. Caithness. Dia. 3". Courtesy of a private collector. $120/200.

Manufacturing problems

It will be clear from reference to chapter one that making paperweights is far from being a simple matter. Apart from run of the mill problems, others can occur from time to time which demand urgent and special attention. Two problems of design forms which were difficult to repeat will now be discussed.

Design difficulties

One of the most difficult weights, as far as consistency is concerned, was Intruder (ref. No. 92). Its history is interesting. The main feature of the weight, a floating matte black bubble, (see figure 166), was

Fig. 166. Intruder, 1977. Technically, a challenging design. Caithness. Dia. 3.25". Height 2.75". Courtesy of Colin Terris, Caithness Glass Ltd. $150/175.

an idea which Colin Terris had as a result of effects created, quite accidentally, while producing Genesis (ref. No. 33).

Genesis was the first weight to be produced without any color, depending for its design effect on the use of a myriad of clear bubbles, interspersed with a few small black bubbles. The effect is achieved by shaking finely divided charcoal powder onto the glass, and then covering it with another gather of clear glass. The fine particles of charcoal flare for a moment and produce minute bubbles. It was then discovered that, if the covering of the charcoal with clear glass was executed very rapidly, some of the air could be trapped so quickly that the charcoal dust did not completely burn, and was left inside the bubble producing a black effect.

Therefore, when it came to producing Intruder, it was thought that it was only necessary to make a large depression in the glass, drop into it a large piece of charcoal, and seal it in as quickly as possible with clear glass. The effect was reproduced on twelve separate occasions, prior to launching, without any difficulty. However, once production commenced an incredible variety of half, and quarter black bubbles, and silvery transparent black bubbles resulted. A four week intensive investigation followed. From this it was realized that three parameters were relevant for success:- 1) the size of the piece of charcoal, 2) the size of the depression into which it was placed, and 3) the time necessary for the charcoal to flare prior to sealing.

Of the traditional weights Snowflake crown shown in figure 167, was a further example of a design which caused problems. The problem here was to produce a weight which was free from bubbles between the alternating strips of colored filigree and latticinio. Colin Terris still feels that this weight, with its silhouette of a snowflake, is one of the most technically and visually interesting weights he has designed.

Certification and base markings

Both the certificates of authenticity, and the markings on the base of weights show considerable variation since Caithness first started production.

Certificates
Early certificates were gold edged, although even within this group the style of printing changed. Figure 168 shows a range of many of the different styles adopted. Some certificates, such as that for the Four Seasons, were signed. Not all certificates of a given edition were necessarily signed, and two variations exist for North Sea.

Fig. 167. Snowflake crown. 1981. Another weight that was very demanding on the maker's skills. Courtesy of Colin Terris, Caithness Glass Ltd. $175/225.

Fig. 168. This shows a wide range of the certificates that Caithness have issued.

Base markings

Starting with Intruder in 1977, bases had the name etched or grit blasted onto the base. From 1983, for reasons associated with production, quality control, and marketing, all unlimited paperweights had a letter and number put on the base with a diamond stylus.

The letter designated the year, and the number represented the number of unlimited weights produced in the said year, up until that time.

Year code

A 1983	H 1990	O 1997
B 1984	I 1991	P 1998
C 1985	J 1992	Q 1999
D 1986	K 1993	R 2000
E 1987	L 1994	
F 1988	M 1995	
G 1989	N 1996	

Thus, for a Moonflower marked G/156, it was the 156th *unlimited weight* made that year (*not* the 156th *Moonflower* made in 1989).

Note the ways in which any identification markings on the base have changed over the years. With the earlier weights, all markings were made by hand using a diamond tipped stylus. Markings typical of those appearing on El Dorado are shown in figure 169.

Colin Terris and William Manson signatures appear on certain of the more important 1970s weights, prime examples being Christmas weight 1977 (the first collector's weight), and Jubilee millefiori crown.

Signature, date, and silhouette canes

The following brief list gives some idea of the vast range of signature and date canes used by Caithness.

A-Z	52
CG	60
PH	77
WM	78
JA	79
A&M	80
A&S	1973
C&D	1980
EIIR	1982
50	1994

In addition, five glassmaker's tools and twelve signs of the zodiac have been used. Figures 170 and 171 illustrate a selection of various canes used.

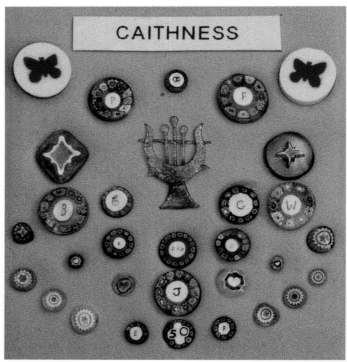

Fig. 170. Just some of the wide range of canes used by Caithness. Courtesy of a private collector.

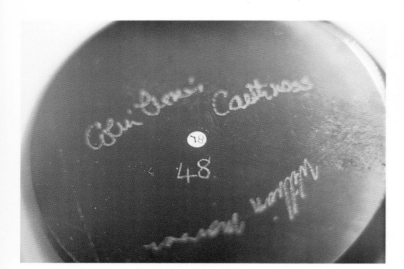

Fig. 169. Base markings on El Dorado. The 78-date cane, William Manson and Colin Terris' signatures, and the issue number (48) all add appeal.

Fig. 171. Close up of the CG, 2000, and C&D (Charles and Diana) canes used in various weights.

Details of Selected Early Weights produced between 1969 and 1979

Mars

Boxed together with Mercury, Saturn, and Venus, Mars was the first weight to be issued by Caithness. Unlike the rest of the Planet sets a single certificate was provided to cover Planets set one.

Coral weights

Of all paperweights manufactured, it is those that give instant recognition of the subject matter that often enjoy the widest appeal. Such is the case with the Coral weights. The finer examples are perfect to the extent of virtually showing the rough, hard structure of Coral, and it is little wonder therefore that these rare weights are amongst many collectors favorites.

Even rarer are the Cased Corals (figure 172). Although the coral design is the same as that in the ordinary weights, the dome of the cased corals are cased with a flash covering of the same color as the design. Rear lighting gives a magnificent effect. Cased corals were the first Caithness weights to be flash covered.

Ink bottles

The earliest design, first issued in 1972, is the only one to have a PH cane incorporated in the stopper. The design in the bottle assumes a growing form not dissimilar to that in the coral weights, except that it is composed of a multitude of colors. The stopper contains a multi-colored layer in to which the green edged, white centered, PH cane is set.

1979 marked the appearance of Sea Lace, the first matching perfume bottle and paperweight set. The Sea Lace bottle has, above a purple ground, an eight segment lacy plant like form, in the center of which are eight stamens. This attractive design is white and crystalline in appearance, and is enhanced by a transparent purple layer that has been imparted to the well.

Jellyfish

Red proved to be the most popular of the three colors issued. Better examples show the abstract form somewhat translucent, thus more truly suggesting a jellyfish.

Fig. 172. Cased coral, damson. 1972. A superb weight that benefits from effective illumination. Caithness. Dia. 2.9". Height 2.3". $225/275.

Shipwreck

If ever there was an award given to an early Caithness weight for being the most sought after it would probably go to Shipwreck, shown in figure 173. Although officially fifty, the actual edition is believed to have terminated at about forty-three. Technically, although not a particularly difficult weight to make, Peter Holmes recalls only too well the main problem of its manufacture. The shipwreck form is actually made from pieces of firebrick, taken from the lining bricks of a glass furnace. However, the coefficient of thermal expansion of the shipwreck is different to that of glass. The result was that many of the weights shattered.

The author has only heard of three Shipwrecks being offered for sale, and it is no surprise therefore that the asking price was high. As one reputable dealer printed in his house journal[1] 'so why not look out that Caithness Shipwreck, and name your price!'

Fish

This was the first engraved weight produced by Caithness. The fish are engraved around the circumference of the weight as two pairs facing each other.

Elements Set (Fire, Air, Earth, and Water)

After the Planets, this was the next set of weights to emerge from Caithness. Although officially a set, the Elements were not boxed as such and this led to many sets being split. One result of this was that Water tended to prove the most popular, and many collectors have only been able to obtain three out of four of the set.

The red used in Fire gives tremendous warmth to the weight. Small brown pieces suggest the presence of slightly cooler embers. No doubt because of the difficulty of depicting Air, this weight is possibly the least interesting of the set. Earth is well represented in the colored swirl, suitably complimented with a green over purple ground. Water is suggestive of the colors and air bubbles that make water come to life.

Genesis

Genesis is well suggested by the gray brown bubble forms that are seen to emerge from the turmoil of the clear bubble froth (figure 174).

Sculpture

Contemporary sculptural art is echoed in this desirable weight. As with many weights, its conceptual background and manufacture will interest collectors. Originally the idea was to depict a bush or tree killed by the effects of atomic radiation, but, feeling this was perhaps too morbid a subject, it was decided to change the theme to its sculptural image.

The method of manufacture is as follows. The sculpture form is fabricated from tin foil which, at the temperature of the molten glass that is applied, melts and is oxidized to leave the characteristic black, white, and gray skeleton. This weight is one of Peter Holmes' personal favorites.

Fig. 173. Shipwreck, 1972. Very few of these effective weights ever re-appear for sale. Caithness. PH cane. Dia. 3.4". Height 2.8". $800/1000.

Fig. 174. Genesis; 1973/4. Another effective early, abstract design. Caithness. Dia. 3". Courtesy of Colin Terris, Caithness Glass Ltd. $400/450.

Stardust

To introduce this paperweight one can hardly do better than quote from the certificate issued: "an interpretation of the mysteries and beauty of space that may be seen by space travelers in the future centuries." An impressive weight by any standards (shown in figure 175), it illustrates what can be achieved when a master craftsman executes a fine design employing thousands of bubbles.

Lovers of abstract paperweights should not pass over the chance to acquire a Stardust.

Flower in the rain

An unlimited weight, but one of very few designed by Jack Allan.

Crown paperweight

Any quality article commemorative of events associated with the British Royal family usually attracts attention. Crown paperweight was no exception. This was the first crown weight ever produced by Caithness, and was issued to commemorate the wedding of HRH Princess Anne to Captain Mark Phillips.

The weight has considerable appeal with its ten main ribbons twisting clockwise (viewing from the top of the weight). Each main

Fig. 175. Stardust, 1973/4. Possibly one of the finest space motif weights ever produced by Caithness. Dia. 3.25". Height 2.4". $300/400.

ribbon is made up of two smaller ones, each of which is red, white, and blue. The top cane contains AM and 1973 in white, surrounded by twenty pink and white cogs. In the base of the weight the ribbons converge to another cane carrying the letters CG and JA, the latter standing for Jack Allan the maker of the weight. Note that whereas the 19th century St. Louis crowns are hollow, the Caithness crown is solid.

Unlike many other crown weights, this design typically forms only about two thirds of the height of the weight. A translucent green background, chosen to intersperse the ribbons, serves to give an added vitality and lightness, while contrasting adequately against the other colors. The weight is shown in figure 176.

Fig. 176. Crown, 1973. Caithness' first crown weight and made, appropriately, for a Royal wedding. Dia. 2.8". Height 2.2". $700/900.

101

Fig. 177. Reflections, blue. 1974/5. Simple, but effective design. Also the name chosen for Caithness Collectors Club journal. Dia. 2.95". Height 2.6". $80/100.

Butterfly

A rare weight, Butterfly is a fine lampwork example of a butterfly. Made by William Manson, Butterfly contains a CG cane.

Reflections

A popular weight, taking as its theme the reflections of a clear bubble, suspended above a colored circular pool, figure 177.

Dragonfly

Caithness revived an old technique of producing a design using a very thin layer of powdered glass. The result was Dragonfly, the first Caithness weight using this technique.

Four Seasons

The seasons are beautifully depicted in this lampwork set by William Manson, illustrated in figure 178, and although when first issued the price appeared to be rather high, paperweight lovers were quick to realize the beauty and quality of the set. One result is that prices have risen steadily.

Each weight has a circle of canes set into the ground, and in one of these for Spring, Autumn, and Winter, is set the WM identifying cane. In the case of the Summer weight the WM cane is set in the center of one of the small flowers.

Spring is defined by the freshness of a daffodil, while Summer uses a blaze of different colors in the flowers. Autumn is illustrated by falling leaves which are cleverly arranged at three different heights. Winter shows two holly leaves set into the ground, together with four berries.

Fig. 178. Four Seasons, 1976. Some paperweights enjoy constant popularity. This set of four is in that group. Fine lampwork by William Manson. Caithness. Average Dia. 3.1". $1350/1500.

Trio

A set of three weights which utilize no color. The effective design is shown in figure 179.

Intruder

Simple in design, but difficult to make. The difficulty lies in applying the coating to the inside surface of the bubble which becomes the Intruder.

The opaque coating is black, buff, or gray in color and one should ensure that the bubble is completely coated. Due to the manufacturing difficulties (see design difficulties) the addition was nowhere near completed. Weights made by Peter Holmes had a black bubble, the lighter shades being the work of other Caithness weight makers.

El Dorado

A weight, shown in figure 180, almost literally was very quickly to become as valuable as gold dust; this is El Dorado which used aventurine in a unique and extremely effective manner. The response to this paperweight was considerable.

Factors contributing to this demand were as follows: the appealing design and the issue size. The aventurine varies in its sparkle, but most weights contain pieces ranging in size from nearly an inch down to minute particles. A "78" cane is set into the base. The "7" is blue, while the "8" is dark green/black, both set in a white surround. Colin Terris' and William Manson's signatures appear on the base.

Fig. 179. Trio, 1976. Effective design resulted in this set of three weights that employed no color. Caithness. Average Dia. 3.1". $500/700.

Fig. 180. El Dorado, 1978. Probably the first modern British paperweight to use aventurine in an abstract manner. A very appealing weight, enhanced by the outer surface. Seldom seen on the secondary market. Caithness. Dia. 3.2". Height 2.6". $500/600.

Lizard

Lizard is the only early weight by this company which uses obsidian as the base, in place of glass. The large silver lizard surmounts the weight. Figure 181 shows this impressive weight.

Fig. 181. Lizard, 1978. Caithness' first weight to use silver set on to an obsidian base. Courtesy of Colin Terris, Caithness Glass Ltd. $1300/1600.

Dawn and Dusk

This pair of weights were the first to utilize an amethyst colored glass for the dome. It proved an admirable choice as it depicts perfectly a typical sky coloring at dawn and dusk, and just masks sufficiently the silhouetted abstract forms which rise from the ground. This interesting set is difficult to obtain, examples are seen in figures 182 and 183.

Fig. 182. Dawn, 1979. A weight made effective by the use of the amethyst tinted dome. Caithness. Dia. 3.3". Height 2.9". Courtesy of Colin Terris, Caithness Glass Ltd. The set with Dusk, $400/500.

Fig. 183. Dusk, 1979. Sold together with Dawn. Caithness. Dia. 3.3". Height 2.9". Courtesy of Colin Terris, Caithness Glass Ltd. The set with Dawn, $400/500.

Queen Elizabeth I

This is one of the early sulphides. An actual sulphide is shown in figure 184 prior to encasement, while figure 185 shows the finished weight.

Fig. 184. Sulphide of Queen Elizabeth I, prior to encapsulation. Very fragile. Width 1.4". Height 1.55". Like examples of canes, and lampwork, this is a useful talking point in any collection.

Fig. 185. Queen Elizabeth I, 1980. Safely encapsulated, the sulphide illustrated in Fig. 184 can now be seen in a completed paperweight. Caithness. Courtesy of Colin Terris, Caithness Glass Ltd. $200/250.

Name	Edition U=Unlimited	Issue Price, $	Value in 1999, $
1969			
1. Mars }	500	}	}
2. Mercury } Planets	500	} 60	} 2925
3. Saturn } Set 1	500	}	}
4. Venus }	500	}	}
1970			
5. Uranus }	500	}	}
6. Jupiter } Planets	500	} 75	} 1875
7. Neptune } Set 2	500	}	}
8. Earth }	500	}	}
9. Orbit	500	13	300
10. Moonflower	U	12	45
1971			
11. Sun }	500	}	}
12. Moon } Planets	500	} 60	} 1500
13. Pluto } Set 3	500	}	}
14. Starbase	500	18	490
15. Spiral	500	18	180
1972			
16. Coral, blue	500	22	260
16. Coral, damson	500	22	260
16. Coral, orange	500	22	340
17. Cased Coral, blue	100	30	165
17. Cased Coral, damson	100	30	210
17. Cased Coral, orange	100	30	165
18. Harlequin single, PH	U	15	75
18. Harlequin single, CG	U	15	60
19. Harlequin double, PH	U	21	135
19. Harlequin double, CG	U	21	105
20. Ink Bottle, PH	U	29	140
20. Ink Bottle, CG	U	29	105
21. Sunflower	500	18	335
22. Tropicana, pink	500	25	170
22. Tropicana, purple	500	25	170
22. Tropicana, yellow	500	25	200
23. Jelly Fish, red	500	13	60
23. Jelly Fish, purple	500	13	60
23. Jelly Fish, green	500	13	60
24. Sea Urchin	500	15	90
25. Shipwreck	50	45	900
26. Fish	500	15	110
27. Ariel	500	15	105
28. May Dance	U	12	50
1973/74			
29. Fire }	1000	}	}
30. Air } Elements	1000	} 78	} 1425
31. Earth } Set	1000	}	}
32. Water }	1000	}	}
33. Genesis	500	22	390
34. Sculpture	500	25	390
35. Stardust	500	30	320
36. Firedance	U	17	60
37. Fulmar	500	19	75
38. Flower in the rain	U	24	53
39. Crown Paperweight	100	68	825
1974/75			
40. Space Rose	1000	30	68
41. Sea Crab	1500	27	150
42. Cascade PH	U	25	105
42. Cascade CG	U	30	90
43. Cascade Rainbow PH	U	25	105
43. Cascade Rainbow CG	U	30	90
44. Butterfly	100	53	375
45. Bullseye millefiori	U	37	150
46. Arctic Tern	500	21	60
47. Space Beacon	500	26	105
48. Reflections	500	23	83
49. Vortex	1000	30	83
50. Sea Kelp	1500	24	120
51. Sentinel	U	18	60
52. Dragonfly	1500	26	410
1976			
53. Sea Base	400	75	410
54. Space Flower	1000	36	143
55. Sea Orchid	1000	36	203
56. Sea Pearl PH or CG	500	45	210
57. Spring }	500	}	}
58. Summer } Four	500	} 375	} 1425
59. Autumn } Seasons	500	}	}
60. Winter }	500	}	}
61. Trio 1	750	}	}
62. Trio 2	750	} 120	} 600
63. Trio 3	750	}	}
64. Puffin	500	26	75
65. Cormorant	500	26	75
66. Gannet	100	90	300
67. Diving Tern	100	90	300
68. Seal	100	90	320
69. Dolphin	100	90	300
70. Spectre	1000	26	112
71. Sundance	3000	30	150
72. Alien	2000	32	83
73. First Quarter PH or CG	1500	32	120
74. Rhapsody	400	45	120
75. Millefiori Reflections	U	30	83
76. Latticinio	U	36	83
77. North Sea	1000	30	173
78. Polar Bear	100	102	232
79. Otter	100	102	232
80. Osprey	100	102	232
81. Eider Duck	500	30	68
82. Black Headed Gull	500	30	68
1977			
83. Stormy Petrel	500	33	68
84. Guillemot	500	33	68
85. Lobster	1500	38	60
86. Jubilee Moonflower	3000	22	105
87. Jubilee Crown Bubble	3000	25	90
88. Jubilee Floating Crown	1000	68	203
89. Millefiori Crown	500	105	710
90. Comet	3000	38	128
91. Plough	3000	38	90
92. Intruder	2000	39	150
93. Zephyr	400	53	188
94. Petal Ink Well	U	75	188
95. Christmas Weight 1977	500	75	563
1978			
96. Angel Fish	1500	38	75
97. Kittiwake	500	36	68
98. Skua	500	36	68
99. Eider Duck	100	120	278
100. Mermaid	100	120	278
101. Aquila	3000	39	90
102. Sagittarius	3000	38	90
103. Asteroid	3000	38	75
104. Spindrift	3000	29	128
105. Sunflare	3000	41	83

Name	Edition U=Unlimited	Issue Price, $	Value in 1999, $
106. Myriad	U	17	45
107. Morning Dew	U	19	53
108. Marooned	3000	41	83
109. Pegasus	1500	41	83
110. Space Pearl	3000	41	83
111. Ice Petal Perfume Bottle	U	83	195
112. Seagrass Perfume Bottle	U	83	203
113. Quartet Perfume Bottle	U	83	203
114. Snow Flower	3000	45	225
115. Cobra 1978	50 Yearly	300	525
116. Salamander 1978	50 Yearly	300	525
117. Octopus 1978	50 Yearly	300	525
118. Manta Ray 1978	50 Yearly	300	525
119. EL Dorado 1978	100	150	563
120. Ladybird 1978	100 Yearly	150	413
121. Swan 1978	100 Yearly	150	375
122. Butterfly and Flower 1978	250	195	450
123. Silver Jubilee Fleet Review	100	113	300
124. Lizard	50	300	1500
125. Mistletoe	500	113	300
126. Journey of the Wise Men	2000	75	150
127. Silver Jubilee Paperweight	1000	42	90
128. Peregrine Falcon	200	99	195
129. Arctic Night	1500	45	105

1979

Name	Edition U=Unlimited	Issue Price, $	Value in 1999, $
130. King Neptune	100	120	233
131. Veil Tail	1500	39	75
132. Humming Bird	1000	53	90
133. Libra	1500	38	75
134. Aries	1500	38	75
135. Sea Lace Perfume Bottle	100	135	525
136. Sea Lace Paperweight	100	135	525
137. Blue petal perfume bottle	U	83	150
138. Silver sentinel	U	22	45
139. Dawn } matching	750	90	450
140. Dusk } set	750	90	450
141. Ice flame	1000	41	98
142. Star flower	1000	41	105
143. Nomad	1000	41	128
144. Triad	1500	38	75
145. Carousel	1000	41	87
146. Ice fountain	1500	38	75
147. Flower form	1500	38	90
148. Ice blossom	1000	45	120
149. Atlantis	1500	38	203
150. Octet	500	56	113
151. Illusion	1000	41	128
152. Mystique	750	68	128
153. Cobra 1979	50 Yearly	300	450
154. Salamander 1979	50 Yearly	300	450
155. Manta Ray 1979	50 Yearly	300	450
156. Octopus 1979	50 Yearly	300	450
157. Ladybird 1979	100 Yearly	150	375
158. Butterfly and Flower 1979	250	195	375
159. Heather bell	100 Yearly	150	323
160. Rosebud 1979	50 Yearly	300	488
161. Floral fountain, red	750	68	180
162. Swan 1979	100 Yearly	150	233
163. Holly wreath	500	120	233
164. Shepherds	2000	83	150
165 Christmas Rose	1000	108	188
166. Henry VIII	1000	114	173
167. Kaleidoscope	U	15	53
168. Black gem	1000	42	83
169. Nucleus	1500	45	68
170. Ocean Spring	1500	45	90
171. Embryo	1500	45	71
172. Ark Royal	500	53	90
173. Year of the Child	250	45	105
174. Puffin	250	113	128
175. King Tutankhamun	250	90	263

1980

Name	Edition U=Unlimited	Issue Price, $	Value in 1999, $
176. Flamenco	U	36	68
177. Bauble, bangle and beads	1500	47	68
178. Black and gold perfume bottle }matching	100	188	450
179. Black and gold paperweight } set	100	188	450
180. Floral fountain, blue	750	89	150
181. Blue rose perfume bottle }matching	100	188	450
182. Blue rose paperweight } set	100	188	450
183. Blue spiral	750	59	113
184. Cosmic rain	750	83	135
185. Contrast	1500	47	68
186. Double spiral	1000	51	75
187. Dream flower	750	63	135
188. Fire flower	1500	47	60
189. Fireworks	1000	53	173
190. Gold throat	1000	65	90
191. Meteor	1000	48	60
192. Moon probe	1000	51	71
193. Nativity 1980 Christmas weight	2000	98	143
194. Night flower	1500	47	113
195. Night venture	1500	47	75
196. Parasol	1000	53	90
197. Sanctuary	500	83	173
198. Satellite	1000	53	105
199. Siamese fighting fish	1500	48	75
200. Skyline	1000	48	60
201. Spaceport	1500	47	68
202. Space orchid	1000	53	120
203. Space traveller	1000	53	75
204. Sunset	1000	48	60
205. Time zone	1500	47	68
206. Twilight	750	59	90
207. Vertigo	1500	47	60
208. Winter moon	1000	48	75
209. Year of the Viking	500	60	90
210. The Rocket	1000	87	120
211. Seal	50	345	525
212. Salamander 1980	50 Yearly	345	450
213. Rosebud 1980	50 Yearly	345	390
214. Manta Ray 1980	50 Yearly	345	375
215. Cobra 1980	50 Yearly	345	398
216. Silent watcher	50	383	450
217. Queen Elizabeth I	1000	123	180
218. Queen Mother sulphide	1000	128	150
219. Thistle and Rose	1000	60	83
220. Royal Arms	80	149	263
221. Glamis Castle	250	75	
222. Pirouette	1000	53	98
223. Royal Birthday	1000	45	75

1981

Name	Edition U=Unlimited	Issue Price, $	Value in 1999, $
224. Springtime	750	68	113
225. Elegance	250	95	210
226. Floral fountain, peach	750	95	180
227. Fantasia	750	75	105
228. Tristar	750	75	105
229. Space shuttle	1000	48	83
230. Touchdown	1000	48	128
231. Lunar III	750	61	173
232. Star Pavilion	750	61	83
233. Jester	1000	48	75
234. Coronet	750	63	75
235. Gazebo	1000	48	75
236. Viking flame	750	63	75
237. Midas	750	63	90
238. Zenith Perfume bottle	150	128	225
239. Faith }set	250	}	}
240. Hope }of	250	} 192	} 488
241. Charity }3	250	}	}
242. Sandsprite	750	63	105
243. Eterna	500	90	143
244. Samarkand perfume bottle	150	128	225
245. Aquaflora perfume bottle	U	83	105
246. Enchanted forest	1000	44	60
247. Coquette	1000	72	90
248. Whirligig, clear	U	20	38
249. Nova; amber, blue, ruby, and topaz	U	17	30
250. Polka; green, orange, and silver	U	21	38

Collectors should be well aware of the difficulties of tracking down weights issued as special commissions, and are reminded that the listing on the previous two pages is incomplete in this respect.

An extensive alphabetical listing of Caithness paperweights was produced by Bevan[2] in 1996, and can be used as an adjunct to the author's data to speed up the search for given weights.

This is far from the end of the Caithness story. Going from strength to strength, up to mid-1999 the company have issued in excess of seventeen hundred different designs[3].

Seconds

Sub-standard weights sometimes appear on the secondary market. These are usually boldly marked "S" or "CIIG," as in figures 186 and 187.

Fig. 186. Second grade weights occasionally appear at boot fairs, collectors fairs, etc. These should be marked in some way. The S signifies the weight is not perfect.

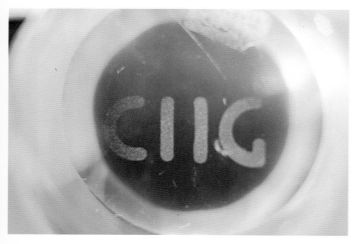

Fig. 187. CIIG. Another way of identifying a weight that is not up to specification.

Brochures

The Company's literature has always been extensive, and to a high standard. In particular, collectors should seek copies of 'Reflections', Caithness' house journal issued regularly since 1985 to members of their Collectors Club. This covers a wide range of topics, with occasional articles of interest on Ysart, and other makers' weights.

Early collectors' guides from c.1979, and early brochures as shown in figure 188, are also now much sought-after.

Fig. 188. Caithness Collectors Guide, Volume 1; and early brochure. Books, manufacturers brochures, and other ephemera form an important part of any fine collection, and are usually keenly sought after. Guide issued 1979 at about $6. Brochure c. 1974. $20/30.

Related Items

Jewelry, and related items, made c. 1970 by Paul Ysart during his time at Caithness are an interesting addition to a collection. Figure 189 shows a paperknife set with a millefiori cane containing a silhouette of a blue butterfly.

The Future

Caithness' future seems assured, and doubtless new innovations will take place. Figure 190 leads the collector to that future with Millennium Dancer.

[1]Paperweights – A Bulletin for Collectors, No. 3, May 1978. Darius Arts Ltd., 105, Clerkenwell Road, London EC1R 5BX
[2]Bevan, Pat and John. Caithness Glass Paperweights – Alphabetical Listing. Privately published, 1996.
[3]Terris, Colin. The Charlton Standard Catalogue of Caithness Paperweights. First Edition. Toronto, Ontario: W.K. Cross, 1999.

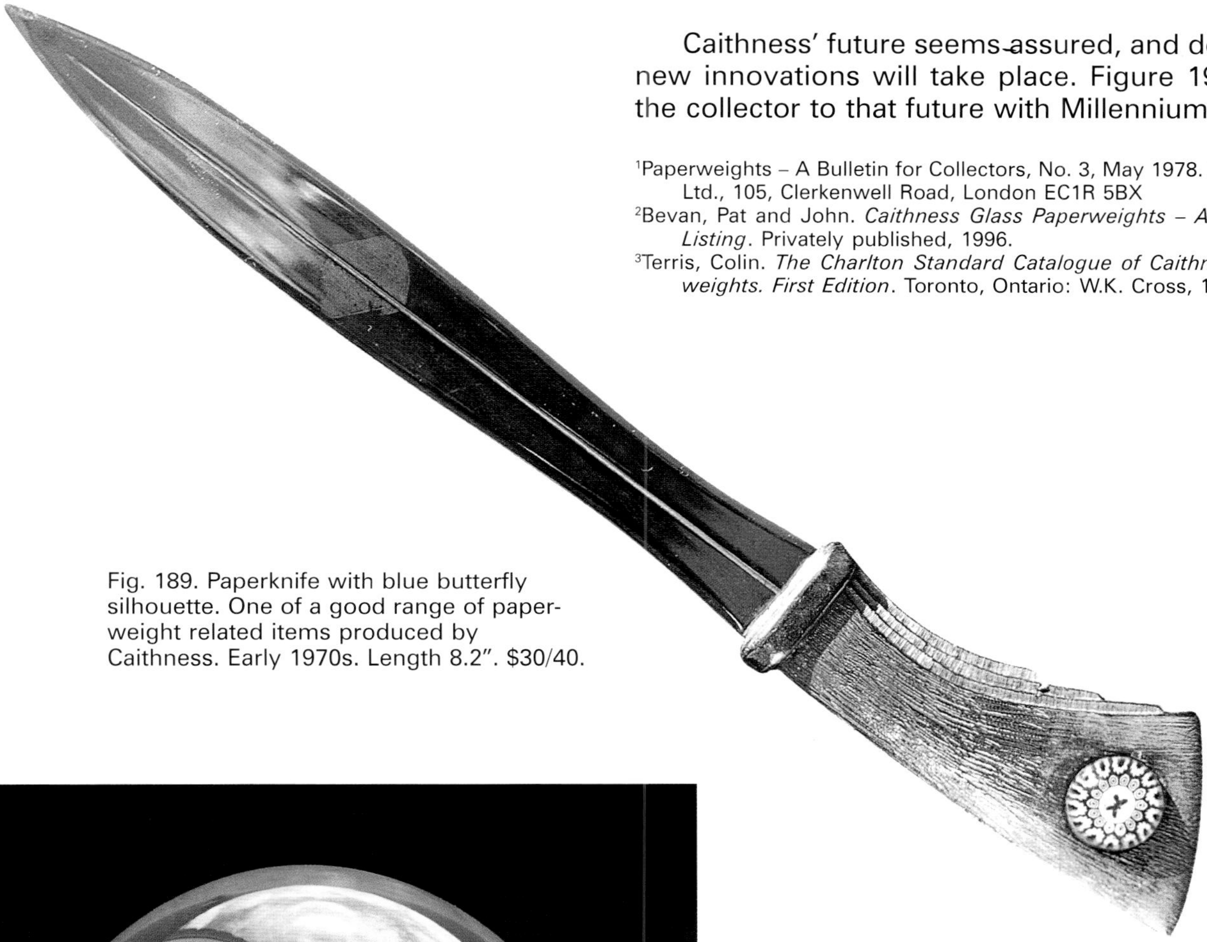

Fig. 189. Paperknife with blue butterfly silhouette. One of a good range of paperweight related items produced by Caithness. Early 1970s. Length 8.2". $30/40.

Fig. 190. Millennium Dancer, 1999. Produced to mark the new millennium. 2000 cane. Caithness. Dia. 3". Courtesy of a private collector. $90.

Fig. 191. Perthshire Paperweights factory in its pleasant setting in Crieff, Scotland. Courtesy of Perthshire Paperweights Ltd.

Chapter 6
Perthshire Paperweights Ltd.

Being one of the older established makers of modern paperweights, it is not surprising to find that even by 1975 Perthshire's background had already been documented by the esteemed authority on paperweights, Paul Hollister, Jr.[1]

In his concise book, Hollister tells us that Stuart Drysdale, a country lawyer, formed Perthshire Paperweights Ltd, Crieff in 1968, having previously been with Vasart Glass Ltd. and Strathearn Glass. Besides covering the full history of Perthshire's development, Hollister's book is commendable to readers who wish to acquire detail of furnace operation, the production of canes, and the renowned millefiori paperweights. The reader is also given an insight into the manufacture of lampwork items and overlay techniques.

Early workers at Perthshire included Jack Allan, Anton (Tony) Moravec, Angus Hutchison, Allan Scott and John Deacons; and in 1979 the names of relevant personnel were listed as: Brilliant cutting, faceting, and development – Anton Moravec, Archie Anderson, and Barry McDougall; Lampwork – Angus Hutchison; Weightmaking – Roy McDonald, Peter McDougall (now General Manager), Harry McKay, Chic Young, and Maurice Crowder.

Allan Scott joined Perthshire Paperweights as an apprentice lampworker on September 8 1975. He was taught by Angus Hutchison who was Perthshire's only lampworker up until that time, and Allan learned not by any vocal instructions but by watching Hutchison's techniques. By Christmas 1976, he was responsible for Perthshire's Christmas weight, Poinsettia. Other weights he remembers doing for Perthshire are Bluebells, and Nosegay. Allan created the lampwork for many Perthshire limited editions up to 1979 when he left to join John Deacons.

Harry McKay started at Perthshire Paperweights on July 21 1969. Harry started his career breaking up lumps of colored glass with a hammer. The resultant smaller pieces of colored glass were ultimately ground, once again by hand, until a chip size suitable for using as colored bases for paperweights, or for making colored millefiori rods was achieved. He did this for two months, then his next step on the career ladder was a move to hot finishing the bases of paperweights and carrying them to the annealing kiln which he did for a year.

As Perthshire worked a team system in those days, his next promotion was to pick up and form the millefiori bases for Perthshire's unlimited range. He gathered the colored glass for the base, picked up the millefiori pattern from the heated base plate, and melted the canes into the base before passing it onto the next person, who would take a further gather of clear glass and shape and finish the paperweight. Four years into his apprenticeship, he started to make limited edition paperweights and also on occasion worked with Jack Allan, Perthshire's top paperweight maker at that time. Harry left Perthshire Paperweights in 1980 and joined John Deacons at J Glass where he stayed for the next three years making both limited and unlimited traditional weights.

Peter McDougall, the present factory manager, was introduced to paperweights while still a teenager. This arose as a result of his next-door neighbor being Jack Allan, a fine glass worker who died in 1996.

Following the death of Stuart Drysdale in August, 1990, the factory is now run by his son, Neil. By 1992 Duncan Scott was the principal lampworker with Gordon Taylor responsible for faceting. By 1999 the number of company employees had grown from its small beginnings to twenty, and figure 191 shows the factory.

Perthshire issues four series of weights: one-offs, annual limited editions, recurring limited editions, and decoratives.

i) **One-off specials** – To date only one to two hundred are believed to have been produced and include encased overlays selling at up to $3000. Many are believed to have been purchased by American collectors. Issue prices of these pieces ranged between $700 and 900 in 1980. Some are listed later and some are illustrated in figures 192 to 195. Two encased overlays are illustrated in the 1979 P.C.A. *Bulletin*.

ii) **Annual limited editions** – produced once only to a specified maximum number of pieces.

iii) **Recurring limited editions** – issued in small editions but re-issued each year with the appropriate date letter, or numerals, inserted. Some are signed P (for Perthshire) and have the year in numerals.

iv) **Decorative weights** – constantly being produced with no specified limit.

As an extension of previously published data[2, 3] the present author has listed all Perthshire's annual limited edition weights. Rather than generally trying to reproduce the weights made by the great names of the mid-19th century, at Perthshire the team endeavor to re-create, and, if possible, improve upon the techniques that are used. The striving to seek perfection, such as the elimination of all un-

Fig. 192. Central skier cane with nine fir tree canes. Perthshire, 1979. A one-off weight. Dia. 3". Courtesy of a private collector. $375/450.

Fig. 193. Upright flowers. Another one-off design. Perthshire, 1989. Dia. 2.75". Courtesy of a private collector. $375/450.

desired bubbles and cording, goes on, and on.

In common with most U.K. manufacturers, Perthshire enjoy a strong export business – typically between 45% and 85% of their production is exported, with a large proportion of this being to the U.S.A.

Perthshire concentrates upon millefiori, lampwork, and traditional design paperweights and their early glass was relatively low lead (about 12% PbO), but from 1992 the use of lead was discontinued with barium carbonate being used in its place. Colored glass used at Perthshire is still purchased from Germany.

Fig. 194. Red and white overlay. One-off. Perthshire, 1999. Courtesy of Perthshire Paperweights Ltd. $600/800.

Fig. 195. Overlay mushroom. Always desirable, this concept originated with the 19th century makers. Perthshire, 1999. Courtesy of Perthshire Paperweights Ltd. $600/800.

113

Unlike many other modern makers weights, only *some* of those issued by Perthshire have any identification markings inscribed on the base. Details are covered by the certificate issued with each weight. An early Perthshire certificate is shown in figure 196.

The Company is noted for having produced an extensive range of silhouette and portrait canes. Although not necessarily complete, the following list gives some idea of the range.

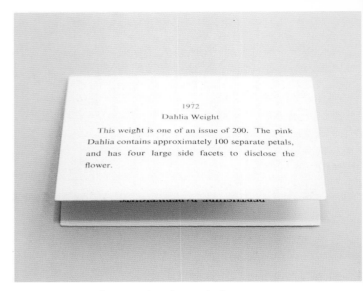

1972
Dahlia Weight

This weight is one of an issue of 200. The pink Dahlia contains approximately 100 separate petals, and has four large side facets to disclose the flower.

Fig. 196. A certificate dating from 1972.

Perthshire Silhouette and Portrait Canes

Aeroplane	Flowers – blue and red	Polar bear
Angel	Frog	Puffin
Balloon	Glass of Guinness	Quail
Berry	Goat	Rabbit running
Bluebells	Golfer and clubs	Red riding hood
Blue tit	Gondolier	Reindeer
Boat	Heather	Roadrunner
Butterfly	Holly and berries	Robin
Camel	Horse	Rooster
Candle	Horse and jockey	Roses
Car	Horses head	Running deer
Cat	Humpty Dumpty	Sailing boat
Cats head	Ice skater	Scottie dog
Chickadee	Insect	Sea horse
Christmas tree	Jockey	Shepherd
Church	Kangaroo	Skier
Clown	Lion	Sleigh
Cockerel	Little Miss Muffet	Snail
Council tree	Mouse	Snowman
Crab	Nativity Mary and child	Soccer player
Crown	Ostrich	Spanish galleon
Desert island	Owl	Squirrel
Dick Whittington	Panda	Swan
Dog	Parrot	Thistle
Donald duck	Partridge	Tiger
Donkey	Peacock	Tulip
Duck	Pelican	Tweetie Pie
Eastern Bluebird	Penguin	Windmill
Elephant	Penny farthing bicycle	Woodpecker
Father Christmas	Pheasant	
Fisherman	Pixie	

Special Canes

Figures 197, and 198 illustrate various portrait canes.

Close-up photographs of many of these silhouette canes have been published by Selman[3] and Mahoney & McClanahan[4], and a further excellent article with illustrations has been published by Jacobsen and Drabeck[5].

Perthshire constantly strive to make even finer products, and amongst their improvements in technique, they have fairly recently tried a new process for the manufacture of multi-colored silhouette canes.

The finished results are said to represent the finest of any cane work ever seen.

To date one of the most complex silhouette canes is that of the peacock featured in the 1991 checker board weight. Complex millefiori canes are a feature of this company's work, and 1989 saw the introduction of a close pack millefiori weight in which every cane was different.

A reflection of the company's striving for perfection is to be seen in the 1983 ruby gingham encased overlay (figure 199) destined for the U.S.A. Only twenty were made at a sales value of $3,700 each.

Fig. 197. Perthshire have always been noted for fine portrait canes, such as these shown here. Courtesy of Perthshire Paperweights Ltd.

Fig. 198. Perthshire portrait canes. Noted for their detail. The tiger (bottom row middle) is a fine example. Courtesy of Perthshire Paperweights Ltd.

Fig. 199. Gingham overlay. A masterpiece from 1983. Courtesy of Perthshire Paperweights Ltd. $3000/4000.

Experimentation proceeds constantly, and sometimes this can result in an unexpected piece showing up at an antiques or boot fair (trunk show). For instance, a glass plate has been found with Perthshire's dragonfly on bouquet design for 1974 (number 23 in catalog section) suitably embedded in the center. The plate was made by Harry McKay at Perthshire – see figure 200.

As a further example, figure 201 shows what was possibly an experimental, and unique piece made in 1969, and marked P1969. The cross cane at the bottom of the illustration is very similar to that produced by Strathearn, as is the spacing of the canes on the latticinio ground. This weight was purchased at an auction in 1983 for $70.

Fig. 200. Rare plate, featuring the design shown in the accompanying 1974 Dragonfly on bouquet weight. Perthshire. Plate dia. 7.5". Courtesy of a private collector. $225/275.

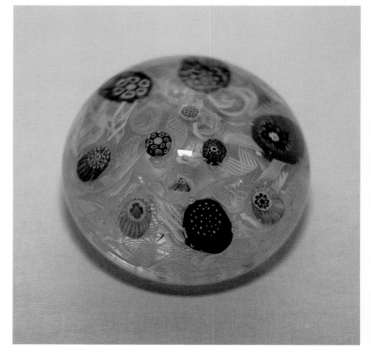

Fig. 201. A very early undocumented spaced millefiori. Dated P 1969. Courtesy of Anne Anderson. $225/350.

The weight shown in figure 202 is also from 1969. An unusual weight shown in figure 203, and made by Jack Allan c. 1970, has the canes on or very near to the surface, making it very reminiscent of designs believed to have originated in Venice as early as the 17th or 18th century.

In view of the popularity of their weights, Perthshire formed a collectors club in 1998. The annual membership fee includes a millefiori paperweight containing a "PPCC" cane (figure 204). A collector's weight is also issued annually, the first of which is shown in figure 205. The first newsletter was issued in January, 1998.

Fig. 202. Early Perthshire millefiori. 1969. Dia. 2.75". Courtesy of Sweetbriar Gallery Archive. $60/90.

Fig. 203. Rare witches ball design by the late Jack Allan. Canes are close to, or on, the surface. Perthshire, c.1969. Dia. 2.75". Courtesy of a private collector. $225/300.

Fig. 204. Weight given to members of Perthshire Paperweights Collectors Club. PPCC cane at center. Courtesy of Perthshire Paperweights Ltd.

PPCC Perthshire Paperweights Collectors' Club

First Annual Collectors' Weight

A large weight containing eight miniature posies between delicate lace twists surrounding a pink centre flower and set on a black background.

Exclusive PPCC cane inserted in base. 3" Diameter.

Fig. 205. 1st collectors club weight. 1998. Dia. 3". Courtesy of Perthshire Paperweights Ltd.

Descriptions of selected Perthshire individual early weights of the Special Limited Editions

1969 Red, white, and blue crown

Ten red, white, and blue, and ten white latticinio canes are used in an alternating fashion in this rare crown weight. These are joined at the top, to a central cane containing eight white stars. In the base is set the 1969 date cane. This crown weight, shown in figure 206, is not hollow.

1972 Miniature flower in basket

This weight shows a small pink flower floating in a basket of composite canes. At the center of the flower, shown in figure 207, a P cane can be seen. Colors vary.

Swan in the Pond

This weight is a replica of an antique paperweight, and some are signed with a P on each wing. Heavily faceted to give reflections. The weight features a green pond, and has a 16 point star cut base. Figure 208 is of a specially sectioned piece designed to show the construction.

1973 Close millefiori

A varied assortment of composite millefiori canes is set on a deep amethyst ground containing a P1973 signature cane (figure 209).

Fig. 207. Miniature flower in basket, 1972. A simple, but attractive design. Perthshire. Dia. 1.75". Courtesy of Sweetbriar Gallery Archive. $180/280.

Fig. 208. Swan in pond, 1972. Specially sectioned to show hollow construction. Courtesy of Perthshire Paperweights Ltd.

Fig. 206. Crown, 1969. Perthshire's first limited edition weight. Dia. 2.75". Courtesy of Sweetbriar Gallery Archive. $550/700.

Fig. 209. Close millefiori, 1973, showing a wide range of canes. Dia. 2.75". Courtesy of Sweetbriar Gallery Archive. $350/400.

1976 Christmas

Consists of a poinsettia on a clear ground (figure 210) surrounded by a ring of alternate green, and white/pink canes. A P cane is behind the flower.

1977 Christmas, Yuletide bells, red ground

With 8 + 1 faceting this weight consists of two bells, made of white, and pink millefiori canes, set on a clear ruby background. The clappers are green, as is the ribbon which joins the bells at the top. A P1977 cane set in the base has blue digits on white (see figure 211).

1979 Sunflower

The large flower weight, shown in figure 212, contains a sunflower set on a golden amber base, surrounded by a garland of green leaves, and matching canes. A P1979 cane is on the base.

Seal

The translucent ruby hollow weight, shown in figure 213, contains a performing circus seal, viewed through the facets. Signed P on base of seal.

Fig. 210. Christmas, 1976. Poinsettia. Dia. 3". Courtesy of Sweetbriar Gallery Archive. $350/550.

Fig. 212. Sunflower, 1979. A popular floral weight with a P1979 cane in the base. Dia. 3". Courtesy of Sweetbriar Gallery Archive. $350/450.

Fig. 211. Christmas, 1977. Another attractive Christmas weight by Perthshire. Dia. 2.9". Courtesy of Sweetbriar Gallery Archive. $450/750.

Fig. 213. Seal, 1979. Example of one of Perthshire's hollow weights. Dia. 2.75". Courtesy of Sweetbriar Gallery Archive. $400/550.

Christmas angel

This Christmas weight, illustrated in figure 214, contains a large colored silhouette of an angel set on a background of the night sky, with stars of varying size scattered throughout. P1979 cane on base.

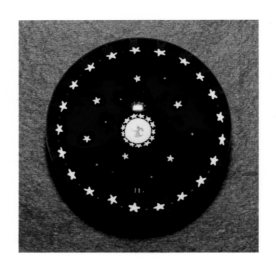

Fig. 214. Christmas 1979. Portrait cane of an angel surrounded by stars. P1979 date cane. Dia. 2.9". Courtesy of Sweetbriar Gallery Archive. $250/400.

Special Limited Editions, 1969 to 1999

Name	Edition limit	Actual No.issued	Issue price, $
*Denotes weights which are known to have increased in value, and have been resold at a premium since first being issued.			
**Denotes weights which are becoming increasingly difficult to obtain.			
1969			
1. Red white, and blue crown*	350	268	45
1970			
2. Dragonfly. Dia. 2.45"*	500	500	45
3. Translucent overlay*	150	150	188
1971			
4. Ribbon*	150	150	65
5. Faceted pansy*	350	350	83
6. Patterned cushion ground**	250	250	56
7. Translucent amethyst overlay bottle*	300	300	101
8. Christmas holly*	250	250	63
9. Ryder Golf Cup commemorative	50		
1972			
10. Faceted cushion ground**	300	300	65
11. Faceted dahlia*	200	200	105
12. Miniature flower in basket**	1000	1000	38
13. Christmas mistletoe*	300	300	56
1973			
14. Swan in the pond**	250	250	113
15. Faceted flower**	600	562	45
16. Faceted carpet ground**	350	348	68
17. Close millefiori**	400	378	53
18. Flower on basket with latticinio. Dia. 2.9"	300	300	72
1974			
19. Flower and bud on lilac base**	350	346	68
20. Scattered millefiori**	500	425	44
21. Garland**	350	334	68
22. Amethyst double overlay millefiori**	300	300	162
23. Dragonfly on bouquet, faceted*	300	300	173
24. Christmas robin, crown**	325	317	57
1975			
25. Penguin on ice, overlay**	350	316	135
26. Patterned cushion ground, six millefiori clusters**	400	400	50
27. Tudor rose*	400	400	69
28. Butterfly*	450	373	89
29. Overlay bottle	250	173	129
30. Christmas, white rose*	350	347	68

Name	Edition limit	Actual No.issued	Issue price, $
1976			
31. Forget-me-not on latticinio**	400	397	89
32. Miniature butterfly, double overlay**	500	488	98
33. Miniature faceted blue and white flower**	400	369	74
34. Blue magnum cushion	300	295	236
35. Moss ground concentric**	300	169	117
36. Christmas flower**	350	316	98
1977			
37. Nosegay on a swirl	400	315	113
38. Plums	500	315	122
39. Yellow triple overlay. Dia. 2.8"*	400	347	213
40. Rooster inside pink cushion**	300	244	173
41. Patterned millefiori, multi-colored base**	400	346	111
42. Carpet ground with silhouettes. Dia. 3.15"**	400	338	120
43. Christmas, Yuletide bells, red ground	325	318	120
1978			
44. Patterned millefiori. Dia. 3"	350	292	89
45. Heather. Dia. 2.5"	500	452	102
46. Bluebell, faceted, star cut base. Dia. 2.25"**	350	350	114
47. Bouquet. Dia. 3"**	350	350	188
48. Blue, and white double overlay garland. Dia. 3.25"**	250	119	195
49. Miniature flower in a basket. Dia. 2.25"**	400	374	105
50. Christmas holly, overlay	325	322	128
1979			
51. Sunflower on amber base. Dia. 3.15"	350	303	120
52. Blue silhouettes, faceted. Dia. 3.25"	450	373	113
53. Miniature blue, and white double overlay, pink flower. Dia. 2.15"	400	351	135
54. Garland on ruby base; silhouettes. Dia. 3.15"	400	293	150
55. Seal, translucent ruby overlay. Dia. 3.3"	400	275	150
56. Overlay bottle, amber or blue. Height 5"	500	331	179
57. Faceted bouquet. Dia. 3.15"	450	332	260
58. Christmas angel	325	307	104
1980			
59. Rose, and bud, faceted. Dia. 2.5"	300	231	207
60. Rose, and bud, faceted, translucent overlay. Dia. 2.5"	200	169	260
61. Floral buds, translucent purple overlay. Dia. 2.5"	300	213	207
62. Fruit on latticinio basket. Dia. 2.65"	350	227	260
63. Triple swirl. Dia. 3.25"	300	245	120
64. Miniature flower. Dia. 2"	450	359	78
65. Garland with silhouettes. Dia. 3.25"	400	283	107
66. Sailing boat silhouette, with millefiori. Dia. 3"	300	194	107
67. Tropical fish in seaweed, faceted. Dia. 3.25"	500	398	207
68. Christmas candle, and holly on latticinio	300	295	110

Name	Edition limit	Actual No.issued	Issue price, $
1981			
69. Swarm of bees, multi-faceted. Dia. 3.5"	200	197	302
70. Aquarium with seahorse. Dia. 3"	350	222	225
71. Miniature swirl with pink flowers. Dia. 2"	350	261	95
72. Patterned millefiori with flower. Dia. 2.75"	250	213	95
73. Acorns, and oak leaves. Dia. 2.35"	300	223	242
74. Gentian blue flower on latticinio. Dia. 2.5"	400	256	141
75. Crown with petaled flower. Dia. 3"	200	191	302
76. Amber on white double overlay	250	143	242
77. Feather, issued to commemorate the wedding of H.R.H. Prince Charles to Lady Diana Spencer	288	282	
78. Crown, issued to commemorate the wedding of H.R.H. Prince Charles to Lady Diana Spencer	145	132	207
79. Christmas, five silhouette canes	300	218	
1982			
80. Millefiori, and flower on translucent color ground	300	243	101
81. Flamingo, and two water lilies	300	188	114
82. Large millefiori on ruby ground	300	165	132
83. Star pattern millefiori	300	238	132
84. Nursery rhyme silhouettes	300	201	147
85. White flowers on aquamarine ground. Dia. 2.5"	250	142	218
86. Pink pom-pom, translucent ruby overlay	300	215	255
87. Floral bouquet, blue, and white double overlay	300	205	
88. Christmas shepherd	350	307	
1983			
89. Yellow flower on millefiori pattern	300	241	120
90. Close millefiori on dark ground	300	212	128
91. Posy ring on latticinio	300	187	144
92. Pink carpet ground with blue flower	300	141	150
93. Faceted bouquet in two millefiori rings	300	194	207
94. Water lily, and butterfly	300	205	239
95. Three ducks on pond	300	255	285
96. Lampwork bouquet, gingham overlay	20	20	3,495
97. Christmas holly wreath, red, and green ribbon	350	343	
1984			
98. Flower pot of three flowers	300	135	113
99. Millefiori petal	300	235	135
100. Caterpillar	300	222	143
101. Floral spray on a double spiral latticinio	400	282	210
102. Ribbon, and flower	300	153	233
103. Squirrel	200	97	300
104. Red petal flower, double overlay	300	294	300
105. Christmas rose with poinsettia, and holly	350	298	
1985			
106. Double clematis over latticinio. Miniature.	400	295	218
107. Upright striped dahlia with leaves. Dia. 3"	300	180	345
108. Polar bear, and cub. Hollow. Flash overlay	300	272	420
109. Flowers, and a ring of canes. Faceted	250	187	
110. Wild pansy, and a ring of canes. Translucent base	350	348	
111. Spray of Scottish Broom on a dark base	350	290	
112. Blue, and white flowers. Triple overlay	250	131	
113. Crown with portrait cane of a candle	300	300	
1986			
114. Close pack millefiori	400	376	143
115. Bouquet of flowers, faceted	300	211	248
116. Dragonfly, upright; in clear glass	300	172	278
117. Strawberries with leaves, and buds	300	222	278
118. Large flower bouquet	250	192	218
119. Mushroom, double green overlay	250	155	375
120. Golden dahlia in clear glass. Dia. 3.25"	300	293	375
121. Red Christmas candle with holly, and berries. Dia. 3.15"	350	338	
122. Royal wedding weight. Prince Andrew and Sarah Ferguson. White rose, bud, stems, and leaves. Date in yellow. Red mottled ground, side facets.	300	132	210
1987			
123. Three small butterflies. Clear ground	300	222	
124. Snowdrops. Double overlay	300	299	
125. Cocoa bean in clear glass	350	190	
126. Humming bird with blue gentian	300	166	390
127. Magnum close millefiori with silhouettes	250	153	
128. American Bald Eagle. Hollow. Overlaid	300	204	465
129. Complicated millefiori with horse, and jockey	250	126	
130. Christmas white rose, 'Noel' in script. Faceted	400	332	233
1988			
131. Kingfisher. Hollow weight. Overlaid pale green	250	147	510
132. Apples, and blossom on deep blue ground. Faceted	200	179	375
133. Bouquet, surrounded by a swirl	350	193	375
134. Pink flower above complex pattern of millefiori	250	194	563
135. Butterfly above a cane basket. Miniature. Dia. 1.9"	400	353	240
136. Scottish thistle, double overlay in green or amethyst	400	316	300
137. Pink flower, and millefiori set on honeycomb canes.	400	205	240
138. Spanish Armada, central ship silhouette. 400th anniversary			
139. Christmas weight showing Three Wise Men. Dark ground	350	307	240
1989			
140. Patterned close millefiori surrounded by millefiori flowers	200	148	435
141. Close millefiori with multi-color complex canes	300	214	600
142. Frog. Hollow weight. Purple flash overlay	250	124	465
143. Millefiori butterfly on a dark ground	300	209	188
144. Three red cherries. All-over faceting. Miniature	300	154	555
145. Lampwork bouquet. Double overlay green or purple	400	216	375
146. Miniature swirl with central flower	600	591	120
147. Christmas – 2 poinsettias with holly leaves. Faceted	350	340	255
1990			
148. Patterned millefiori on selenium red ground. Faceted	300	193	99
149. Central lampwork blossom, and 6 buds with millefiori	300	249	156
150. Miniature crown. White alternating with blue, yellow, and white	400	224	173
151. Multi-colored lampwork bouquet on black ground. Faceted	350	260	294
152. Butterfly, blossom, and bud. Ruby, and white double overlay	300	132	345
153. Three dimensional bouquet with 2 rows of facets	300	295	345
154. Magnum pedestal close pack millefiori. Latticinio base	200	163	518
155. Partridge in a pear tree. Dia. 3.25"	400	341	278
1991			
156. Lampwork bouquet surrounded by canes, and latticinio	300	300	176
157. Columbine within millefiori garland on ruby or clear ground. Dia. 3.2"	300	234	312
158. Pink, and white rose with 2 buds on amethyst basket	300	241	405
159. Checker board weight with 9 silhouettes, white lace ground	350	350	210
160. Close millefiori with latticinio spokes, faceted	300	300	185
161. Bouquet with translucent blue overlay, faceted	300	178	446
162. Three dimensional bouquet, faceted, star cut base	300	170	498
163. White turtle dove	375	288	338
1992			
164. Bouquet of yellow buds	300	254	

Name	Edition limit	Actual No.issued	Issue price, $
165. Bouquet of pink, and white flowers on trellis, green ground Dia. 3.15"	300	277	338
166. Concentric millefiori	350	350	
167. Yellow flower	350	350	
168. Bouquet over latticinio. Overlay	300	300	
169. Five circlets of millefiori. Dia. 3.5"	300	160	
170. Panda, and eucalyptus leaf. Flash overlay. Faceted	300	126	645
171. Snowman within 2 rings of complex canes. Black ground	250	224	353
172. Gold millefiori cross on translucent blue ground. Designed exclusively for L.H. Selman Ltd.	300		95
173. Star of David. White canes on blue ground. Designed exclusively for L.H. Selman Ltd.	300		95

1993

Name	Edition limit	Actual No.issued	Issue price, $
174. Square pattern of complex millefiori	350	191	
175. Amber flower within 5 cane clusters. Dia. 2.5"	300	198	270
176. Barber pole, complex canes surrounded by ruby, and white muslin rods	350	258	
177. Honeycomb faceted millefiori on blue ground	300	156	
178. Pink, and amethyst fuchsia on white lace ground. Dia. 3.15"	300	300	
179. Lampwork bouquet, black single overlay. Dia 3.15"	300	199	540
180. Three dimensional bouquet, blue flash base	250	250	
181. Magnum with complex square, and bullseye canes. Central 12 petaled flower. Signed	50	40	
182. Nativity scene – Mary, and child portrait cane within millefiori, and latticinio. Dia. 3"	250	250	
183. 25th Anniversary weight, to commemorate Perthshire's founding. Central pink flower surrounded by complex, and cluster canes. Blue translucent ground. 25th Anniversary cane, P25 in base. Dia. 3"	200	200	180

1994

Name	Edition limit	Actual No.issued	Issue price, $
184. Amethyst, and yellow pansy. Lace background	400	280	263
185. Carpet ground including 5 portrait canes	300	150	278
186. Intricate millefiori canes on a double spiral latticinio basket	300	145	330
187. Five thistles within white stardust canes. Blue or black ground. Dia. 3.05"	300	220	383
188. Intricate bouquet set on a unique royal blue webbed cushion ground. Dia. 3.05"	300	187	435
189. Fruit weight containing oranges, grapes, a pear, lemon, and cherries. Dia. 2.95"	300	266	600
190. Three-dimensional bouquet. Gold ruby overlay	300	214	660
191. Intricate three-dimensional bouquet of flowers, and buds. Stems tied with an amethyst-striped bow. Dia. 3.35"	35	29	1,898
192. Two white Christmas bells with a sprig of holly, all in a circle of ruby, and blue canes. Green translucent ground. Top facet. Dia. 3"	200	200	195

1995

Name	Edition limit	Actual No.issued	Issue price, $
193. Complex millefiori. Chain of blue, and white half canes. Ruby ground. 6 + 1 faceting. Dia. 3"	300	191	180
194. Four red or blue lampwork flowers on lace. Three silhouette canes. Dia. 3"	300	204	185
195. Flower over a base of double twisted canes. Dia. 2.75"	350	284	212
196. White daisy, and bud on amethyst blue ground. 6 + 1 faceting. Dia. 3"	300	140	228
197. Rose bouquet. Top, and 24 side facets. Star cut base. Dia. 2.75"	300	251	278
198. Two butterflies, and bouquet. Top, and 12 side facets. Amethyst red, and white double overlay. Dia. 3.5"	300	228	423
199. Blue flash overlay encasing various flowers tied with a yellow bow. Highly cut. Dia. 2.5"	250	143	443
200. Multi-faceted magnum millefiori weight. Complex canes, and 6 colored portrait canes around a central cane of a horse, and jockey. Ruby ground. Dia. 4.25"	50	35	1,275
201. Pasque flower. Six petaled mauve flower with stem, and foliage. Clear ground, and star cut base. CPC 1995 cane. Dia. 2.9"	40		135

Name	Edition limit	Actual No.issued	Issue price, $
202. Robin portrait cane, sprig of holly, and nine 5-point white stars on translucent ruby ground. Peripheral circles of pink and white, and, green and white canes. 6 + 1 faceting. Dia. 3"	250	250	203

1996

Name	Edition limit	Actual No.issued	Issue price, $
203. Lampwork flower, with two rows each of 6 petals, encircled with blue or green canes. 6 + 1 faceting. Eight point star cut base. Dia. 2"	400	258	131
204. Ten petaled blue flower within 2 rows of daisy canes, all on a lace ground. Signed, and dated on the base. 6 + 1 faceting. Dia. 3"	250	141	180
205. Crown style weight in blue, ruby, and white encasing a 6 petaled white flower with leaves. Signed, and dated on base. Dia. 2.5"	300	297	162
206. Pink flower, and bud with yellow, and orange stamens. Translucent blue ground. Dia. 2.75"	250	246	278
207. Three blue flowers set on light green leaves. A ladybird is positioned to the left of the blooms. Clear ground. Signed at base of stem. 12 + 1 faceting. Dia. 2.75"	250	250	293
208. Green over white double overlay encasing an array of flowers set on a cushion ground. Signed, and dated on base. 12 + 1 faceting. Dia. 3"	200	159	443
209. Profusion of pink buds, and flowers with yellow stamens together with a bed of small leaves. Signed at base of stem. 16 + 1 faceting. Star cut base. Dia. 3.25"	200	182	488
210. Bouquet of 8 deep blue buds cascading between delicate roots, and leaves. 40 + 1 faceting. Unusual feather cut base. Dia. 3.25"	25		653
211. Bouquet of mistletoe, holly, and poinsettia on opaque white ground. P1996 cane. 5 + 1 faceting	250		

1997

Name	Edition limit	Actual No.issued	Issue price, $
212. Blue or pink lampwork flower set in a ring of matching color canes. Overlaid with thin basket canes. Top facet. Dia. 2"	350	350	
213. Two lampwork flowers surrounded by complex canes, and filigree. Amethyst ground. Signed, and dated on base. 9 + 1 faceting Dia. 3"	250	219	
214. A garland of white stardust canes around 6 blue florets. Rich gold-ruby ground. 12 + 1 faceting. Signed, and dated on base. Dia. 3.15"	250	188	
215. Three dimensional bouquet of 6 blue flowers with dark green leaves. Signed with a 'P' cane. 24 + 1 faceting. Strawberry cut base. Dia. 2.75"	300	183	
216. Bouquet of flowers with marine blue flash overlay. 60 + 1 faceting. Star cut base. Dia. 3"	250	190	
217. Three dimensional bouquet of flowers, and buds set on a delicate latticinio swirl basket. 24 + 1 faceting. Dia. 2.75"	200	175	
218. Coiled yellow, and brown diamond back rattlesnake on sandy ground with a cactus, and wild flower. Dia. 3.15"	150	138	
219. Close millefiori mushroom with a yellow, and blue stalk. Rings of circular facets. Dia. 3.75"	25		
220. Two lampwork snowmen within a frosted glass dome. Two 8-point stars engraved in the background. Dia. 2.5"	250		278

1998

Name	Edition limit	Actual No.issued	Issue price, $
221. Ruby lampwork flower on latticinio twists over a blue, and green ground. Signed, and dated on the base. Dia. 2.5"	250	196	147
222. Green, and white double overlay encasing a bouquet. 12 + 1 faceting. 12-point star cut base. Dia. 2.65"	200	200	213
223. Thistle with 3 flower heads, and 4 leaves. P cane at base of stem. 16-point star cut base. Dia. 2.75"	200	200	228
224. Amethyst, and yellow pansy within a circle of red flowers. 5 + 1 faceting, and 10 flutes. Strawberry cut base. Dia. 2.9"	200	124	309

Name	Edition limit	Actual No.issued	Issue price, $
225. Two roses, and bud surrounded by blue complex canes. Set on a white latticinio base. 24 + 1 faceting. Dia. 2.75"	200	150	360
226. Blue, and white bouquet, and 6 portrait canes set on a ruby, and black spiraled ground. Signed, and dated on the base. Dia. 3.25"	200	180	390
227. Single flash overlay hollow weight containing a smiling clown. 16 + 1 faceting. Signed, and dated on the base. Dia. 3"	175	114	653
228. Encased double overlay bouquet with very intricate cutting. Dia. 3.5"	30		1,478
229. Boy with sledge on snow, and owl in tree. 5 + 1 faceting. Dia. 2.75"	200		326
1999			
230. Miniature bouquet on black ground. 6 + 1 faceting. Signed, and dated on base. Dia. 2"	300		147
231. Tropical fish swimming between reeds. Turquoise blue ground. 5 + 1 faceting. Signed, and dated on base. Dia. 2.75"	200		195

Name	Edition limit	Actual No.issued	Issue price, $
232. Amber flowers, and buds cascading from a central flower. Amethyst red ground. Signed, and dated on base. Dia. 3"	200		228
233. Three dimensional amethyst petaled flower with multiple stamens, and 5 veined leaves. Translucent ruby ground. 12 + 1 faceting. Dia. 2.25"	175		263
234. Bouquet of multiple flowers, and buds on a blue ground. 7 + 1 faceting. Signed, and dated on base. Dia. 3"	175		293
235. Three dimensional bouquet on clear ground. 12 + 1 faceting. Unusual star, and feather cut base. Dia. 3"	150		420
236. Double overlay pedestal (amethyst red over white) with bouquet on a blue ground. 18 + 1 faceting. Hexagonal base. Height 3"	150		555
237. Foxglove, and buds on clear ground. 32 + 1 faceting. Star cut base. Dia. 3.15"	25		735
238. Three Christmas candles on bracken, all on a latticinio ground. 6 + 1 faceting	200		300

Perthshire have issued over 200 recurring Limited Edition and Decorative designs. These have been well documented by Mahoney and McClanahan[4]. The weights, issued at prices ranging from $12 in the early 1970s to about $200 in the 1990s, cover a very wide range of lampwork, and millefiori designs.

This range of weights are prefixed PP. Three examples are shown in figures 215 to 217. PP19 and PP33 are a further good illustration of how some weights have appreciated in value, being originally issued at $20, and $67 respectively.

Fig. 216. Pattern PP19, 1974. A good scrambled weight, such as this, can add variety to a collection of more formal designs. Dia. 2.5". Courtesy of Sweetbriar Gallery Archive. $120/150.

Fig. 215. Pattern PP13, 1977. Spaced canes on lace, on an attractive colored ground. Dia. 2.5". Courtesy of Sweetbriar Gallery Archive. $170/200.

Fig. 217. Italian garden, 1979. Pattern PP33. Dia. 3". Courtesy of Sweetbriar Gallery Archive. $130/180.

Typical Current Value dollars ($) of selected Perthshire weights

Ref. No.	Value	Ref. No.	Value	Ref. No.	Value
1	750	48	560	101	485
2	300	50	420	103	440
3	660	51	450	104	435
5	475	54	450	105	375
6	225	55	400	106	220
7	180	56	410	107	350
8	400	57	400	108	400
9	255	58	400	112	480
11	470	59	280	113	660
12	280	60	450	114	280
13	330	61	420	115	330
14	400	62	435	116	350
15	225	63	280	117	375
16	375	64	210	118	300
18	285	65	450	119	730
19	255	67	660	120	600
20	270	68	290	121	650
21	280	69	1750	122	210
22	615	70	490	125	350
23	555	72	420	126	400
24	825	73	400	127	400
25	400	75	430	129	450
26	190	76	410	134	510
27	540	77	560	135	300
30	750	78	490	139	450
31	210	79	650	140	585
32	310	80	225	143	225
33	180	81	360	147	305
36	540	83	230	149	360
37	330	84	430	150	375
38	225	85	410	152	470
39	510	88	390	155	460
40	375	91	240	157	460
42	450	93	270	164	470
43	750	96	4100	169	490
44	210	97	525	181	1560
45	330	98	195	183	260
46	210	99	335	187	460
47	500	100	260		

One-off Specials

1. A sprig of bluebells with a diamond cut purple over white double overlay, encased in clear glass and overlaid a second time with purple over white. Star cut base. Unsigned.
2. A central silhouette cane of a rooster surrounded by two concentric circles of canes including five animal silhouettes. Unsigned.
3. A hollow faceted weight with a pale blue flash overlay enclosing a performing circus seal. P cane on base. This is very similar to the seal issued in 1979 (reference number 55).
4. A central silhouette cane of a sailing boat surrounded by eight canes each bearing an animal silhouette. All on a pink, and white upset muslin ground. Unsigned.
5. A lampwork '25' in yellow centrally placed, and surrounded by six five petaled flowers. Translucent green ground with a blue over white double overlay. Unsigned. Presumably designed to commemorate a birthday or anniversary.
6. Upright bouquet of tulip-like flowers with a red over white fancy cut double overlay, encased in clear glass. Faceted. P1982 cane on base.
7. Upright bouquet of roses with a purple over white double overlay, encased in clear glass. Faceted. P1982 cane on base.
8. A pink, and a blue flower, and bud, on a green latticinio cushion with a purple, and white double overlay encased in a flash overlay. Signed.
9. Three pink rosebuds on a white disc surrounded by double overlaid petals, all encased within a double overlay of ruby on white, with a double row of oval printies. Made in 1980.
10. A central portrait cane of a Christmas tree surrounded by four sprigs of holly, and berries. All above a lace ground. Circular top facet. P1977 cane. Diameter 2.8". At Selman's Spring 1993 auction, this weight realized $413.
11. Multi-color close millefiori mushroom in clear glass. Top printie, and 2 rows of oval printies around the side. P1983 cane. Dia. 3" Housed in the Bergstrom Mahler Museum (at least five other one-off specials are housed in this museum).
12. Of special importance is the Stuart Drysdale commemorative weight, figure 218. An exquisite piece made to commemorate Stuart Drysdale's considerable contribution to modern Scottish paperweights. Made in 1994, the weight is now housed in the Bergstrom Mahler Museum.

This list does not purport to be complete.

Fig. 218. Stuart Drysdale commemorative weight, 1994. An absolutely superb magnum, produced in honor of the considerable contribution that Perthshire's founder made to paperweights. Housed in the Bergstrom Mahler Museum, U.S.A. Courtesy of Perthshire Paperweights Ltd.

Special Commissions

These are occasionally undertaken. For instance, in 1986 - 7 a weight showing a lampwork Teddy Bear was produced in an edition of fifty for the prestigious London store Harrods Ltd. The weight is shown in figure 219, and in 1995 an example sold for $200.

Fig. 219. Teddy bear, 1986/87. An appealing, and rare weight made in an addition of 50 for Harrods. Dia. 3". Courtesy of Sweetbriar Gallery Archive. $250/350.

In 1995 Perthshire Paperweights Ltd. were commissioned to produce a weight exclusively for members of the Cambridge Paperweight Circle. The design for the weight is based upon the Pasque flower (*pulsatilla vulgaris*), which flowers in April and May, and hence derives its name from the French word pâques (meaning Easter).

The issue was restricted to one weight per member, and figure 220 shows an example, from which it will be observed that the coloring of the flower, and the fern-like foliage has been accurately reproduced. Figure 221 shows the signature cane. Each weight is numbered on the base.

An interesting commission is that initiated by the manufacturers of Guinness. The company approached Perthshire, and the trial result was that shown in figure 222. Not entirely happy with the result, Guinness are believed to have then contacted another maker. Fortunately, this trial piece was retained.

Fig. 220. Pasque flower, 1995. Special commission of forty weights made for members of the Cambridge Paperweight Circle. CPC 1995 cane. Dia. 2.8". Height 2". $225/300.

Fig. 221. The good signature cane that complements the weight shown in Fig. 220.

Fig. 222. A trial piece, commissioned by Guinness, and a one-off. c.1992. Dia. 2.4". Courtesy of a private collector. $150/250.

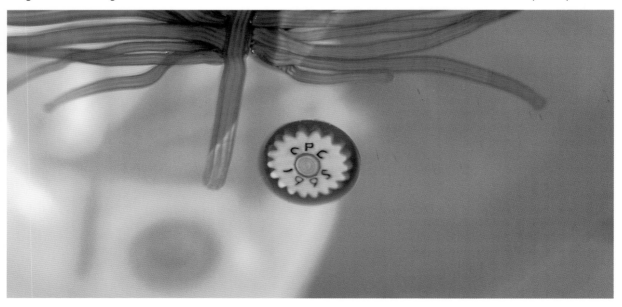

Canes

Date, and signature canes

By no means all of Perthshire's recurring limited edition and decorative weights carry a cane which gives the year of manufacture, many simply have a 'P' for Perthshire (figure 223). However, some weights are dated via a lettering system which Stuart Drysdale introduced from the very first year of production.

This system adopts the following letters for the respective years of issue:

A	1969	J	1978	S	1987
B	1970	K	1979	T	1988
C	1971	L	1980	U	1989
D	1972	M	1981	V	1990
E	1973	N	1982	W	1991
F	1974	O	1983	X	1992
G	1975	P	1984	Y	1993
H	1976	Q	1985	Z	1994
I	1977	R	1986		

In general, individual artists were not allowed to sign weights. However, one weight which is signed by the artist is the blue, and white double overlay garland made in 1978. This weight has a JD cane on the bottom showing that it was made by John Deacons.

Perthshire's range of canes is extremely vast, and figure 224 will serve to show a further selection of their designs.

Fig. 224. A good selection of Perthshire canes. The bottom row includes those used for special items or occasions. Courtesy of a private collector.

Paperweight Related Items

In common with most makers, Perthshire made related items such as doorknobs (figure 225), earrings, and paperknives which can all add interest to a collection.

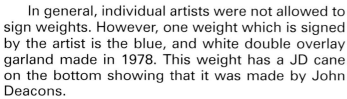

Fig. 223. P signature cane found in many Perthshire paperweights.

Fig. 225. Perthshire doorknob. Design PP18. A useful paperweight related item with brass fitting. Dia. 2.4". Height 3.4". $80/130.

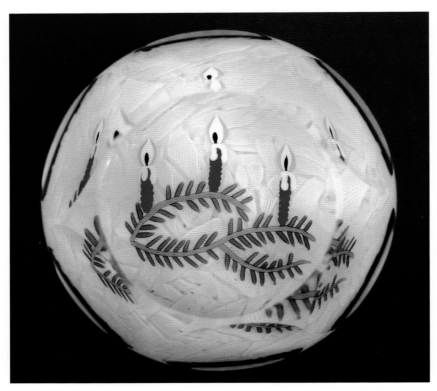

Fig. 226. Christmas, 1999. Perthshire. The latest in the annual series of attractive Christmas themes. Limited edition of 200. Courtesy of Perthshire Paperweights Ltd. $300.

Some people collect only weights with a Christmas motif. Perthshire's pieces are impressive and their example for 1999 is illustrated in figure 226.

[1]Hollister, Paul. *Glass Paperweights – An Old Craft Revived*. Coupar Angus, Perthshire: William Culross and Son Ltd., 1975.

[2]Selman, Lawrence H. and Linda P. *Paperweights for Collectors*. Santa Cruz, California: Paperweight Press, 1975.

[3]Selman, Lawrence H. *The Art of the Paperweight – Perthshire*. Santa Cruz, California: Paperweight Press, 1983.

[4]Mahoney, Colin and McClanahan, Gary. *The Complete Guide to Perthshire Paperweights*. Santa Cruz, California: Paperweight Press, 1997.

[5]Annual Bulletin of the Paperweight Collectors Association, 1977.

Chapter 7
Selkirk Glass Ltd.

In 1977, at the age of twenty-nine, Peter Holmes (Head of Paperweight Making Dept.) and Ron Hutchison (Sales Manager) decided to leave Caithness Glass Ltd., to set up their own company which was to concentrate mainly on low edition paperweights of high quality. They headed south and settled in Selkirk to form Selkirk Glass Ltd. An old, disused factory was located and with skillful re-styling by the Borders Regional Authorities, converted to a clean, modern unit of pleasing appearance.

Peter Holmes was born on December 3 1947. His father was in the Royal Air Force, and stationed in Northern Scotland near to where Caithness had their first factory.

As a teenager, Peter had a part-time job at a local blacksmiths where Paul Ysart traded for his ironwork. It was as a result of this that Paul got to know Peter, and suggested that he become an apprentice at Caithness. Peter's career in glass had begun.

The reliable operation of glass furnaces and annealing ovens is, of course, essential if production is to run smoothly, and an electric light was appropriately coupled to the relevant heating circuits, and sited on top of the original factory building to act as a visual aid. Peter Holmes (figure 227) acquainted the author with the fact that by standing on a bed, in his first residence, he could just see the light, and could thus sleep peacefully, safe in the knowledge that all was well!

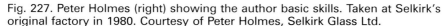

Fig. 227. Peter Holmes (right) showing the author basic skills. Taken at Selkirk's original factory in 1980. Courtesy of Peter Holmes, Selkirk Glass Ltd.

A further humorous story related by this master paperweight maker concerns hypodermic syringes. Peter Holmes uses these in the production of certain weights to blow into, and thus expand, certain bubbles incorporated in the design. Working late at night, and with doors wide open to improve the air circulation, Peter received a visitation from the police checking up to see that everything was in order. Seeing the hypodermics lying around, the expressions on the policemen's faces gave Peter the impression that, momentarily, they thought he was using them for something far less savory!

Such are the light-hearted stories that this maker can tell, but, let no one be under the misapprehension that Peter Holmes takes the making of his weights in similar vein. Although to witness him making a complex weight may give an air of casualness, in fact, everything is conducted based on a wealth of experience. In 1980 Peter told the author that his reject rate was of the order of only 3%. Here then is a man whose total life appears to revolve around paperweights. He admires the fastidious perfection with which Paul Ysart, his mentor, made his paperweights, and respects the detail that his American contemporary Paul Stankard puts into his floral weights.

Nothing succeeds like success, and Peter Holmes and Ron Hutchison's hard work is paying off. Even in the early days order books were frequently full, with significant exports to France, Germany, and the U.S.A. Other countries exported to include Australia, Switzerland, and Japan. Business expanded, and in 1990

Selkirk moved into a new factory which is about two hundred and fifty yards away from the original.

While Peter Holmes is associated first and foremost with abstract design and experimentation, it is interesting to note that Selkirk Glass were probably the first company, after Ysart and Strathearn, to produce sulphide paperweights in Scotland since the 19th century.

What then does Peter Holmes foresee as a challenge for the future? To quote his own words he is "faced with many challenges, primarily in being able to do things that other people cannot and will not be able to copy. My aim really is to make beautiful and artistic pieces of work that people will study a hundred years from now, and find just as much pleasure as collectors do now, and that glassmakers of the future will use them as a goal to aim for." A further challenge Peter says is to "get things into paperweights to make them exactly as nature intended them to look." As an example of this, collectors should study his Primrose weight (figure 228) – a three-dimensional vertical flower. One of these weights sold for $517 in 1994.

Peter has had to develop many techniques to enable him to produce some of his weights. Some of these have taken literally years to perfect and details regarding them are, not surprisingly, confidential. Further examples include the perfection and production of gold effects, as in Argonaut (shown in figure 229). See also Chapter 1, The Manufacture of Glass Paperweights.

Fig. 228. Primroses, 1980 Selkirk. A good example of Peter Holmes' lampwork. PH cane.. Courtesy of Sweetbriar Gallery Archive. $400/500

Fig. 229. Argonaut, 1981 Selkirk. This shows the gold effect which took Peter Holmes a long time to perfect. Courtesy of Peter Holmes, Selkirk Glass Ltd. $200/250.

Canes and Lampwork

Quite a wide range of canes and lampwork has been produced over the years, and a selection of these is to be seen in figures 230 to 235.

Fig. 230. Selection of typical Selkirk canes, and a lampwork flower.

Fig. 231. More fine Selkirk canes, including the shamrock and daffodil in the bottom row. Courtesy of Peter Holmes, Selkirk Glass Ltd.

Fig. 232. Lampwork flowers. Just some of the many lampwork items produced by Peter Holmes. Courtesy of Roy and Pam Brown.

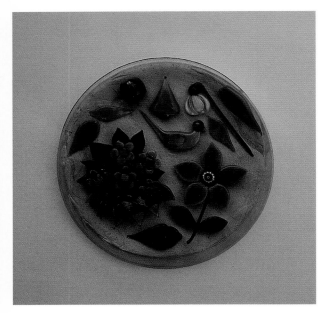

Fig. 233. Further lampwork by Peter Holmes. Notice the detail in the floral arrangement. Courtesy of Roy and Pam Brown.

Fig. 234. Signature canes. Two forms of PH cane used by Peter Holmes. Courtesy of Peter Holmes, Selkirk Glass Ltd.

Fig. 235. The H cane Peter Holmes did not use, to avoid confusion with H canes in certain Ysart weights. Courtesy of Peter Holmes, Selkirk Glass Ltd.

Brochures
These are issued yearly by the company. Figures 236 and 237 show the earliest brochure known to the author dating from 1978.

Fig. 236. Selkirk brochure, 1978. As stated elsewhere, brochures should form an important part of a collector's items. This is the outside of Selkirk's first brochure.

Fig. 237. Selkirk brochure, 1978. This shows many of Selkirk's early designs and provides a useful reference.

List of Selkirk Weights Issued

Name	Issue price $	Edition size

1978

Name	Issue price $	Edition size
1. Atlantis	53	400
2. Candor	22	U*
3. Dragonfly	90	250
4. Ink bottle 1978, PH cane in stopper	83	150
5. Ink bottle 1978, PH cane in base	83	150
6. Merlin sky, cauldron	38	U
7. Merlin sky, wizards eye	38	U
8. Nebula	53	400
9. Red mirage	39	500
10. Rubor	22	U
11. Scylla	53	400
12. Space pool	36	500
13. Summer Magic, lovebirds	38	U
14. Summer Magic, butterfly, see figure 238	38	U

Fig. 238. Summer Magic Butterfly. First issued in 1978. A good example of motifs placed near the outer surface. PH cane. Courtesy of Sweetbriar Gallery Archive. $100/120.

Name	Issue price $	Edition size
15. Robert Burns	113	250
16. John Knox	113	250
17. Mary Queen of Scots	113	250
18. Sir Walter Scott	113	250
19. Holly	150	75
20. Pond life, frog and water lily	135	30
21. Pond life, trout	135	30
22. Pond life, otter	135	30
23. Pond life, great crested grebe	135	30

1979

Name	Issue price $	Edition size
24. Aquarius	105	350
25. Aurora	45	500
26. Butterfly and flower	180	200
27. Electra (Blue, green, ruby, and silver)	22	U
28. Frog	150	200
29. Fruit basket	180	200
30. Ice pool	68	350
31. Ink bottle 1979	83	150
32. Marbrie, pink, see figure 239	44	450
33. Marbrie, blue	44	450
34. Millefiori emblem, thistle	30	500
35. Nova	38	500
36. Edinburgh Military tattoo	98	250

Name	Issue price $	Edition size
37. Rose	83	450
38. Sea bed	135	200
39. William Shakespeare	113	250
40. Winter dream	53	350
41. Triton	89	25
42. Christmas rose	150	75
43. Partridge in a pear tree	53	500
44. Pond life, Dragonfly	144	30
45. Pond life, Sedge warbler	144	30
46. Pond life, Kingfisher	144	30
47. Pond life, Perch	144	30

1980

Name	Issue price $	Edition size
48. Chameleon	41	500
49. Christmas 1980, two turtle doves	56	500
50. Dark Star	63	450
51. Fission	50	350
52. Gemini Ruby	22	U
53. Gemini Blue	22	U
54. Ink bottle 1980	95	150
55. Little owl	56	350
56. Mariner	27	500
57. Minaret	63	350
58. Millefiori emblem, English rose	33	500
59. Miniature flower 1980	29	500
60. Moonglow	63	450
61. Northern lights	47	500
62. Oracle	56	400
63. Primrose	209	200
64. Scent bottle	120	150
65. Slipstream	63	450
66. Space probe	29	500
67. Summer magic, dragonfly	51	U
68. Tranquility, Ruby	15	U
69. Tranquility, Purple	15	U
70. Wren	56	350
71. The Queen Mother		350
72. The Queen Mother (faceted)	95	100

1981

Name	Issue price $	Edition size
73. Argonaut	50	350
74. Aquamarine	27	500
75. Citadel	57	350
76. Cyclone	27	500

Fig. 239. Marbrie, pink. A fascinating design first issued in 1979. French workers in the 19th century were the forerunners of this effect. Courtesy of Sweetbriar Gallery Archive.

Name	Issue price $	Edition size	Name	Issue price $	Edition size
77. Christmas 1981, Three French Hens	57	500	145. Perfume bottle 1983	105	150
78. Dragonfly	95	250	146. Perfume bottle, blue flower	120	75
79. Love, ruby and purple	32	U	147. Seaburst, blue	18	U
80. Ink bottle 1981	95	150	148. Seaburst, purple	18	U
81. Jet stream	50	350	149. Solitaire, burgundy	26	U
82. Midas	57	350	150. Solitaire, ruby	26	U
83. Millefiori emblem, daffodil	38	500	151. Solitaire, blue	26	U
84. Millefiori flower	50	250	152. Solitaire, green	26	U
85. Millefiori ring	50	250	153. Sonar	56	350
86. Miniature flower 1981	32	500	154. Starship	39	350
87. Neptune's crown	57	350	155. Talisman	35	500
88. Olympus	57	350	156. Triad	27	500
89. Sanctuary (blue, damson)	45	350	157. Typhoon	30	500
90. Saturn	63	350	158. Tulip	45	250
91. Scent bottle	120	150	159. Zenith	30	500
92. Sceptre	57	350			
93. Song thrush	57	350	**1984**		
94. Sorcerer	30	500	160. Bluebells	69	250
95. Tranquility (silver)	15	U	161. Blue ice	36	500
96. Voyager	27	500	162. Carousel	33	500
97. Vulcan	38	450	163. Cavalcade	42	450
98. Whirlpool	29	500	164. Christmas 1984, 6 geese	62	500
99. Millefiori bubble	29	450	165. Christmas 1984, 2 bells	160	75
100. Engraved CD	53	250	166. Chiffon	36	500
101. Coronet	57	250	167. Clematis	69	250
102. Millefiori crown	68	250	168. Futura	30	500
103. Double sulphide	102	100	169. Ice station	56	450
104. Orange Blossom	180	75	170. Ice spiral	30	500
			171. Inca	33	500
1982			172. Latticinio flower, pansy	105	100
105. Alpha (Matching	45	450	173. Mercury	59	350
106. Omega (set	45	450	174. Mirage	36	500
107. Aztec	41	400	175. Nautilus	30	500
108. Butterfly, miniature	41	250	176. Nymph	56	450
109. Centurion	32	500	177. Perfume bottle	105	150
110. Christmas 1982, Four Calling Birds	60	500	178. Quintet	33	500
111. Helios	27	500	179. Sand Sprite	56	450
112. Ice fountain	29	500	180. Sea Fern	56	450
113. Invader	63	250	181. Space station	42	500
114. Lovebirds, miniature	41	250	182. Spindrift, blue, burgundy, or ruby	21	U
115. Millefiori crown, green	69	150	183. Starburst	29	500
116. Millefiori crown, blue	69	150	184. Tornado	30	500
117. Millefiori emblem, shamrock	41	500			
118. Millefiori flower and bud	45	250			
119. Miniature flower 1982	41	250			
120. Mistral	29	500			
121. Moonstone	29	500			
122. Mystic	56	350			
123. Orbiter	56	400			
124. Perfume bottle, pink flower	120	75			
125. Perfume bottle, 1982	101	150			
126. Sea Spray	56	350			
127. Tempest	30	500			
128. Wild Rose	225	75			
129. Angel Fish, engraved	56	250			

1983

Name	Issue price $	Edition size
130. Bouquet	56	150
131. Christmas 1983, Five gold rings	62	500
132. Christmas 1983, Three candles	144	75
133. Cosmos	78	75
134. Crocus, see figure 240	45	250
135. Emperor	27	500
136. Firecrest	53	350
137. Five Moons	60	350
138. Harmony	30	500
139. Labyrinth	53	350
140. Latticinio flower	95	100
141. Maritime	27	500
142. Miniature flower 1983	45	250
143. Pegasus	56	350
144. Penguin	120	75

Fig. 240. Crocus. First issued in 1983, the lampwork is well framed by the latticinio. Selkirk. Dia. 2.75". Courtesy of Sweetbriar Gallery Archive. $200/250.

Name	Issue price $	Edition size	Name	Issue price $	Edition size

1985

Name	Issue price $	Edition size
185. Arabesque	39	500
186. Basket flower, see figure 241	128	100
187. Blossom	57	450
188. Christmas 1985, 7 swans	63	500
189. Christmas rose	177	75
190. Daffodils	69	250
191. Ice coral	63	450
192. Latticinio bouquet	209	100
193. Mikado	45	500
194. Millefiori bouquet	69	250
195. Moondance	32	500
196. Perfume bottle	113	150
197. Pirouette	45	500
198. Saracen	63	450
199. Snowdrops	69	250
200. Space pearl	30	500
201. Springtide	57	450
202. Symphony	36	500

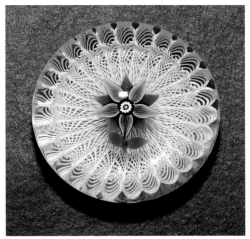

Fig. 241. Flower in basket, 1985. A good design with great visual depth in the basket, an effect also created by Paul Ysart (Peter's mentor). Courtesy of Sweetbriar Gallery Archive. $250/320.

1986

Name	Issue price $	Edition size
203. Basketflower	128	100
204. Calypso	45	500
205. Christmas 1986, 8 maids	69	500
206. Christmas flower	180	75
207. Garland	56	450
208. Haley's comet	69	500
209. Ice petal	63	450
210. Moondust	39	500
211. Moonmist	39	500
212. Mosaic	33	500
213. Paladin	63	450
214. Pastelle pink, or green	27	U
215. Perfume bottle	113	150
216. Quadro	53	450
217. Serenade	33	500
218. Sovereign	56	500
219. Spiral galaxy	42	500
220. Sunburst	30	U
221. Whirlwind	39	500

1987

Name	Issue price $	Edition size
222. Basket flower	144	100
223. Carnival	45	500
224. Christmas 1987, 9 pipers	69	500
225. Christmas mistletoe	209	100
226. Ebony	63	450
227. Ebony perfume bottle	128	150
228. Emerald star	45	500
229. Fantasy magnum	57	500
230. Lace fountain	45	500
231. Lotus	69	450
232. Melody ruby, purple, or turquoise	27	U
233. Midwinter	69	450
234. Midwinter perfume bottle	128	150
235. Minstrel	35	500
236. Monsoon	39	500
237. Moonshadow	35	500
238. Nimbus black and orange, or lilac and blue	24	U
239. Pastelle blue	29	U
240. Peace	72	450
241. Phantom	54	500
242. Samurai	45	500
243. Shangri-La	69	450
244. Stratos	33	500
245. Triton blue or ruby	33	U

1988

Name	Issue price $	Edition size
246. Autumn breeze	33	U
247. Constellation	56	500
248. Flamenco	39	500
249. Ice dance	45	500
250. Jester magnum	72	500
251. Matador	57	500
252. Oasis	36	U
253. Pansy	173	250
254. Pastelle black and white	30	U
255. Scimitar	60	500
256. Seasprite	95	150
257. Silver star	53	500
258. Skyhawk	39	500
259. Space orchid	69	500
260. Space orchid perfume bottle	128	150
261. Stardust	45	500
262. Summer bouquet	270	100
263. Warrior	48	500
264. Wayfarer	56	500
265. Whispers lilac	36	U
266. Christmas 1988, 10 Lords		

1989

Name	Issue price $	Edition size
267. Arctic lights	72	500
268. Arctic lights perfume bottle	137	150
269. Cabaret	36	U
270. Cauldron	45	750
271. Chrysalis	80	500
272. Fiesta	45	750
273. Filigree	45	750
274. Masquerade	35	U
275. Nocturne	39	U
276. Pastelle coffee and cream	32	U
277. Paradise magnum	78	500
278. Phoenix	80	500
279. Rendezvous	39	U
280. Rockpool	105	500
281. Scotia	80	500
282. Sea Pearl	42	750
283. Snapdragon	72	500
284. Troubadour	36	U
285. Whispers crimson	38	U
286. Winter breeze	35	U
287. Spiral star	56	500
288. Christmas 1989, 11 pipers		

Name	Issue price $	Edition size	Name	Issue price $	Edition size
1990			**1993**		
289. Fireglow	72	500	358. Crimson	102	350
290. Firestar	51	750	359. Fire Coral	84	500
291. Golden orchid	89	500	360. Jasmine Green	45	U
292. Hawkwind, magnum	144	500	361. Jasmine Purple	45	U
293. Lagoon	80	500	362. Pageant	60	500
294. Marrakesh	45	750	363. Reflections	53	500
295. Melody blue or gold	30	U	364. Sea Jade	95	500
296. Midnight lace	45	U	365. Sea Jade perfume bottle	171	150
297. Monarch, magnum	89	500	366. Seven Stars	74	500
298. Pastelle, coffee and cream	33	U	367. Spindrift Lilac	39	U
299. Pulsar	89	500	368. Sun Prince	53	500
300. Rainbow star	69	500	369. Tapestry	74	500
301. Sapphire, magnum	95	500	370. Tiger Lily	42	U
302. Scimitar	69	500	371. Windsurf	51	500
303. Seaburst, green	32	U	372. Amberlight	33	U
304. Spindrift, black and white or rainbow	32	U	373. Electra Ruby	33	U
305. Springbreeze	38	U	374. Mascot Pink	24	U
306. Silver mist	78	500	375. Mascot Rainbow	24	U
307. Silver mist perfume bottle	144	150	376. Windswept Black	24	U
308. Starfrost	56	750	377. Windswept Blue	24	U
309. Stormforce	33	U	378. Sculpture 93	225	75
310. Sunburst	36	U	379. Juggler	105	500
311. Tiger's eye	45	U			
312. Whispers, lilac	42	U	**1994**		
313. Caress, miniature	23	U	380. Acrobat	78	500
314. Satin, miniature	23	U	381. Azure	51	U
315. Starstream, miniature	23	U	382. Beacon	95	500
316. Tristar, miniature	23	U	383. Carmine	66	500
317. Christmas 1990, 12 drummers			384. Discovery	62	500
			385. Medusa	95	500
1991			386. Nightshade	62	500
318. Concerto	48	U	387. Pagoda	84	500
319. Emerald dance	48	U	388. Sea Gems	59	U
320. Enchantress	80	450	389. Seascape	48	U
321. Evening star	60	500	390. Silhouette	84	500
322. Fanfare	80	450	391. Sun Princess, see figure 242	59	500
323. Galleon	68	500	392. Topaz	59	500
324. Illusion	45	500			
325. Mandarin	53	500			
326. Sea mist	53	500			
327. Sea nymph	68	350			
328. Silver cascade	68	500			
329. Soothsayer	89	450			
330. Summertime	272	75			
331. Sun king	45	500			
332. Winter crocus	89	500			
333. Winter crocus perfume bottle	158	150			
334. Electra, miniature	26	U			
335. Ice mist, miniature	26	U			
1992					
336. Ballerina	53	500			
337. Coronet	74	500			
338. Equinox	102	500			
339. Eternity	48	U			
340. Explorer	84	500			
341. Merlin	74	500			
342. Mystique	95	500			
343. Mystique perfume bottle	171	150			
344. Neptune	60	500			
345. Panache	60	500			
346. Sculpture 92	225	75			
347. Scanner	60	500			
348. Silver Rhapsody	120	500			
349. Space Orbit	84	500			
350. Spinnaker	75	350			
351. Starlight	65	500			
352. Summer breeze	45	U			
353. Titania	74	500			
354. Traveller	74	500			
355. Firecracker	29	U			
356. Melody	29	U			
357. Satin blue	29	U			

Fig. 242. Sun Princess, 1994. Fine abstract designs are one of Peter Holmes' specialties. A good, but not expensive, example. Dia. 3.25". Courtesy of Sweetbriar Gallery Archive. $60/70.

Name	Issue price $	Edition size	Name	Issue price $	Edition size
1995			438. Pink latticinio	233	100
In 1995 the average diameter of standard weights was 3.15″ with miniatures at 2.6″.			439. Ribbons, blue	47	U
			440. Ribbons, ruby	47	U
393. Crusader	117	150	441. Ribbons, yellow	47	U
394. Cyclone	71	500	442. Sculpture 96	270	75
395. Electra, blue, miniature	36	U	443. Spring tide	65	500
396. Elegance	36	U	444. Sultan	117	350
397. Eternity, green	54	U	445. White spiral	270	100
398. Festival	47	U			
399. Firedance, miniature	36	U	**1997**		
400. Firefly	54	500	446. Blue vortex	86	500
401. Guardian	81	500	447. Daydream	73	500
402. Harlequin	65	U	448. Genie	86	500
403. Indigo, miniature	36	U	449. Inferno	53	U
404. Mardi Gras, miniature	36	U	450. Intrigue magnum	145	350
405. Millefiori flower, ruby, scalloped petals	125	100	451. Lacewing	86	500
406. Millefiori flower, ruby, pointed petals	125	100	452. Mantle	117	500
407. Moondrops, miniature	54	U	453. Minuet	117	500
408. Neptune's star	78	500	454. Nightfrost	126	350
409. Night Hawk, black	62	500	455. Nomad	83	500
410. Night Hawk, blue	62	500	456. Patriot	104	500
411. Pastorale	59	U	457. Spectrum	44	U
412. Pierrot	47	U	458. Twilight	53	U
413. Satin, crimson	36	U	459. Wavetide	59	U
414. Seafarer, miniature	36	U	460. Zephyr	68	U
415. Seaquest	78	U	461. Anniversary Bouquet**	712	20
416. Spellbound	54	U	462. Stargazer (limited to the number sold in 1997)**		
417. Stardance	78	500	463. Bouquet '97	450	75
418. Starflower	99	500	464. Flower and bud '97	300	75
419. Sun Queen	65	500	465. Romance	59	U
420. Tiger Lily, purple	47	U	466. Sculpture '97	255	75
421. Vision	135	150	467. Charisma	41	U
422. Windswept, green, miniature	29	U			
423. Windswept, pink, miniature	29	U	**1998**		
424. Windswept, blue, miniature	29	U	468. Galaxy	74	500
			469. Highland spring	60	500
1996			470. Jazz	53	500
425. Apollo	75	500	471. Myriad	53	500
426. Celebration	47	U	472. Moon crystals	60	500
427. Cocoon	143	500	473. Overture	75	500
428. Corona	105	350	474. Shadows, black	45	U
429. Crimson star	65	500	475. Shadows, blue	45	U
430. Daffodils	233	100	476. Snow queen	97	500
431. Fire fountain	89	500	477. Butterfly	300	75
432. Golden reef	48	500	478. Fantasia	112	150
433. Goldstream	65	500	479. Romance, lilac	60	U
434. Lotus flower	99	500	480. Rose bottle, and weight	262	50
435. Meteor	98	350	481. Rose petal (uncut)	100	200
436. Midsummer	99	500	482. Ruby cascade	112	150
437. Millefiori crown	89	100	483. Ruby flower	262	75

Detailed Aspects of selected early weights from 1978 to 1981

Atlantis

The rich blue ground of this abstract weight contrasts vividly against the four pinnacled, white, crystalline motif. Viewed from above, the motif can be clearly seen in the bubble. A PH cane set in the base has dark colored letters set in white, with a green surround. Identification markings on the base of the weight are shown in figure 243.

Fig. 243. Atlantis, 1978. Typical base markings on a very early weight. PH cane. Dia. 3.3". $100/120.

Dragonfly

A fine weight both from the technical and aesthetic points of view. The wafer thin dragonfly makes use of a specialized technique. Peter Holmes feels that this weight was more challenging technically than many other weights he has made.

Unlike most other dragonfly weights which have been produced, the dragonfly in this weight is seen hovering above a five petaled yellow water lily, set onto two green leaves. This lily is in turn floating on a sporadic blue coating, which expertly conveys the impression of water. Peter Holmes finally created an attractive ground, which resembles stones at the bottom of a pond. A PH cane is set amongst these stones and faces upwards. The three-dimensional result, and water effect, in many examples of this weight is excellent. Figure 244 shows this exciting weight.

Fig. 244. Dragonfly, 1978. The delicate dragonfly is an interesting departure from lampwork/millefiori types, and a good addition to a collection. Dia. 3.25". Height 2.7". $200/300.

Ink bottles

1978 issue. The purple form echoes that used in the Caithness purple coral paperweights.

Of particular interest is the positioning of the PH cane. Due to technical difficulties during manufacture only a very few bottles had the cane inserted into the stopper, thus making such specimens rare. The remainder of the issue had the PH cane inserted into the base of the bottle.

1979 issue Generally similar in form to the 1978 issue, this ink bottle features a pink abstract form in the base. It differs from the 1978 issue in having the pink form, in miniature, included also in the stopper (figure 245). A PH cane is set into the base.

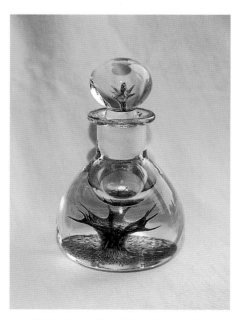

Fig. 245. Ink bottle, 1979. One of the earlier abstract design bottles by Peter Holmes. Dia. 3.1". Height 3.9". $100/120.

1980 issue Delicate blue swirling forms and a central bubble fill the base of this bottle, and a similar form is present in the stopper. The rim of the bottle contains small flecks of the same blue, and gives a subtle enhancement.

Scent bottles

First introduced in 1980, the scent bottle, shown in figure 246, is generally somewhat smaller than the ink bottles, and more elaborate regarding its cutting. The 1980 issue contains a flat bouquet of seven red, blue, yellow, and mauve flowers with stems and five leaves. Eight scal-

Fig. 246. Scent bottle, 1980. An excellent bouquet in the base gives this scent bottle much appeal. Star cut base. PH cane. Dia. 2.6". Height 4". $200/250.

loped cuts run from the middle of the bottle up to its neck. A footed base is star cut (16 points). An attractive stopper contains a five petaled flower (similar to those in the base), but with the addition of a PH cane at its center. Six facets complete the stopper.

Merlin sky – cauldron and wizards eye; and Summer Magic – lovebirds, butterfly, and dragonfly

Although produced in unlimited editions, these five weights are appealing due to the fact that the art work is applied to the surface of the paperweight, and is translucent.

Nebula

The swirling orange nebula form, set reasonably high in the dome, is suggestive of plenty of movement.

Rubor

Red swirling and bubbly design is reminiscent of the blue design used by Caithness in their Spindrift weight.

Scylla

The murky depths of the ocean are well represented in Scylla. Very subtle use of tinges of orange, often missed at a first viewing, serve to break up the black forms. Bubbles of various sizes rising up the sides of the black forms are well placed.

Space pool

Virtually all clear glass, save a small region of bubbly golden brown eruption, and a large adjoined bubble. See also Chapter 1 – The manufacture of glass paperweights.

Sulphides

Robert Burns
John Knox
Mary Queen of Scots
Sir Walter Scott
William Shakespeare
H.M. Queen Elizabeth the Queen Mother
(faceted and plain), see figure 247
H.R.H. Prince Charles and Lady Diana Spencer

Collectors should note that, whereas Peter Holmes made the actual sulphides for the first five weights listed, those of the Royal family were of French origin.

Fig. 247. H.M. Queen Elizabeth, the Queen Mother, 1980. Produced in celebration of her 80th birthday. Set on an attractive royal blue ground. Dia. 3". Height 1.75". $200/300.

Holly

A sprig of holly and berries (in lampwork) surmounts a bundle of three yule logs in this attractive weight. The snow-white ground, with a few flakes and drifts onto the logs, makes a beautiful background. PH cane is set into the end of one of the logs.

Footed weights

Aquarius and Rose were the first two footed weights to be produced by this company. Aquarius shows spike-like forms radiating outwards from a large bubble. Rose shows lampworked petals in dark red.

Aurora

A faceted weight of abstract form making dramatic use of orange and pink to depict the aurora borealis.

Frog

A charming weight with a lampwork green frog sitting on algae covered rocks. It is shown face to face with a water snail, with both looking as though they have surprised each other.

Ice pool

A most fascinating, clever weight, Ice pool has a white, just translucent layer immediately below the dome surface which conveys the impression of a frozen cavern, or igloo. Through a ragged window one sees a chunk of ice, complete with entrapped air bubbles, and oddments of debris (figure 248).

It was Jacque Cousteau's underwater exploits

Fig. 248. Ice pool, 1979. A superb representation of ice, frozen within an equally impressive igloo surface effect. Dia. 3.1". Height 2.5". $200/300.

which inspired Peter Holmes to create Ice pool; and he recounts how, having seen some breathtaking shots on television one evening, he enthusiastically hurried to the factory the next morning to conduct some trials. How glad we should be that he did just that! The effect is superb, combining the natural

beauty and coldness associated with ice. A PH cane is present in the base. See also Chapter 1, The Manufacture of Glass Paperweights.

Millefiori emblems

Over a period of four years Selkirk depicted, in four weights, the national emblems of Scotland, England, Wales, and Ireland; namely, the thistle, rose, daffodil, and shamrock respectively. The profile of these weights differs markedly from weights issued hitherto by this company, in that the dome is very low.

Five clusters of composite millefiori canes are evenly spaced, and a variety of canes and colors are used. A sixth cluster at the center of the weight features the cane after which the weight is named. Canes are set flush with the ground.

Sea bed

Considered by a number of collectors as one of the finest early Selkirk weights, Sea bed depicts many of the things its title would suggest. Weathered rocks abound, many covered with green plant life. Behind one of the rocks the collector's eyes will suddenly perceive a PH cane, probably half buried in the sandy ground. A variety of pointed sea shells in different colors are to be seen, and sometimes these are of skeletal form, as if eroded by the passage of time. The shells are made by working thin ribbons of glass to form the cornucopia shape.

The first thing that the eye will observe in the weight is the orange-brown five legged starfish. Better examples of this fine weight even show texture and a degree of veining in the legs, and some illustrate a leg that has re-grown following damage to the original limb – again copying nature almost to perfection (figure 249). For paperweight enthusiasts, and nature lovers, this is indeed a weight to be keenly sought after and treasured.

Fig. 249. Sea Bed, 1979. A fine weight that seldom re-appears on the secondary market. PH cane. Dia. 3". Height 2.5". $300/400.

Winter dream

Collectors who appreciate abstract forms and seek weights with a Christmas theme will probably like 'Winter Dream'. The brilliant white ground is similar to that found in 'Holly', while the tree-like form has many golden baubles hanging from its branches.

Triton

This rare weight (figure 250) combines the superb engraving by David Gulland with the mastery of the weight manufactured by Peter Holmes. Its irregularly curved smooth surface does much to enhance its appeal, and is the forerunner of a few later weights, which Selkirk made to a similar shape. The shape is achieved by prodding with a suitable tool before the weight is too cool.

From Greek mythology, Triton, a descendant of minor sea-gods represented as men with fishes' tails, and occasionally with fore-feet of a horse, and carrying a shell trumpet, is well depicted on the engraved facet. Only about ten Triton weights were made.

Pond life

Issued as two sets of faceted weights, four weights to each set, Pond Life again illustrates the marrying of the skills of the paperweight maker (Peter Holmes), with those of the engraver (David Gulland).

Originally shown at the Birmingham Trade Fair in 1978, where it attracted much attention, the edition of the first set of Pond Life was rapidly fully subscribed. Its popularity continues, and collectors will now be lucky to purchase a set at the issue price.

The green abstract forms within the weights are suggestive of the plant life that is to be seen swirling in a country stream.

David Gulland's engraving cleverly adds the master's touch by including other items which are ancillary to the main subject, but which do so much to contribute to the total beauty of the finished weight. For example, above the 'Otter' a shoal of small fish is to be seen, as shown in figure 251, and the 'Great Crested Grebe' appears gracefully amongst some rushes. The 'Frog' is set well to the foreground, and amongst some of the lily leaves some open blooms are to be seen. Finally, the 'Trout' is shown to perfection, appearing to leap out of the weight.

Fig. 250. Triton, 1979. This shows the combined skills of Peter Holmes, and David Gulland the engraver. Dia. 3.7". Height 2.75". $100/150.

Fig. 251. Otter (Pond life series 1), 1978. One of a set of four weights with David Gulland's engraving. Dia. 3.3". Height 2.4". $150/200.

Collectors should note the markings on the base. Here we have two distinctly different types of styli used by David Gulland, and Peter Holmes. The former's signature appears as a smooth, fairly broad style, which Gulland follows with 78 (the year of manufacture), the name of the weight, and number. A much finer and sharper line results from Holmes with the inscription "Selkirk Glass made by Peter Holmes," see figures 252 and 253.

Fig. 252. David Gulland's signature on the base of Great Crested Grebe. Selkirk, 1978.

Christmas Rose 1979

A very attractive lampwork weight, and shown in figure 254. Towards the center of the petals some yellow ochre, and gold variegation has been introduced. The center of the flower consists of thirteen canes, the six outer being plain orange, and the seven inner bordered with orange.

Partridge in a Pear Tree

Sets of weights usually prove popular, and this is often particularly the case where the weights have themes associated with Christmas. Partridge in a Pear Tree is the first of a series of twelve weights which depict the Twelve Days of Christmas. On the engraved facet the partridge can be seen taking a bite out of a pear. Although the pink tree-like abstract form is perhaps somewhat unconventional in color, the white ground does much to set the Christmas scene.

Fission

The fission mushroom like cloud is depicted in a rich purple, which is also used in other weights first issued in 1980. Through the center of the cloud the main vertical blast can be seen. In the best ex-

Fig. 253. Peter Holmes' signature on the base of Pond Life weights. Selkirk, 1978.

amples this just penetrates the top of the cloud, thus adding greater interest. The surface shape is similar to that which was first used on this company's 'Triton' weight. A PH cane is inserted in the ground.

Minaret

Pinnacled, flattened, multi-colored bubbles characterize this weight, and make it very distinctive. Five of the bubbles form a circle, and surround a sixth, slightly larger bubble. All are set on a mottled ground which is mainly white, green, and deep red.

Minaret is especially appealing as a result of the color imparted to the surface of the bubbles. The effect is not dissimilar to the rainbow effect observed on thin-walled soap bubbles, or that of an oil film on

Fig. 254. Christmas Rose, 1979. Selkirk – Lampwork flower with delicate, mottled petals, on attractive broken turquoise ground. Dia. 2.7". Height 1.9". $200/250.

142

water, and red, green, yellow, pink, gray, and white are all clearly visible. The result is even more impressive because reasonable translucency has been maintained.

Oracle

Often one observes that the appeal of a fine paperweight is in no small way due to the nature of its faceting. This is certainly the case with 'Oracle'. Four facets, each of different size, and placed asymmetrically, give this weight much intrigue and interest.

The Oracle is a purple colored, transparent, slightly flattened bubble with a small pip on the top. Its shape is reminiscent of the forms in Minaret, and the main form surmounts four smaller ones. Internal reflections are plentiful, and this weight is commended to collectors who like unusual weights.

Saturn

A masterpiece for lovers of space theme weights. It is significant that this superb weight was issued in 1981, as it was on August 25 that Voyager 2 passed

closest to this planet, and sent back to earth the most detailed pictures seen up until that time.

Peter Holmes depicts the planet together with its multi-colored rings. In the finer examples the rings are not parallel with the base of the weight.

Royal Wedding – H.R.H. The Prince of Wales to Lady Diana Spencer

The distinctive cane in the base of the weight (figure 255) is basically formed within a white seven-pointed star, with a red three-pointed crown at the apex. Below the crown is a red heart surrounded in blue by "C.D." and "1981." The segments between the points of the star contain shaped canes which, in total, make the whole appear circular. Each of these pieces are in white, and contain a minuscule pink heart. As for the two orange blossoms with their delicate stamens, these are a delight.

Fig. 255. Thistle cane, and the CD 1981 cane used for the weight shown in Fig. 256. Courtesy of Peter Holmes, Selkirk Glass Ltd.

Following the tragic death of Lady Diana in 1997, the demand, and value, of these weights has already started to show a significant increase. The example (figure 256) is special in that it is number 29 of the edition of 75; the Royal couple was married on July 29, 1981.

Fig. 256. Orange blossom, 1981. A low edition to commemorate the wedding of H.R.H. Prince Charles and Lady Diana Spencer. Very good lampwork flowers, with well executed stamens all go to make this a very desirable weight. PH and CD 1981 canes in base. This piece is numbered 29, the date of the wedding. Dia. 2.6". Height 1.9". $400/600.

Other weights

In addition to his wide range of limited and unlimited editions, Peter, like most artists, has also issued various one-offs, two examples of which are shown in figures 257, and 258.

Finally, in figure 259, Peter captures the imagination with a controlled internal fracture to produce Silicon Chip.

Fig. 259. Silicon chip, c.1983. a cleverly controlled abstract design. Courtesy of Peter Holmes, Selkirk Glass Ltd. $90/150.

Fig. 257. Kite, c.1991, Selkirk. A kite is realistically depicted in this abstract one-off weight by Peter Holmes. Dia. 3". Courtesy of a private collector. $180/220.

Fig. 258. Magnum flower, c.1997. Selkirk. Magnum weights of this quality are relatively rare. PH cane. Dia. 3.75". Courtesy of a private collector. $300/400.

Chapter 8
William Manson

Born on November 1, 1951, at Wick, Caithness, William Manson (figure 260) was educated at Wick High School where his best subjects were art and navigation. He had intended joining the merchant navy until a school trip to Caithness Glass Ltd. sparked his interest in glass that was to result in his pursuing a career in glass paperweights.

Without further ado he was granted an interview with Graeme Brown, the managing director of Caithness Glass Ltd. at the time, and began his four year glass blowing apprenticeship there in 1966. It was here that he first met Paul Ysart who was employed as training supervisor, but it was some time before he realized Paul also made paperweights.

In 1970 he went to work with Paul Ysart at Harland where his duties included mixing the batch, furnace maintenance, as well as learning basic lampwork, cane making, and weight making skills. In fact, to quote William's words, "it was a whole new apprenticeship and much more involved than glass blowing." Although an intensive training program, William thoroughly enjoyed his time with Paul Ysart and they had many light-hearted moments together.

As an example of an amusing story involving William Manson, the following is worth quoting. One Saturday, while at Harland, Paul Ysart entered the factory and told William that an order for twelve Ysart weights with PY canes had been received from Paul Jokelson in the U.S.A. Paul instructed William to grind and polish these weights, wrap them carefully, and pack them in a carton ready for collection. Graeme Brown, who was a partner in the company, was to collect them and dispatch them to America first thing on the following Monday morning.

By 3:30 pm William had finished attending to these twelve double fish weights, and the carton was placed on the floor for safety. Ready for a break, William decided to stop for tea. About fifteen minutes later George Brimms, the farmer at Harland, came into the factory carrying something in his hands. At his side was Ginny, his pet labra-

Fig. 260. William Manson giving a weight a thorough inspection prior to dispatch. 1998. Courtesy of William Manson Paperweight Studio, Friarton Road, Perth PH2 8DF, Scotland.

dor. The something in his hands was one of the carefully polished, wrapped PY weights.

George explained that while on his way home past the factory, he met Ginny emerging from the side door with the paperweight in her mouth. A recount of the carton revealed that nine weights remained – two were still missing!

William was just beginning to think his future with Paul Ysart looked very dim when he spotted Ginny take another weight out of the carton and disappear out of the side door. George and William quickly followed Ginny across the farmyard to a trailer, behind which was a ventilation duct leading to a grain store. Suddenly all was revealed. Not only did the missing weights come to light, but a few others as well!

When told about the incident Paul was very amused and delighted that a labrador dog had liked his work enough to start collecting it. Needless to say, after that, Ginny's visits to the factory were closely guarded.

William can still recall the very first weight he made at Harland – a harlequin multi-colored piece. Ironically this is a single deck version of a weight he had seen Paul Ysart make nine years earlier. He re- counts that in 1969 when Lord Thurso, chairman of Caithness Glass Ltd, was showing some important guests around Caithness, Paul Ysart was asked to make a paperweight – a double harlequin with one central and six peripheral air bubbles. This is one of the few occasions that Paul made a weight in public.

By 1974 Manson had rejoined Caithness. In 1979 William decided to work more independently and so, together with Graeme Brown, formed William Manson Paperweights at Kilwinning, Ayrshire. Many collectors were advised of the new venture by The Collectors Investment Guild[1], which provided a color brochure illustrating the first three weights being issued, figures 261 to 263.

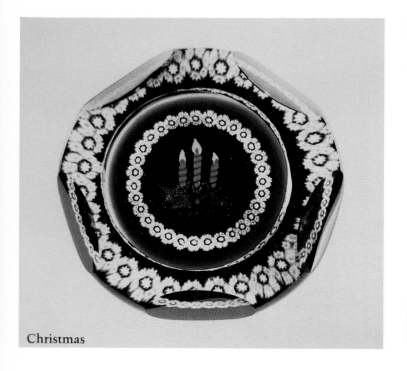

Butterfly and flower

Fig. 261. Butterfly and Flower, 1979. The first of three weights issued when William formed William Manson Paperweights at Kilwinning. Dia. 2.5". Height 2.5". Courtesy of William Manson Paperweight Studio. $250/350.

Manta Ray

Fig. 262. Manta Ray, 1979. Second of the earliest weights from Kilwinning. A fine lampwork fish. Dia. 2.5". Height 2.5". Courtesy of William Manson Paperweight Studio. $400/500.

Christmas

Fig. 263. Christmas, 1979. Another fine example of lampwork, this time combined with aventurine holly, and millefiori. The third of the early Kilwinning weights. Dia. 2.5". Height 2.5". Courtesy of William Manson Paperweight Studio. $200/300.

With the cessation of this venture in September, 1981, William returned again to Caithness. Since August, 1991, William Manson has again been producing his own weights. Four distinct types have been produced:

1. Upright miniatures signed William Manson.
2. Standard size featuring flora and fauna in editions of 150. These are signed and dated.
3. Standard size upright weights in editions of 50, 100, and 150, also signed and dated.
4. One-offs.

Figures 264 to 266 are reproduced from Manson's brochure for 1992 and serve to give some idea of the range. The upright weights are of flat-tened profile, rather more like thick circular discs than the conventional spherical dome appearance. Production prices ranged from $97 - 320.

In 1997 William Manson once again parted from Caithness, and in July of that year started William Manson Paperweights at the present factory (figure 267) in Friarton Road, Perth, where he continued to complete some outstanding orders for Caithness until December 23. Work at Friarton Road is now very much a family business, for working with William are Joyce (his wife), William Jr. (his son) who can be seen in figure 268, and his daughter, Carolyn. Figures 269 to 272 show the weights issued in 1997 and 1999.

Fig. 264. 1992 Brochure illustrating more recent production. Courtesy of William Manson Paperweight Studio.

Fig. 265. 1992 Brochure. Note the range of superb lampwork pieces. Courtesy of William Manson Paperweight Studio.

Fig. 266. 1992 Brochure. The last of the range illustrated in 1992. Courtesy of William Manson Paperweight Studio.

Fig. 267. William with Carolyn (daughter) and Joyce (wife) at the new factory at Friarton Road, Perth. 1997. Courtesy of William Manson Paperweight Studio.

Fig. 268. William Manson Jr., 1998. An up and coming artist to be watched. Very able, and following in his father's footsteps. Courtesy of William Manson Paperweight Studio.

Fig. 269. Two weights issued in 1997, in commemoration of the tragically short life of H.R.H. The Princess of Wales. Both named Diana – England's Rose, the one on the left is of standard size, and that on the right is a miniature. Courtesy of William Manson Paperweight Studio. $300 and $106 respectively.

Right:
Fig. 270. Seventeen weights from 1997. Courtesy of William Manson Paperweight Studio.

Far right:
Fig. 271. Twelve weights from 1997 showing some fine examples of William's skills in lampworking. Courtesy of William Manson Paperweight Studio.

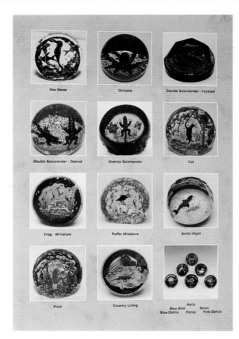

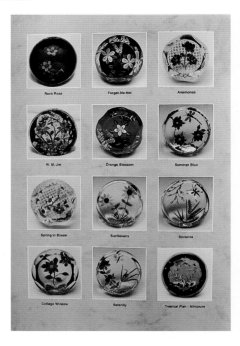

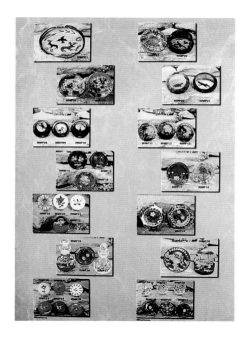

Fig. 272. This gives some idea of the range of weights issued in 1999. Courtesy of William Manson Paperweight Studio.

William Sr.'s paperweights have always had many admirers and in November, 1998, the William Manson Paperweights Collectors Club was formed. Figures 273 and 274 illustrate the club members' weights for 1998 and 1999 respectively.

The formulation of Manson's early glass was identical to that of Caithness with the exception that the lead monosilicate was omitted and replaced by additional sodium carbonate. This produced a workable glass which was not so harmful to the furnace lining.

Manson's early weights, not surprisingly, closely resembled the later weights with which he had been associated at Caithness. For example, many weights have a royal purple ground, and similar cog canes. Similarities to Ysart weights can also be seen.

Fig. 273. First Collectors Club members weight, 1998. Dia. 3". Courtesy of William Manson Paperweight Studio. $150.

Fig. 274. Collectors Club members weight, 1999, complete with its wooden packing case. Dia. 2.75". Courtesy of William Manson Paperweight Studio. $115.

In addition to his 1980 - 1981 range of limited edition weights, figure 275, Manson also issued a lower priced unlimited series of weights – the Scotia range – shown in figure 276. It is believed that two to three hundred of each of the more popular Scotia designs were issued, these included numbers 30,

33, 34, 38, 40, and 46 (see list of weights issued), many of which were purchased by L.H. Selman Ltd., U.S.A. Numbers 28, 29, 32, 35, 42, 43, and 47 proved to be the least popular. Figure 277 shows a Scotia label and cane on the base of Snowman.

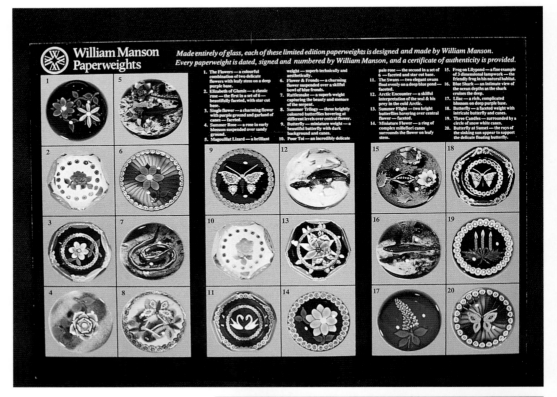

Fig. 275. The importance of preserving any literature associated with paper-weights should not need to be stressed. This is the first brochure ever produced by William Manson in 1980/81. Courtesy of William Manson Paperweight Studio.

Fig. 276. This shows the Scotia unlimited editions issued in 1980/81. Courtesy of William Manson Paperweight Studio.

Fig. 277. Scotia label and cane on the base of a weight. Courtesy of a private collector.

Manson lists two paperweights which, looking back over his career to date, he found particularly difficult to make.

The first of these was Octopus, made at Caithness in 1978. One problem here was the difficulty of attaching the tentacles to the body. Slightly too much heat would result in burning the color, with a resulting blackening of the glass. The other problem occurs during the encasement of the lampwork octopus. Molten glass is required to flow over the lampwork from above. To achieve this, a great deal of pressure has to be applied to force out any entrapped air from the lampwork. Applying too much pressure can cause two additional problems: a) distortion of the lampwork, and b) the pontil rod being forced too far into the glass, making it impossible to withdraw it without causing even more distortion. The solution was to raise the temperature of the molten glass to make it more fluid.

The other difficult weight was the Charles and Diana sulphide. This was particularly difficult to make because as well as the sulphide, two lampwork flowers and a ring of canes were included in the design. To be successful, sulphides have to be heated to a much higher temperature than lampwork. In order to accommodate the different temperatures, two separate steel plates, with locating marks scribed onto them, were used. The sulphide was placed onto one of these and heated to its high temperature, while the lampwork was located on the other plate and heated to a lower temperature. It was then simply a question of encasing the sulphide first, followed by the lampwork. Twenty-five double overlays of the same weight also caused quite a few headaches.

William Sr. has always been noted for his lampwork, and figure 278 shows some fine examples. Figures 279 and 280 show some of his canes.

Fig. 278. Lampwork items made by William Manson, including a particularly fine reptile. Courtesy of Roy and Pam Brown.

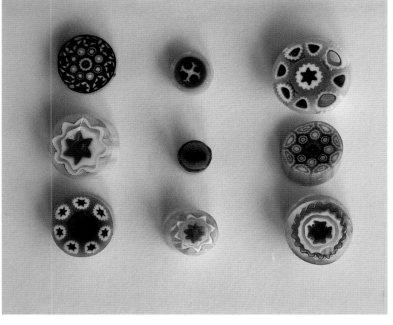

Fig. 279. A selection of William Manson's canes, including a WM signature at the center.

Fig. 280. Close up of two different WM signature canes.

Details of selected limited edition weights issued between 1979 and 1981

Butterfly and flower
Very similar to the Caithness butterfly and flower weights of this period, but the wings are yellow/green with white centers.

Manta ray
The Manta ray being blue is very similar to the lampwork form that appeared in Caithness' Manta ray that Manson made in 1978. The sandy colored base differs by not being flat and contains a number of irregular peaks.

Christmas
Three red candles with two green holly leaves and a bow that appears to be in green aventurine form the central flat motif of this attractive weight. A circle of white (central cog) canes surrounds the motif. Being a cross between Caithness' Hollywreath and Xmas weight 1977, the side and top printies of Christmas all serve to make this weight very reminiscent of those Manson produced with his former employer.

Elizabeth of Glamis
A classic rose, named after H.M. Queen Elizabeth the Queen Mother, this theme was used for the first of what was intended to be a series of six rose weights. Elizabeth of Glamis was issued in a suitably printed presentation box (figure 281) to commemorate the 80th birthday of The Queen Mother.

With the design and circle of canes being on a clear ground, the weight assumes a very clean, simple beauty. The sixteen point star-cut base coincides with the circle of sixteen canes, one of which contains a WM80 cane.

Magouillat Lizard
The coloring of this lizard is very striking. As with many of Manson's weights aventurine is used – this time for the blue body. An orange spotted head and yellow spots underneath the body give the lizard much character, and the claws are well executed.

Three flowers add interest to the very pale turquoise ground, and the small white rocks have a very natural appearance. Figure 282 shows the red and black WM81 cane set in the base – note by contrast the WM and 80 are both black in the weights made in 1980. The weight is shown in figure 283.

A little known point regarding this weight concerns its actual content in relation to that shown in Manson's illustrated brochure. The original idea was to place a red ladybird on top of one of the flowers. In practice however, it is believed that only one weight was ever made which included a ladybird. Technical difficulties, believed to be associated with disintegration, precluded the continuation of the ladybirds presence.

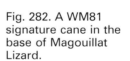

Fig. 282. A WM81 signature cane in the base of Magouillat Lizard.

Fig. 281. Elizabeth of Glamis, 1980. A fine rose issued on the occasion of the 80th birthday of H.M. Queen Elizabeth the Queen Mother. $300/380.

Fig. 283. Magouillat lizard, 1981. An excellent example of an early William Manson reptile weight. $350/425.

Flower and fronds

Possibly one of the most popular of all Manson's early limited edition weights, flower and fronds was purchased by some people wanting a one-off gift, thus denuding the number available to collectors. These are fine weights, the cane basket creating the illusion of considerable depth with the flower suspended as if in mid-air (figure 284). A WM80 cane is at the base of the stem, see figure 285.

Fig. 284. Flower and Fronds, 1980. A flower in a superb canework basket. WM80 cane. $275/325.

Although a fine and striking weight the idea is not new. For instance, Perthshire issued a somewhat similar weight in 1978, and they in turn were preceded by Paul Ysart who used this design (see also Butterfly at Sunset).

Summer Trilogy

Butterflies are frequently featured in Manson's weights. Perhaps this reflects back to his early days at Caithness when he made their butterfly weight in 1974 - 5. As William Manson Paperweights, he has now made weights containing up to three butterflies. It is the three different colored butterflies, at various levels, that form the basis of Summer Trilogy shown in figure 286.

One wonders whether Manson put three butterflies in this weight not to follow a suggested name for a weight, but to illustrate a peak of technical expertise. While it does indeed reflect achievement, it gives a slightly confused appearance, particularly when viewed from above; or is this intentional camouflage? For instance, the pink butterfly is rather lost against the background of the pink clematis flower which lies in the base.

Fig. 285. WM80 cane in Flower and Fronds.

Fig. 286. A selection of William Manson's early butterflies, including Summer Trilogy (bottom right). Average dia. 3". $350/450.

Fig. 287. Summer Trilogy, 1981. Side view showing the excellent vertical separation between the butterflies. $450.

Butterfly at Sunset

Lovers of the 'Flower and fronds' weight will probably also appreciate Butterfly at Sunset. The basket of canes is in a beautiful gold sunset shade with white centers. A blue winged butterfly appears to be hovering at the center of the basket.

Pour Toi

A delicate pale yellow rose, with leaves, forms the central motif of this paperweight. Like the Elizabeth of Glamis weight, the Pour Toi rose is on a white base and is the second weight in what was to have been a series of six.

The Swans

A pair of white swans facing each other are set on a deep blue ground and are enclosed within a circle of canes. Apart from containing two swans, as opposed to one, this weight is very similar to the Swan weights that Manson made when he was first with Caithness Glass Ltd.

Butterfly

A miniature weight introduced in 1981. The body is usually green aventurine, and this is complimented by green complex cane wings and yellow antennae. Complex canes encircle the insect. The base contains the identifying cane with WM in red and 81 in black.

Aventurine is used in various colored forms for the bodies, and all the heads and antennae are yellow. Side viewing, in the author's opinion, shows the butterflies in a more realistic and individual form – figure 287. A WM81 cane is positioned centrally underneath the flower.

Summer flight

The two butterflies with wings made from canes have bodies, heads, and antennae similar to those in Summer Trilogy. The clematis and surrounding circle of canes, together with the purple base, are similar to those in Caithness' Summer weight of The Four Seasons.

Butterfly

Although only containing one butterfly, after looking at Manson's Summer Trilogy and Summer Flight, the simplicity of butterfly is immediately apparent. One can therefore concentrate fully upon the solitary butterfly and note, for instance, the detailed structure of its cane worked wings, see figure 288.

Three Candles

An attractive weight with three lampworked candles, holly, and goldstone bow, surrounded by a circle of white canes. The weight is almost identical to this makers Christmas weight.

Fig. 288. Butterfly, 1980. A close up showing the detailed cane wings, and the green aventurine body.

Orange flower

Introduced in 1979, the orange flower has a WM cane at the base of the stem. A 79 cane is in the base of the weight, and some bases are inscribed WM as well as carrying the weight number and issue limit of 150.

154

Christmas single candle

A single candle, identical in form to those in Three Candles, within a wreath of six holly leaves with berries and goldstone ribbon all set in a circle of white canes. The purple ground contains a WM80 cane. Cane work is similar to that in the weights he produced at Caithness.

Sea Encounter

A blue aventurine manta ray with a white underside, has yellow and black eyes and a long brownish black tail. It is accompanied by a green aventurine fish with yellow spots, and eyes which are identical to those in the manta ray. The fish is very similar to some of those that Paul Ysart made. A WM80 cane is in the purple base (figure 289).

Salamander

A green bodied salamander with small yellow spots is set on a sandy base, in the presence of white sharp looking rocks.

Fig. 289. Sea Encounter, 1980. The influence of Paul Ysart, (William Manson's mentor) can be clearly seen in the spotted fish. Dia. 2.9". $300/400.

Edition size and price data for 1979 – 81 issues

Name	Edition Issue	Price $	Value $ in year stated	Features
			1979	
1. Butterfly and flower	150	240		Lampwork butterfly on 8 petaled pink flower. 5 + 1 faceting.
2. Manta Ray	150	300	412/1996	Blue lampwork manta ray above undulating sandy ground.
3. Christmas	150	120	198/1996	Three lampwork candles set into two holly leaves all surrounded by a circle of white millefiori canes. 5 + 1 faceting.
4. Orange flower	150		358/1996	Orange flower on dark ground WM and 79 canes.
			1980	
5. Elizabeth of Glamis	200	210		Lampwork rose on white ground star cut base. 5 + 1 faceting.
6. Flower and fronds	150	195	303/1996	Lampwork flower suspended above blue cane basket.
7. Summer flight	150	240		Two butterflies on a flower. 5 + 1 faceting.
8. Butterfly	150	102		Butterfly surrounded by circle of canes. 5 + 1 faceting.
9. Christmas single candle	150	160		Single lampwork candle and spray of holly. Circles of canes. 5 + 1 faceting
10. Sea encounter	150	300		Blue manta ray and spotted green fish above sandy ground.
11. Salamander	150	300	613/1992	Yellow spotted green salamander on sandy ground with white rocks.
			1981	
12. Summer Trilogy	250	240		Three butterflies and a flower. Outer circle of canes.
13. Magouillat Lizard	250	300	960/1995	Lizard amongst leaves and a flower.
14. The flowers	250	102		Two delicate flowers with stem and leaves. Deep purple ground.
15. Single flower	150	138		Flower with stem and leaves. Purple ground. 5 + 1 faceting.
16. Summer Rose	150	240		Pink rose with leaves over a sandy ground.
17. Rattlesnake	150	337		A snake slightly reared up over a sandy ground.
18. Pour Toi	250	240	460/1998	Pale yellow rose. 5 + 1 faceting.
19. The swans	150	159	330/1996	Two swans. Deep blue ground. 5 + 1 faceting.
20. Arctic encounter	250	345	535/1991	A seal and his prey. White ground.
21. Miniature flower	150	102		Yellow flower, stem and leaves. Outer circle of canes.
22. Frog on Lily pond	150	240	427/1994	Lampwork frog amongst leaves and flowers. Blue ground.
23. Blue shark*	150	337	585/1995	Shark above a textured sandy ground.
24. Lilac	150	195		Complex blossom, with stem and leaves. Deep purple ground.
25. Butterfly	150	159		Butterfly with cane wings. Outer circle of canes. 5 + 1 faceting.
26. Three candles	150	159		Candles. Leaves and ribbon, within circle of white canes.
27. Butterfly at sunset	250	210		Blue winged butterfly within basket of canes.
28. Charles and Diana sulphide	150			
29. Charles and Diana sulphide	25			double overlay

*Although not officially listed until 1981, a Blue shark weight exists with a "79" (for 1979) date cane inserted. This could possibly be a prototype.

Unlimited editions (Scotia range)
1980 – 81

Name	Issue price $	Value $ in year stated
30. Atlantis	27	
31. Sandfish	33	
32. Red flower	66	
33. Fountain	33	
34. Springtime	27	
35. Dragonfly and canes	66	
36. Satin chain	48	
37. Jellyfish	27	
38. Garland	48	
39. Winter rose	66	
40. Thistle and canes	66	145/1991
41. Snowman	42	
42. Father Christmas	36	384/1999
43. Three mice	39	
44. Effervescence	30	
45. Crocus	27	
46. Palm tree	27	
47. Star	48	
48. Dahlia head	39	
49. Scent bottle	75	

Certification and Base Markings

In contrast to early Caithness and Selkirk paperweights, which typically carry a reasonable amount of engraving on their bases, Manson's early weights typically have the weight number and the edition size. Bases are polished flat.

A certificate of authenticity accompanies each weight, and takes the form of a circular piece of paper which consists of five segments that can be opened to display the full details. Figure 290 shows the wording and layout of a 1981 certificate for Summer Trilogy.

Fig. 290. A typical early certificate.

Collectors should note however that various forms of early certificates were issued. The weights issued in an edition limit of 150 had this number printed on the relevant segment and the year was later written in by hand. These certificates were cream colored. 1981 saw the appearance of the 250 edition limit being written in by hand, and the use of a white paper. These certificates are marked with the month of issue as well as the year, see figure 291. All certificates were signed by Graeme Brown. It should be observed that these certificates are somewhat delicate as a result of being printed on a medium weight paper, and thus deserve special care to ensure they are preserved in fine condition.

Before leaving Manson's certificates, the wording of sections 3 – 5 (figure 290) should be observed.

These invite the owner to place his/her name and address on sections 4 and 5 and return it as a registration form to William Manson Paperweight Collectors Society. It goes onto say that owners can then, as relevant, be put in touch with other collectors when wishing to sell or extend a collection of paperweights. Thus, it is quite clear that even in the early days Manson had gone some way towards realizing the various advantages of collectors' societies.

By 1999, William Jr.'s skills in lampwork were already becoming evident, as can be seen in figure 292 which also shows fine examples of his father's work. Figures 293 to 295 show a range of William Sr.'s current work, while figure 296 illustrates just how well William Jr.'s paperweight-making ability has developed.

Fig. 291. This shows the typical variation in the way early certificates were signed.

Fig. 293. William Sr.'s. inventiveness is shown here with his Web Spinner (1992), and depicts well the angularity, and nature of a spider's web. Courtesy of Anne Anderson. $280/400.

Fig. 292. Lampwork by father and son team. William Sr.'s examples are at the bottom, while the top shows the fine achievements of William Jr. Courtesy of William Manson Paperweight Studio.

Fig. 294. Lady's Slipper Orchid, 1998. The first flash overlay from the Friarton Road Studio. Exquisite top faceting adds to an already fine weight. Edition of 15. Courtesy of William Manson Paperweight Studio. $600/ 700.

Fig. 295. Pigs, 1998. Made as a special commission for L.H. Selman Ltd., U.S.A., this scene, like many of William Manson's captures much humor. Courtesy of William Manson Paperweight Studio. $475.

Fig. 296. Secret Garden, 1998. William Manson Jr. Tremendous skills are already being shown in this weight, commissioned by L.H. Selman Ltd., U.S.A. Courtesy of William Manson Paperweight Studio. $390.

It is interesting to observe how father and son have started working together on collaborative ideas and weights (figure 297 shows an example). An unusual idea for a paperweight is the collaborative piece of Cave Drawings in figure 298.

Fig. 297. Monarch butterfly/Yellow flowers, 1998. A one-off lilac and white overlay collaborative weight. William Jr. made the flowers, and his father the butterfly, and weight. Courtesy of William Manson Paperweight Studio. $585.

Fig. 298. A collaborative weight of unusual design. Cave drawings, 1998. Father and son both thought of the idea, and William Sr. made the lampwork, and weight. Edition of 15. Width 5". Height 3.5". Courtesy of William Manson Paperweight Studio. $850.

Finally, as a sign of the high regard collectors have for William Manson's work, the Cambridge Paperweight Circle chose him to produce one of the two designs for their Millennium paperweight. This single green overlay, called Peace Lily, and limited to fifty pieces, is shown in figure 299, while figure 300 shows the same weight, with trial weights either side which were rejected due to the overlay failing to show off the motif to maximum advantage.

[1]The Collectors Investment Guild, 39 Derwent Avenue, Kingston Vale, London SW15 3 RA.

Fig. 299. Peace Lily, 1999. Edition of 50. Specially commissioned by the Cambridge Paperweight Circle, following a members design competition, to mark the millennium. Courtesy of William Manson Paperweight Studio. $300.

Fig. 300. Peace Lily. The interest here is to compare the final selected design (center), with those either side which were rejected due to color, and contrast considerations. Courtesy of William Manson Paperweight Studio, Friarton Road, Perth PH2 8DF, Scotland.

Chapter 9
Jay Glass –John Deacons

John Henry Deacons, born September 12, 1950, studied at the Edinburgh College of Art, and duly became a skilled designer.

Having spent some time with Strathearn Glass, John left the company in 1968 to join Perthshire Paperweights Ltd. In 1978 he felt that he wanted to venture into setting up his own business to develop his own ideas, and so he departed from Perthshire. Thus Jay Glass was formed, operating from a small glass house – Ladymill, Dallerie, near Crieff, Scotland.

Since his early involvement with glass paperweights, John Deacons has admired the masterly achievements of the makers of the 19th century classical period, particularly when bearing in mind their lack of the technological facilities which, today, are taken for granted.

Although the classical period was dominated by the three great French houses of Baccarat, Clichy, and St. Louis; John Deacons, like others, realizes that they were not responsible for the foundation work. This foundation work, John feels, is probably in part the result of one maker who put a lower case 'j' cane in his weights. These weights are sometimes referred to as J-weights. Inspired by this background, it is hardly surprising that John Deacons named his new venture Jay Glass and inserted a 'J' cane in his weights[1, 2].

Another worker from Perthshire Paperweights Ltd. was to join Jay Glass in 1979. This was Allan Scott. Allan was responsible for making many of the lampwork pieces, and in recognition of this an 'A' cane (as well as a 'J' cane) was inserted in some of his weights, and, in particular, those pieces that were exported to the U.S.A. from 1979 to 1981, which included Dragonfly bouquet, Spring wildflowers, Pink clematis set on swirl latticinio, Pink flower on radial latticinio, and Garland royal primrose.

The 'A' cane consisted of the 'A' at the center of a white rod. This was surrounded by various numbers of white stars, each covered with Kugler moosgrun to give the finished dark green cane. Seven stars were common.

Date canes were used for the years 1980, 1981, and 1982. These canes consisted of a 'J' cane surrounded by four separate numerals. The numerals were reminiscent of those used by Baccarat in the 19th century in that they were made in any combination of red, blue, and green. Some weights exist with a black numeral.

A 'J' cane is shown in figure 301, and figure 302 shows a typical date as used in design J16.

Base cutting was initially carried out by John Deacons and Allan Scott. Bases, at this stage, were flat. Concave bases followed a year or so later, and these and faceting was often conducted by Brian Lawson and Harry Mckay.

Fig. 301. J cane in a 1978 J Glass weight by John Deacons.

Fig. 302. J 1979. Signature, and date cane in the base of Bouquet on a ruby base (design J16). Like Baccarat in the 19th century, note the date is made from red, blue, and green.

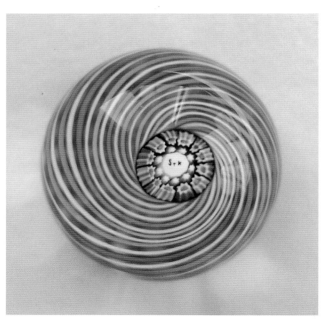

St. Kilda is an island some forty miles west of the Outer Hebrides, and John Deacons was thinking, long and hard, before deciding on how to identify weights that were to be sold to Decora Imports in the U.S.A. Then the idea of "StK" came to him. As he says, "I thought it would get people thinking." Figure 303 shows one familiar design, a swirl with the "StK" cane at the center. The cane typically shows green letters on a white background, as in figure 304. Sales to Decora ceased in 1987.

Fig. 303. J Glass. Swirl with StK cane. Late 1970s. Dia. 2.35". Height 1.7". $150/200.

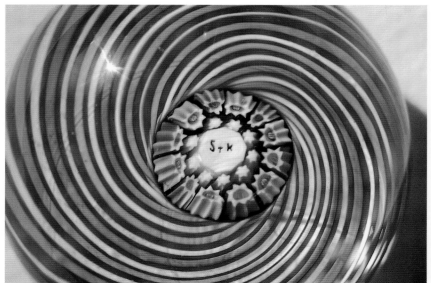

Fig. 304. This shows the detail of the StK cane shown in Fig. 303.

Early Jay Glass weights were all miniatures, and limited editions were restricted to a maximum issue of 101, each accompanied by a signed certificate. Examples of weights issued in 1978 and 1979 are shown in figures 305 and 306. The diameter of early weights, such as JO1, is 2.15 to 2.25". As with some other manufacturers products, the price of 'J' weights did not remain at the issue figure; by 1986, for instance, a small flower (JO1) was retailing at $100. Jay Glass made extensive use of lampwork designs, sometimes combined with millefiori, while a few weights were entirely millefiori in design.

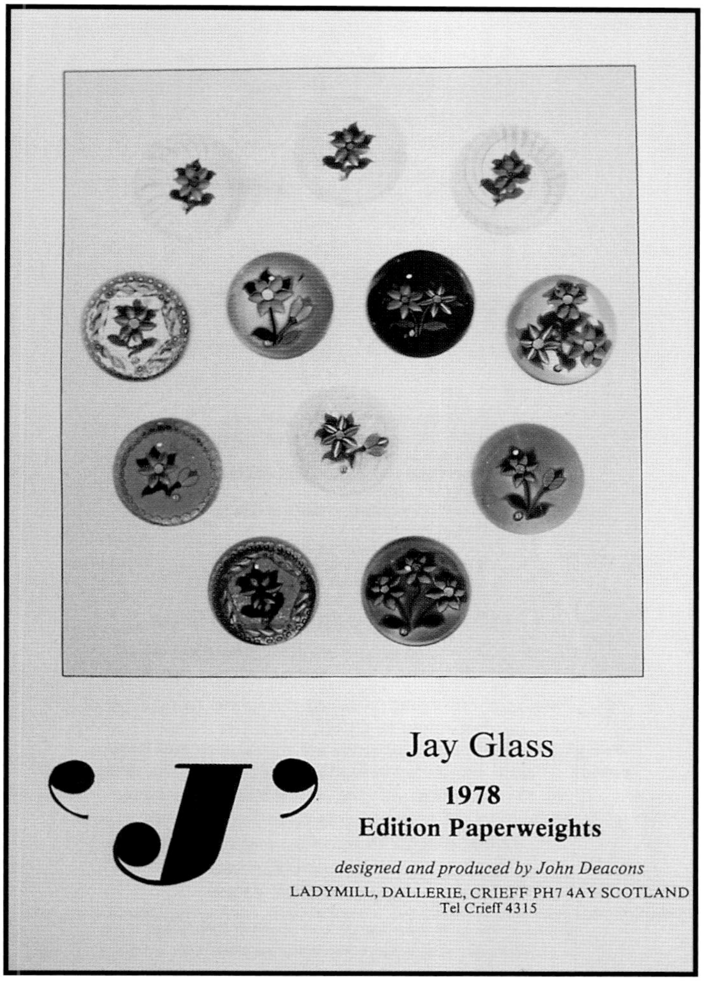

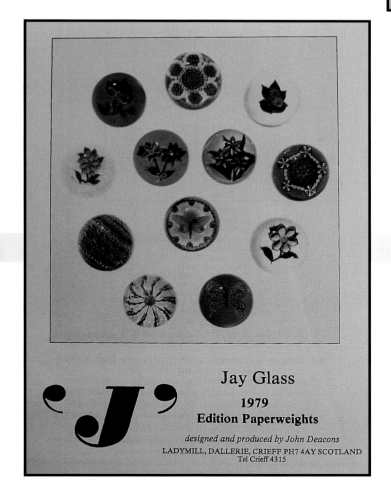

Jay Glass
1978
Edition Paperweights

designed and produced by John Deacons
LADYMILL, DALLERIE, CRIEFF PH7 4AY SCOTLAND
Tel Crieff 4315

Fig. 305. Jay Glass 1978. The company's first brochure showing their range of miniature weights. Courtesy of John Deacons.

Jay Glass
1979
Edition Paperweights

designed and produced by John Deacons
LADYMILL, DALLERIE, CRIEFF PH7 4AY SCOTLAND
Tel Crieff 4315

Fig. 306. Jay Glass. 1979 Brochure. Like the 1978 issues, these weights are all miniatures, and approximately 2" in diameter. Courtesy of John Deacons.

Unfortunately John Deacon's venture was not to last long, and by 1983 Jay Glass ceased trading.

John quite often worked by himself in his own small studio, and weights produced around 1990 and 1991 contained a cane showing a thistle. A paper label on the base also shows a thistle and the words 'Made in Scotland.' Figure 307 shows a range of John's canes which include names. The name canes are used in paperweights made to order for a special occasion, such as an anniversary gift. A JD cane has been widely used which can have the letters surrounded in white within a blue outer circle – see figure 308.

John has a large rockery at his present property and a while ago this became the home of his reject weights. It is covered with StK, J, and JD weights that failed to make the grade!

Like most paperweight makers John can tell many a humorous story, but one that easily comes to his mind relates to when he was at Strathearn working under Jack Allan who he greatly respected.

An important party of visitors had come to the factory and after looking at a fine millefiori paperweight, one of the female guests turned to Jack and said, "now tell me how exactly do you get those little pieces into the glass?" "Well," said Jack, with his typical charisma and sense of humor, "we take a mouthful of pieces of cane and blow them down one of those metal tubes!" Apparently satisfied with the weird reply, she then went onto ask how the filigree twists were made. "Ah," said Jack, "to do that we have to take one of these tubes which has spirals cut on the inside like a rifle barrel. We blow the canes down the rifled tube and it gives us the twisted effects!" The well to do lady then walked away happy with her newly acquired knowledge.

Since the cessation of Jay Glass, many of John's weights have risen steadily in value, as can be seen from the list that follows.

Fig. 307. A selection of canes by John Deacons, including his name canes introduced in the late 1990s.

Fig. 308. A good flower over a latticinio swirl. JD cane, for John Deacons, at base of stem. Courtesy of Anne Anderson. $150/200.

164

Fig. 322. Christmas 1981. Courtesy of a private collector. $30/55.

Fig. 324. Christmas 1983. Courtesy of a private collector. $30/55.

Fig. 323. Christmas 1982. Courtesy of a private collector. $30/55.

Fig. 325. Christmas 1984. Courtesy of a private collector. $30/55

Floral Motifs

These attractive Coalport flowers, issued in 1979, are set within the hollow blown glass weight. The weights are 2.9" in diameter and valued at $105. One is shown in figure 326.

Fig. 326. Wedgwood, Coalport flower. An attractive addition to any collection. Dia. 2.9". Courtesy of Sweetbriar Gallery Archive. $105.

Cameos of Famous People

At least four famous people have been depicted as cameos set onto a full lead crystal base. The faceting and cutting are different in each case. Known examples are:

Julius Caesar – produced between 1967 and 1983. Current value $100.

Lord Mountbatten of Burma – engraved 'In Honour Bound' produced c. 1970, the cameo is set on a glass disc 3" in diameter by 1.5" high. Current value $100.

Sir Winston Churchill – a beautifully faceted piece with a current value of $240.

Queen Elizabeth II – Silver Jubilee. Issued in 1977 in two distinctly different styles:

1. Probably the finest of all the cameos, and produced in a limited edition of one thousand. The blue and white jasper cameo is encircled with the inscription H.M. Queen Elizabeth II, 1952 Silver Jubilee 1977. Around the top of the weight is a hallmarked sterling silver ring. Fine hand cutting and a 16-point star cut base complete the perfection and appeal of this piece. Each piece was issued with a well docu-mented certificate. Issued at $40, the current value is now $320 - 500. This paperweight is shown in figure 327.

2. The same cameo is set onto a crystal base of squat barrel form to make this very attractive weight. Around the circumference the date 1977 and twenty-five stars are etched, and on the base Queen's Silver Jubilee 1952 – 1977, Wedgwood, made in England. Although unlimited, the weight now has a value of $150 - 320. The weight is shown in figure 328.

Fig. 327. Queen's Silver Jubilee, 1977. A beautifully cut weight with a cameo of H. M. Queen Elizabeth II, and a heavy ring of hallmarked sterling silver. Dia. 3.1". Height 1.9". $320/500.

Fig. 328. Queen's Silver Jubilee, 1977. The same cameo as in Fig 327, but set on an attractive cut squat barrel-shaped base. Dia. 3". Height 2.3". $150/320.

Chapter 11
Langham Glass

A beautifully converted Norfolk barn, dating from 1722, is the home of the dedicated team of glass workers headed by master glass maker Paul Miller (figure 329), who operate as Langham Glass.

Langham Glass has descended directly from King's Lynn Glass, a company started in King's Lynn, Norfolk, by Ronnie Stennet-Willson, which Paul joined as a young man.

King's Lynn Glass was later acquired by Wedgwood. It was during the Wedgwood period that Paul was to design and develop many of the animals and paperweights that collectors of Wedgwood are now so keen to acquire.

Deciding they would like their own glass business, Paul and his partner, Ronnie Stennet-Willson, joined by businessman Jim Middleditch, realized when they saw the Norfolk barn that they had found the perfect location for their new venture. Thus, in 1979 Langham Glass was born.

Fig. 329. Paul Miller, F.R.S.A. Courtesy of Langham Glass Ltd.

Left:
Fig. 330. The attractive premises, and setting of Langham Glass Ltd., in Norfolk. Courtesy of Langham Glass Ltd.

The delightful setting of this barn and its outbuildings, shown in figure 330, attracts many visitors who can now enjoy excellent close-up views of the glass working processes from a fine gallery that extends around the perimeter of the glasshouse.

A healthy export trade enjoyed by the company is made up in no small measure by the wide range of glass animals, birds, fruit, and fish that Paul continues to make. In 1998, for example, around three thousand glass fox paperweights were exported to the U.S.A. where business with companies such as Winterthur Museum (Winterthur, Delaware, 19735) is brisk. In 1999 this is being followed by an equally large number of apple paperweights.

With his skills, knowledge and devotion to the subject, it should come as no surprise that Paul is now a Fellow of the Royal Society of Arts.

For many years Langham produced their own clear glass, but, in common with some other artists, they now purchase and use pre-compounded material, Phillips pellets 20/30. This change was made partially for reasons associated with health and safety.

Glass paperweights form part of a wide range of glass items made by Langham which include candlesticks, decorative vases, animals, birds, fish, and wine glasses. Earlier designs until the late 1980s had the company logo, showing a glassblower, sandblasted onto the base (figure 331). However, it became difficult to maintain a well-defined image and was soon discontinued. All paperweights are now marked Langham, England and, as relevant, are signed by Paul Miller, as in figure 332.

Current production paperweights cover a range of abstract and lampwork designs and are shown in figures 333 to 337. Black Horse is unusual in being a limited edition weight that contains canes made by Langham, a close-up of which is shown in figure 338.

Fig. 331. Langham's attractive logo of a glassblower to be seen sandblasted on earlier items. Courtesy of Langham Glass Ltd.

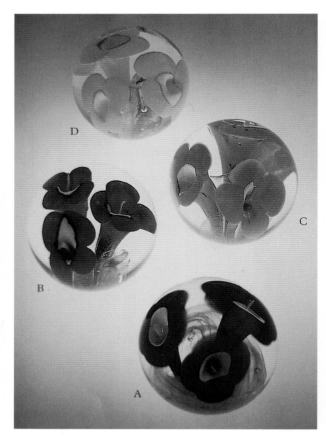

Fig. 333. Crocus designs, A-Sapphire, B-Poppy red, C-Orange, D-Yellow. Courtesy of Langham Glass Ltd. $61 each.

Fig.332. Paul Miller's signature, (together with the Langham England mark), to be found on the base of later items. Courtesy of Langham Glass Ltd.

174

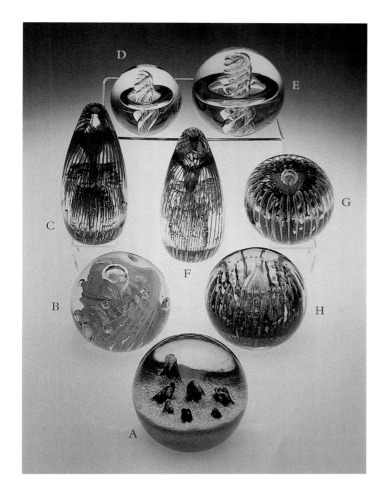

Fig. 334. A-Desert Mystery, B-Eastern Tears, C and F-Summer Fountain, D and E-Astral cub and standard, G-Summer Cascade, H-Mardi Gras. Courtesy of Langham Glass Ltd. $39/115.

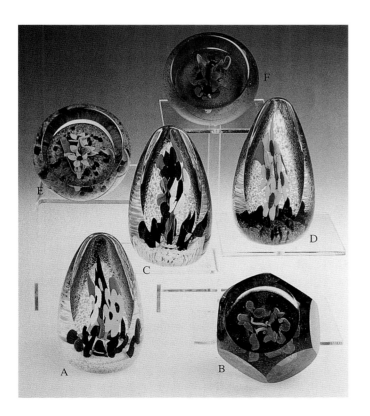

Fig. 335. A-Mini, B and H-Eastern Tears, C-Mardi Gras, D-Apple, E-Pear, F-Summer Fountain, G-Arctic Ice. Courtesy of Langham Glass Ltd. $20/115.

Fig. 336. Limited edition designs. A-Pansy Twist, B-Orientale, C-Bridal Spray, D-Irish Eyes, E-Rudbeckia, F-Papaver. Courtesy of Langham Glass Ltd. $180/190.

Fig. 337. Limited editions. A-Black Horse, B-Polar Bear, C-Desert Scorpion, D-Mallards, E-Penguins, F-Jungle Panda. Courtesy of Langham Glass Ltd. $215/265.

Fig. 338. Close up detail of the canes used in the Black Horse design shown in Fig. 337. Courtesy of Langham Glass Ltd.

Designs Issued

Unlimited Editions

STD = Standard Size, CUB = Small Size, LGE = Large Size.

Design	Type	Size	Issue price, $
Air	STD	3.15" dia.	47
Air	CUB	2.6" dia.	32
Astral	STD	3.15" dia.	61
Astral	CUB	2.6" dia.	39
Celeste	STD	3.15" dia.	47
Celeste	CUB	2.6" dia.	32
Confetti	STD	3.15" dia.	39
Confetti	CUB	2.6" dia.	25
Crocus	STD	3.15" dia.	61
Eastern Tears	STD	3.15" dia.	47
Manhattan	LGE	7.5" high	66
Manhattan	STD	6.3" high	52
Manhattan	CUB	4" high	37
Mardi Gras	STD	3.15" dia.	66
Marina	STD	4" high	47
Marina	CUB	3.15" high	32
Melody	STD	3.15" dia.	47
Streamer	STD	3.15" dia.	47
Streamer	CUB	2.6" dia.	32
Summer Cascade	STD	3.15" dia.	66
Summer Fountain	STD	4" high	63
Apple/Pear	STD	3.15" dia./ 4" high	47
Mini		2.4" dia.	17

Limited Editions

Design	Edition Size	Dimensions	Issue Price, $
Anemone Collection	250	3.15" dia.	190
Anemone Sapphire	250	3.15" dia.	
Arctic Ice	250	3.15" dia.	115
Bridal Spray	250	4.3" high	190
Desert Mystery	250	3.15" dia.	115
Duke	150	3.15" dia.	
Fuchsia	150	3.15" dia.	210
Jungle Panda	150	3.15" dia.	265
Mallards	150	3.15" dia.	265
Orientale	250	3.15" dia.	
Pansy Twist	250	4.3" high	
Pauls Scarlet	150	3.15" dia.	205
Polar Bear	150	3.15" dia.	265
Royal Majesty	200	4.5" high	167
Spell Bound			167
Spring Flowers	250	3.15" dia.	190
Woodland World	150	3.15" dia.	
Black Horse	150	3.15" dia.	225
Desert Scorpion	150	3.15" dia.	215
Destiny	250	3.15" dia.	320
Evolution	250	3.15" dia.	320
Irish Eyes	250	4.3" high	180
Lost in Time	200	4.3" high	167
Mystique	200	3.5" high	167
Pacific	200	3.15" dia.	167
Papaver	250	3.15" dia.	180
Penguins	150	3.15" dia.	262
Royal Highness	200	4.5" high	167
Rudbeckia	250	3.15" dia.	180
Spirit	450	4.1" high	110
Swiss Giants	250	3.15" dia.	180
Blue Bell	150	3.15" dia.	180

Chapter 12
Other Makers and Studio Artists

Some additional British paperweight companies and individuals are presented, regardless of their size or output. Hopefully, this brings the broadest possible range of paperweights to the attention of the collector. The list is not intended to be complete.

Jane Beebe

Items include spiral design weights with no pontil mark. Original issue price was about $55.

Margaret Burke

Margaret's attractive Athletics design from c. 1990 is shown in figure 339.

Edinburgh Crystal

This established company has been well documented by other authors. A number of different designs were made for the company, in 1986 and 1987, by Caithness, who incorporated an 'E' cane (figure 340) in all weights produced. Figure 341 shows the weights featured in the company's 1986 brochure, and figure 342 a close-up of 'Aquamarine.'

Fig. 339. Athletics. A surface decorated weight suggesting movement. c.1990. Margaret Burke. Dia. 2.75". Courtesy of a private collector. $110/130.

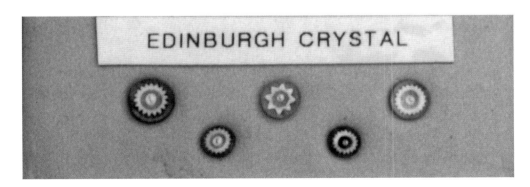

Fig. 340. Five E signature canes used in Edinburgh Crystal weights. Courtesy of a private collector.

The Foundry

Running from 1975 until the early 1980s, the Foundry was located next to the gift shop in the Royal Brierley factory. Figure 343 illustrates their Graffiti design.

Island Glass, Guernsey

Produce attractive abstracts, and overlays in gold leaf. The trademark is three rabbits impressed into the base.

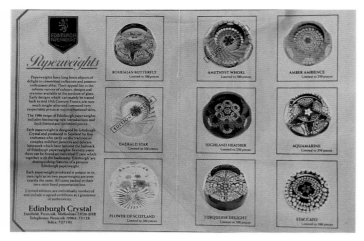

Fig. 341. A selection of weights shown in Edinburgh Crystal's catalog for 1986. Courtesy of a private collector. $200/500.

Fig. 342. Aquamarine, 1986. An attractive paneled design, with an E cane at the tip of the top panel. Edinburgh Crystal. Dia. 2.75". Courtesy of a private collector. $150/200.

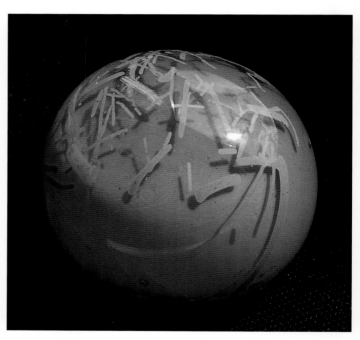

Fig. 343. Graffiti, The Foundry. 1975 – early 1980s. Dia 3.25". Courtesy of a private collector. $35/45.

Liskeard Glass

In the 1960s Murano canes were used in the company's weights. Abstract designs dated 1976 exist. These include a design very similar to Strathearn's P1 and incorporate a piece of Cornish agate quartz. A distinctive feature of these particular weights is a very clear mark impressed on the base within a circle, together with a scratched number. Produced as a limited edition of 1000, the weights were made with orange or blue swirling grounds. See figures 344 and 345. The 'ST' stands for St. Tudy, a village in Cornwall. Similar weights containing a large bubble have a 'Y' for Yelverton. Later dates are known.

Fig. 345. Impressed mark ST, and date 1976 on base of a St. Tudy weight.

Fig. 344. A signed St. Tudy weight containing agate quartz. 1976. Dia. 3.15". Height 2.25". $45/65.

Siddy Langley

Siddy Langley served an apprenticeship under Peter Layton at the London Glassblowing Workshops, and in the mid-1980s set up her own workshop Alchemy Glass at her residence.

Siddy specializes in paperweights that have iridescent surface patterns (figure 346). This iridescence is produced by spraying the weight, while it is still hot on the pontil rod, with stannous chloride and then re-heating it. In the case of the weight named Brideshead the weight is also rolled into

pieces of white glass, which stay on the surface. This is an unlimited but attractive weight, which is produced in reasonable numbers – one dealer, for instance, sold about twenty in 1988 retailing at about $50 each.

Equador, also iridescent, is rolled into green powdered glass prior to the working of heart shaped designs in mixed pink and white glass on the surface. Up until 1990 only about five of these had been made.

All paperweights are signed Siddy Langley together with the year on the base. The pontil mark is clearly visible.

Fig. 346. A range of weights by Siddy Langley. Courtesy of Sweetbriar Gallery Archive. $40/50 each.

Peter Layton

Born in Prague in 1937 Peter Layton's career achievements have been impressive. An important milestone was clearly his founding of The London Glassblowing Workshop, currently operating at 7, The Leather Market, Weston Street, London SE1 3ER.

Various abstract paperweight designs have been produced, but to collectors perhaps the type most normally associated with Peter is that shown in figure 347.

Those wishing to learn much more about this man and his work should read his book *Glass Art*.[1]

Fig. 347. A signed weight by Peter Layton. Courtesy of Anne Anderson. $100/200.

James Maskray

Operating at Poole Pottery, in c. 1996 James produced the toadstools featured in figure 348.

Okra

Famous for its surface iridescent effects, figure 349 shows this to advantage with attractive flowers internally.

Fig. 348. Double toadstools, c. 1996. An attractive design by James Maskray. Dia. 3.25". Courtesy of a private collector. $30/40.

Fig. 349. Secret Garden, a good floral design with a typical outer surface finish. Okra. c. 1990. Dia. 2.75". Height 4". Courtesy of a private collector. $180/220.

Obsidian Glass

Run by Pardeep Sodera in Littlecote House, near Hungerford, Berkshire, uses blanks, and sandblasts them to produce attractive designs like the example in figure 350.

Sally Penn-Smith

Sally's weights are often large, and encased. Figure 351 is an example of her 'Frosted Orchard.'

Sunderland Glass

Philip Chaplain and Stuart Cumming, both ex Caithness employees, now operate at the National Glass Centre on the banks of the River Wear, in Sunderland.

Formed in 1988, the company use a lead free glass, containing barium, to produce a range of about fourteen unlimited, and fourteen limited edition abstract designs. Limited editions are marked on the base, and edition size is between 50 and 500. Prices range from $20 - 280.

Fig. 350. Elephants, c. 1997. Obsidian Glass. A very attractive surface design. Dia. 3". Courtesy of a private collector. $70/80.

Fig. 351. Frosted orchard, c. 1995. Sally Penn-Smith. One of Sally's bold designs. Dia. 3.75". Courtesy of a private collector. $110/130.

Patrick Stern

Patrick became fascinated by glass as a result of watching his brother, who had set up a studio around 1977. After training under him for about three years, he worked with Peter Layton. Some excellent, and unusual, canes have been made by Patrick, and some of these, shown in figure 352, feature in the weight illustrated in figure 353.

Fig. 352. Canes, Patrick Stern. Patrick's canes are often very different, but extremely good, and interesting. Note the wonderful chessboard on the left. Courtesy of a private collector.

Fig. 353. Cube, c. 1996, Patrick Stern. An interesting, and rarely seen weight, utilizing Patrick's chessboard cane. Width 1.9" Courtesy of a private collector. $70/90.

A.J. Thorneycroft

Al Thorneycroft produces abstract designs using glass with a high lead content. Latticinio typically twists down from left to right. The bases usually show a partially ground out pontil, and are signed AJT together with the year of manufacture. Figures 354 and 355 show examples of his weights, and a typical base.

Fig. 354. Selection of weights by A.J. Thorneycroft. Courtesy of a private collector. $30/40 each.

Left:
Fig. 355. Scratch signature A JT on base of a weight by A.J. Thorneycroft. Courtesy of a private collector.

Tweedsmuir

An attractive transfer weight of a stag's head, shown in figure 356, was made c. 1997 by Chris Dodds. Plain abstract designs with low domes are also produced.

Hartley Wood

Victorian green dump weights by John Kilner and other makers will be well familiar to the average collector. In the early 1990s Hartley Wood in Sunderland produced a range of about thirteen reproduction designs. The glass was usually slightly bluer and cleaner than that of the 19th century originals. Prices ranged from $20 - 80.

[1]Layton, Peter. *Glass Art*. Huntingdon, Cambridgeshire: A. & C. Black, 1996.

Fig. 356. Stag's head, c. 1997. A transfer weight by Chris Dodds of Tweedsmuir. Dia. 3". Courtesy of a private collector. $25/30.

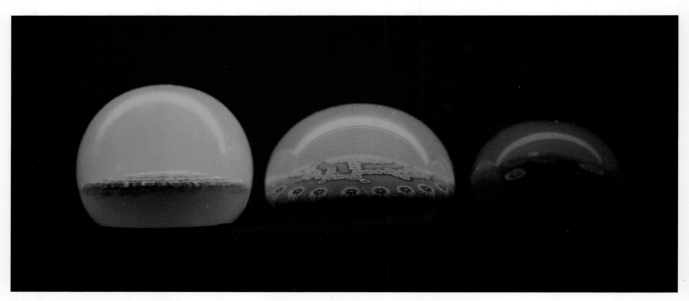

Fig. 357. From left to right, 1930s-40s Ysart, post 1946 Ysart, and a fake. Post 1946 are a different shade of color, and of lower luminosity. Note particularly the very dull color of a fake.

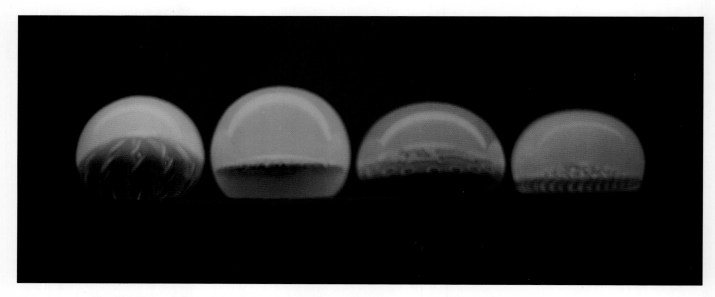

Fig.358. From left to right, Caithness, 1930s-40s Ysart, post 1946 Ysart, and Whitefriars. The dull straw color of Caithness is clearly visible, and the brilliant blue of Whitefriars is unmistakable.

Chapter 13

Identifying Unknown Paperweights
using scientific tests

In addition to canes, pontil marks, and so forth, there are three scientific tests which singly, or better still collectively, can be conducted on paperweights in order to establish their identity more conclusively. These are:

Ultra-violet (U.V.) fluorescence;

Refractive index (R.I.), and

Specific Gravity (S.G.). Of these, the first ,although subjective, is by far the cheapest to conduct.

Ultra-Violet (U.V.) Fluorescence

In common with many other substances, glass fluoresces under U.V. light emitting a color and brilliance which is dependent upon its composition. Thus it will readily be appreciated that such a property can frequently be used as a clue to the identity of a paperweight, particularly as many makers use glass of different composition. The classic weights of the 19th century, for instance, produced by Baccarat, Clichy, and St. Louis, all emit distinctive colors, and various authors have documented their findings.[1, 2, 3]

Briefly, the technique involves examining a paperweight in a darkened room under an ultra-violet light of the appropriate wavelength. Lamps most frequently used for this work emit their maximum energy at a wavelength of 365 nm., sometimes referred to as long wave.

Typical fluorescence colors emitted by modern paperweights are as follows:

Caithness – Pale orange, straw.

J. Glass – Dull orange, but a few very early weights (1979) are pale blue.

Langham – Pale straw.

Manson – Pre 1981, dull yellow similar to some Ysart. Post 1997 dark straw.

Perthshire – Pre 1992, pale sandy straw. Brilliance varies from dull to medium.

Selkirk – Pale sandy straw, but slightly green.

Strathearn – Very similar to Perthshire, although some are distinctly yellow like early Ysart.

Whitefriars – Bright blue. The highest luminosity of all the makes tested.

Paul Ysart – Pre-1946, quite bright yellow. Post 1946, green and mauve. The yellow fluorescence has been observed typically, but not exclusively, in those weights which have tinted domes.

Salvador Ysart – Identical to pre 1946 Paul Ysart.

Paul Ysart, fakes – Very dull orange. The luminosity of fakes is by far the lowest of all the makes tested.

It should be stressed that a number of parameters are very relevant, and experience must be coupled to the results of tests when making any assessment. Figures 357 and 358 give some idea of the colors observed under U.V. light.

An interesting survey of antique and modern weights has been conducted by the Cambridge Paperweight Circle.[4] The perception of color is highly subjective, and for their assessment up to twenty-three observers were selected. Their results for Whitefriars and Ysart weights were as follows:

Maker	Observed Color	No. of observers
Whitefriars	Bright blue	21
Whitefriars	Mauve	2
Ysart, pre-1946	Variations of green	18
Ysart, pre-1946	Yellow	4
Ysart, post-1946	Variations of mauve	8
Ysart, post-1946	Variations of pink	4
Ysart, post-1946	Variations of gray	4
Ysart, post-1946	Variations of brown	2
Ysart, post-1946	Variations of green	2
Ysart, post-1946	Blue	1

It is believed that Paul Ysart used three different formulations at Perth during the manufacture of his early weights. Different formulations were also used by him at Caithness; and at Harland two different compositions were used.

Refractive Index

Another parameter which can be used as an aid in characterizing different weights, is the refractive index of the glass. This value typically shows slight variation from one manufacturer to another, and is influenced, for example, by the lead content of the glass.

The value can be determined by applying liquids of known refractive index to minute scratches such as are often found on the base of a weight. For those interested, Hollister gives fuller details of this method.[5]

Refractive Index Values for British manufacturers paperweights are as follows:

Maker	Refractive Index
Caithness	1.514
J. Glass	1.495
Manson	1.49 – 1.50
Perthshire	1.51 – 1.52
Selkirk	1.52
Strathearn	1.49 – 1.50
Sunderland	1.52
Whitefriars	1.55 – 1.56
Ysart, pre-1946	1.48 – 1.50
Ysart, post-1946	1.514

All values relate to the colorless glass, such as is used for the dome. The most significant differences are between early and late Ysart weights, and Whitefriars.

Revealing peripheral canes which are normally invisible

Due to the refractive properties of glass, it can sometimes be very difficult, or even impossible, to see canes which are at or near the periphery of a weight.

Fortunately, sometimes such areas can be seen more clearly, by taking advantage of the difference in the refractive index of glass and water. To achieve any improvement possible, the problematical weight should be viewed while immersed in water. Typical improvements can be gauged by reference to figures 359 and 360.

Fig. 359. A Strathearn close pack but with some peripheral canes which, due to the refraction of the glass, cannot be seen.

Fig. 360. The weight shown in Fig. 359, but this time photographed under water. Notice that peripheral canes, from the 9 o'clock to 2 o'clock position, are now totally visible. This is extremely significant as it is by no means uncommon to find an important cane, such as a signature or silhouette, in the outer row.

Specific gravity

The specific gravity of glass is the ratio of its weight compared with that of an equal volume of water.

Results of specific gravity tests can be highly significant when trying to establish the identity of unknown paperweights. Like the refractive index results, all S.G. values are quoted at 20°C.

The difference in the values for early and late Whitefriars weights is significant, and is of use for identifying the period of unknown or undated examples. Specific gravity should certainly be used as an aid in deciding whether an Ysart weight is genuine or a fake.

Company	S.G.
Caithness	2.51
J. Glass	2.53
Langham	2.56
Manson, post-1997	2.47
Monart/Vasart	2.55
Perthshire, pre-1992	2.57
Selkirk	2.465
Strathearn	2.56
Sunderland	2.55
Whitefriars 1951–1953	3.24
Whitefriars 1970–1980	3.19
Paul and Salvador Ysart	2.50
Paul Ysart, fakes	2.59

[1]Boore, J.P. Hobbies, Old Glass Paperweights, The Ultra-Violet light. March 1961.
[2]Hollister, Paul and Lanmon, Dwight P. Paperweights: Flowers which clothe the meadows. U.S.A., 1978.
[3]Elville, E.M. Art of the French Paperweight, Annual Bulletin of the Paperweight Collectors Association. 1959.
[4]Cambridge Paperweight Circle. Newsletters no. 6, April 1983 and no. 7, July 1983.
[5]Hollister, Paul Jr. The Encyclopedia of Glass Paperweights. U.S.A., Bramhall House, 1969.

Glossary

Annealing – process of cooling hot paperweights at a controlled rate, to avoid cracking.

Aventurine – sparkling glass made by processing glass with metal particles.

Block – piece of wood, or other material, used to shape the dome of a weight.

Cane – piece of glass which has been pulled while molten to reduce its diameter. Usually contains a pattern, and is of circular section.

Cording – striations occasionally observed in the dome, usually more visible when viewing from the side.

Dome – the clear glass which is above the design.

Facet – flat or concave cuts on the outer surface.

Filigree – colored, spiral like effect, short lengths of which are used in a wide range of designs.

Flash – a thin outer coating of colored glass.

Gaffer – a master glass craftsman.

Gather – a variable quantity of molten glass picked up on the end of a pontil rod.

Glory hole – relatively small unit, heated to a high temperature, in which glass on a pontil rod can be re-heated as necessary.

Goldstone – a gold colored aventurine.

Ground – the base, often colored, on which a paperweight design rests.

Jasper ground – a mixture of small pieces of glass in two or more colors, scattered randomly to form a ground.

Lampwork – glass which has been worked by a hot burner to produce such items as flowers, fish, and insects, etc.

Latticinio – woven like, spiral twisted white canes.

Lehr – a furnace for melting glass.

Magnum – paperweight which is greater than 3.25" in diameter.

Marbrie – a marbled like design, with colored curved forms usually originating from a top central cane, and extending to the base. The design is near the surface.

Marver – flat steel plate on which molten glass can be rolled.

Millefiori – the multitude of various cane designs that go to make up a finished design.

Miniature – a paperweight which is less than 2" in diameter.

Overlay – a paperweight coated in one or more layers of white or colored glass. Facets are then cut to re-expose the internal design.

Pontil mark – mark, often roughly circular, at the center of the base where the weight was broken away from the pontil rod.

Pontil rod – a metal rod, a few feet long, and usually of iron, on the end of which paperweights are built up.

Portrait cane – a multi-colored picture design, such as a golfer, tiger, etc. formed by bunching together many very thin colored rods in a mosaic fashion.

Printy – another word for facet, but often reserved to describe a concave cut.

Priscillas – tong like tool used for cutting in at the back of a paperweight, prior to tapping it off the pontil rod.

Refractive index – a measure of the degree to which a ray of light is bent on entering glass from air.

Servitor – an assistant to the gaffer.

Set up – the assembly of canes, and/or lampwork prior to encasement.

Silhouette cane – a single color shape in a cane of a butterfly, or animal, etc.

Star cut – a star, of various numbers of points, cut into the base of a weight to enhance its appearance.

Sulphide – a white ceramic like three-dimensional motif set into a paperweight. Often of famous people, or to commemorate a special event. Colored versions are rare.

Bibliography

Andrews, Frank; Clarke, Alison; Turner, Ian. *Ysart Glass*. London: Volo Edition Ltd., 1990.

Annual Bulletin of the Paperweight Collectors Association, 1959, 1971, 1977, 1983, and 1997 – 99.

Bergstrom, Evangeline H. *Old Glass Paperweights*. London: Faber and Faber Ltd., 1948.

Bevan, Pat and John. *Caithness Glass Paperweights – Alphabetical Listing.* Privately published, 1996.

Boore, J.P. *Hobbies, Old Glass Paperweights, The Ultra-Violet light.* March 1961.

Caithness Glass Ltd. Newsletters, September 1981, and Spring 1982.

Cambridge Paperweight Circle, Newsletter no. 6, April 1983, no. 7, July 1983, and no. 63 March 1998.

Evans, Wendy; Ross, Catherine and Werner, Alex. *Whitefriars Glass – James Powell and Sons of London*. London. The Museum of London. 1995.

Hall, Robert G. *Scottish Paperweights.* Atglen, Pennsylvania: Schiffer Publishing Ltd., 1999.

Hollister, Paul. *Glass Paperweights – An Old Craft Revived*. Coupar Angus, Perthshire: William Culross and Son Ltd., 1975.

Hollister, Paul and Lanmon, Dwight P. *Paperweights: Flowers which clothe the meadows*. U.S.A., 1978.

Hollister, Paul Jr. *The Encyclopedia of Glass Paperweights*. New York: Bramhall House, 1969.

Jackson, Lesley. *Whitefriars Glass – The art of James Powell and Sons.* 1996.

Johnson, Glenn S. *The Caithness Collection.* U.S.A. 1981.

Jokelson, Paul. *One hundred of the most important paperweights.* London: John Wallace Printing, 1966.

Kovacek, Michael. *Paperweights.* Vienna: Michael Kovacek, 1987.

Layton, Peter. *Glass Art.* Huntingdon, Cambridgeshire: A. & C. Black, 1996.

Mahoney, Colin and McClanahan, Gary. *The Complete Guide to Perthshire Paperweights*. Santa Cruz, California: Paperweight Press, 1997.

McCawley, Patricia K. *Glass Paperweights.* London: Charles Letts Books Ltd., 1982.

McClanahan, Gary W. *The Printy, Vol.3, No.3.* Fountain Valley, California: G.W. McClanahan, 1995.

Pavitt, Trevor. *Paperweights – a bulletin for collectors, number 3, May 1978*. London: Darius Arts Ltd.

Selman, Lawrence H. *Mail auction catalogs and price guides, 1990 – 99.* Santa Cruz, California: Paperweight Press.

Selman, Lawrence H. and Linda P. *Paperweights for Collectors*. Santa Cruz, California: Paperweight Press, 1975.

Selman, Lawrence H. *The Art of the Paperweight – Perthshire*. Santa Cruz, California: Paperweight Press, 1983.

Terris, Colin. *The Charlton Standard Catalogue of Caithness Paperweights. First Edition*. Toronto, Ontario: W.K. Cross, 1999.

Three hundred years of glass making. Whitefriars publication.

For an extremely comprehensive listing of books and articles on glass paperweights, the reader should refer to:-

Dohan, Andrew H. *The Dictionary of Paperweight Signature Canes.* Santa Cruz, California: Paperweight Press, 1997.

Index